S0-AHB-271

Teaching Teens Religion

Teaching Teens Religion

How to Make It a Favourite Class

Danny Brock

NOVALIS

© 2009 Novalis Publishing Inc.

Cover: Blair Turner
Layout: Audrey Wells

Novalis
10 Lower Spadina Avenue, Suite 400
Toronto, Ontario, Canada
M5V 2Z2
www.novalis.ca

Library and Archives Canada Cataloguing in Publication

Brock, Danny, 1950-
    Teaching teens religion : how to make it a favourite
class : information and inspiration for high school religion
teachers / Danny Brock.

ISBN 978-2-89646-126-4

    1. Christian education of teenagers. 2. Religious education
of teenagers. 3. Catholic Church--Education. I. Title.

BX926.3.B76 2009   268'.433   C2009-901408-4

Printed in Canada.

All rights reserved. No part of this publication may be reproduced, stored in a retrieval system, or transmitted in any form, or by any means, electronic, mechanical, photocopying, recording, or otherwise, without the written permission of the publisher.

We acknowledge the financial support of the Government of Canada through the Book Publishing Industry Development Program (BPIDP) for our publishing activities.

5   4   3   2   1   13   12   11   10   09

Dedication

This book is dedicated to the students of
O'Grady Catholic High School, Prince George, B.C., Canada
Eastside Catholic High School, Sammamish, Washington, USA
Saint Andrew's Regional Catholic High School, Victoria, B.C., Canada
(I tried to write what you taught me.)

Acknowledgments

Heartfelt thanks to Gerry Daigle, Peter Bagnall and Rob Fuller, who said to me, more than a few times, "You should write a book." From the vantage point of many years, your words were much more than friendly advice; they were benedictions from the heart.

To my wife, Philomena, who helped edit this book as she has edited me since the day she decided I was worth putting time into. My book and my life are better for it.

To Flo Follero-Pugh, who typed the manuscript whenever little Kimberly was sleeping. Your joy and enthusiasm are infectious.

To my son, Dominic, whose tumultuous adolescence was always more about the heart than the theories in my head — where he often found me hiding.

To Kevin Burns, for supporting this work at its initial stages.

To Grace Deutsch of Novalis, for her promotion of this book and my confidence.

To Anne Louise Mahoney of Novalis, for her belief in the ministry of teaching teens Religion and her editorial skill in bringing clarity to the text.

Contents

Introduction

*You have asked me, brother Deogratias, to write something to you
on the instructing of candidates for the catechumenate that may be
of use to you ... because you are supposed to possess great ability in
catechizing, by reason both of your thorough training in the faith and
the charm of your style: but that you are almost always perplexed ...*

—St. Augustine, *De catechizandis rudibus*
(written to a Religion teacher between 398 and 405 CE)

So you want to teach Religion and you want to teach it to teens. Or you don't want to teach Religion to teens, but your principal wants you to. Or you didn't want to teach Religion, but now, after thinking about it, your curiosity has been piqued, and you have been recollecting your religious upbringing, checking in with your spirituality, and recalling any formal Religious Education or close fac-simile thereof (I took an Ethics course in university!), so you're actu-ally getting excited about teaching Religion. But deep inside a question looms and in small, muted whispers you hear, "*How* do you teach Religion to teens?"

Drag that question into the daylight, hold onto it, turn it over and examine it. Eureka! You've just asked the most important question.

Most new Religion teachers begin by asking the second most important question: *What* do I teach? This question is answered when the principal, Director of Religious Education, department head or a colleague gives you the teacher's manual and says something like, "Mostly the Beatitudes and the Ten Commandments, but also a review of the Sacraments and some basic knowledge of Scripture ... No big deal; you'll be fine!"

The reason the first question is not asked is that new Religion teachers assume they know the answer. How do you teach Religion? The same way you teach Math, English, Social Studies, Geography, or any other subject … except it's just Religion. Right? Wrong. Too much heat is generated around the question of *what* teens should learn in Religion, but not enough on *how* they should learn it. Knowing the *what* of Religious Education has contributed to *your* faith development; knowing the *how* of Religious Education will contribute to *your students'* faith development. The goal of Religious Education is not for students to say at the end of the year, "Mr. Hughes and Miss Baron are very religious people." The goal is to help students see that *they* are very religious people.

Is teaching Religion really the same as teaching any other subject, with only a few cosmetic changes? Ask any seasoned and effective Religion teacher – teaching Religion is not only very different, it is also very difficult.

What? I thought the only qualification was being a baptized Catholic and then it's like … well … anybody can teach Religion, right?

Wrong!

Too many reluctant Religion teachers are chosen to fill in blocks on a timetable, and are thrown into the lion's den unprepared, ill equipped and oblivious. Some survive, licking their wounds. For others, it is a beneficial work-study program, a self-conducted workshop in Religion, a let's-all-learn-this-together enterprise. Still others, unaware and a poor fit for the task, incite a third-millennium version of a 1960s-style student rebellion. Believers in the class become lukewarm, agnostics become atheists, and self-proclaimed "I'm not religious" types sabotage the classroom and use it as their popularity pump-up training room. They ask outlandish questions to get a rise and a laugh. "I heard the Pope said all Anglicans are going to hell." The class devolves into a barrage of banter and barbs, and another lesson plan is derailed.

Other classes, usually the early morning ones, lapse into a spiritual stupor. Seven rows of teens staring at you – through you – as you ramble on and on, the Religion teacher's equivalent of a long Sunday sermon.

Some are staring into the void; others are sleeping; some whisper to friends, pass notes clandestinely or do their Math homework. You scan the class and realize – they're gone; I've lost them. Now what do I do?

Welcome to the Fellowship! I wrote this book for you.

Few people realize how hard it is to teach Religion to teens. Religion teachers I ask say flatly, "It's the most difficult subject to teach." They may love teaching Religion, as I do, but having taught History, Law, and Social Studies at the high school level (and a medley of subjects in upper elementary), I say, unreservedly, Religion is the hardest. It is also the most rewarding, when done well.

Religion is different. Consider the reaction you get when you tell others, "I teach Religion," as opposed to "I teach Math." You're at a party, in a circle of strangers. Someone inevitably asks, "What do you do?" You want to tell a white lie and say, "I work for the Department of Wildlife." But instead you declare, "I teach." "What do you teach?" predictably follows. You hesitate. You want to say, "teens," but acquiescing to the call for transparency, you tell it like it is: "I teach Religion to high school students." There are seven people in the circle with you; here are their reactions.

- Person One: "That must be easy – one big rap session." (Clarification: a rap session is a mid- to late 20th-century term for a meeting in which everyone just says whatever they want and the teacher keeps saying, "I hear you.")

- Person Two: "That sounds interesting, teaching about all the different religions in the world. You don't teach just one, do you?" (Clarification: there is great merit in teaching a World Religions course in high school, but this person wants to tell you all about his idea of the many paths to the one truth and how we don't need to go to a church, mosque, temple, or synagogue to pray to God – we can go to the top of a mountain.)

- Person Three: "That must be a real break from teaching all those hard, factual courses, you know, like science and math. I guess you get to relax, kick back – I mean, you don't give them tests or anything like that … do they get credit for that course?" (Clarification: No, it isn't a break; yes, it is factual; no, we don't kick back; yes, we do give tests … more on this later.)

- Person Four: At first he doesn't say anything; he just looks at you. But you feel unnerved, like you are about to get hit in the back of the head with a paintball. Finally, Person Four can't hold it in any longer. "Give them the truth. Teach them the Universal Catholic Catechism, Church history, Apologetics, the Church Fathers. Teens today are religious illiterates. They know nothing. They don't even know who Saint Angelina Faustus Guterio is!" (Clarification: I just made up that saint, but Person Four will tell you of the latest saint they are reading about, and reveal to you that they just started reading Church history not long ago, and demand, "Why didn't I get this when I was in high school?" I'll answer that one later, too.)

- Person Five: When you first saw Person Five in the group, she was a congenial, somewhat deferential person with a pleasant but guarded smile. But when you said the word "religion," you noticed her eyes instantly dart to the wall, her feet shift, and her wine glass impulsively rise to her mouth. Your Religion teacher sensor triggers the alarm (all Religion teachers develop this), and you just know this person has a BIG ISSUE with ORGANIZED RELIGION. The best way to defuse this potential explosion is to follow "I teach Religion" with a shrug and a joke. "This person dies. After he passes through the pearly gates, St. Peter shows him lots of rooms with fun-loving people partying. Then Peter takes him to a separate room down the hall and says, "Shhh! These are the Catholics; they think they're the only ones here. Ha ha ha ha ha!" (No clarification.)

- Person Six: She looks at you. There is absolutely no change of expression on her face. Five seconds go by and she says, "Do you think the housing market has peaked?" She is saying this to the guy next to you who revealed previously that he is a realtor. (Clarification: Person Six cannot relate, cannot compute, cannot process this information. The term "Religion teacher" is off her radar and has flown by.)

- Person Seven: This person is a mother of a teenage son. She wants him to grow up to be a responsible, compassionate, virtuous, spiritually sensitive person who respects girls. Lately, however, he spends a lot of time playing video games, watching movies and asking, "What's for dinner?" This person is very interested in what you do and can talk to you for hours. (Clarification is found in the rest of this book.)

The art of teaching teens Religion has changed dramatically over the past 40 years. Parents of my students are happy that their child is enjoying Religion class, but often do not understand what makes it enjoyable. All the reflection, discussion, discernment, wisdom and prayer over the last four decades has reached an apex. The stars have aligned and presented what American Archbishop Donald W. Wuerl has called a "new moment in the Church in terms of the renewal of catechesis." The publication of the revised *National Directory for Catechesis* (2005) in the US, the revised *General Directory for Catechesis* (1997), the *Catechism of the Catholic Church* (1992) and the *U.S. Catholic Catechism for Adults* (2006) has provided a set of clear and solid resources for Religion teachers. The call for a "new evangelization" by Benedict XVI and his predecessor, John Paul II, has given Religion teachers a deeper and broader vision of their ministry. *Build Bethlehem Everywhere* (2002), a statement on Catholic education by Fr. Erik Riechers, SAC, has become, according to Joanne Rogers, President of the Canadian Catholic Trustees' Association, "a major resource in the renewal and encouragement of Catholic educators across Canada." Fr. James Mulligan's recently revised *Catholic Education: Ensuring a Future* (2006) summons us in Canada to realize once again that we are in the throes of a defining moment, whether we like it or not.

Still, there is another reason for this "new moment" beyond the Church's desire to engage youth in catechesis: the readiness, and indeed eagerness, of youth to receive it.

Young people today are more in touch with their deeper longings than their peers of the previous 40 years. The place where their heart speaks to them is also where they have been most hurt. This generation has been burned. They have experienced family disruption, close relatives broken by addiction, friends sexually abused or harassed or just plain used. They have experienced inner emptiness in the midst of abounding wealth, have witnessed moral collapse on the part of adults they once considered models, and have touched that place that asks, "Why should I live, anyway? Who would miss me? Why would it matter if I were gone?" They have been asking religious questions for a while now – the false promises of a relativistic and consumer culture have driven them to it.

Youth today are more open, more forthcoming and less discreet than youth in the past. They tell you their struggles, their hurts, their fears, and their sins. They do this because they want help. They want something different, something real, something that lasts. Teens see the crack in the glitzy veneer of our self-absorbed culture, and they want something better. They want congruence between their inner world and their outer actions. They want integrity, conviction, character and faith. They are crying out for joy, goodness, community and good old-fashioned fun. Above all, they want real love.

They tell you they are drowning because they want you to be a lifeline. More than needing a lecture on the meaning of life, *they want an experience of the fullness of life*. They want you to be a witness that such a life really exists. Pope Paul VI said, "Modern people listen more willingly to witnesses than to teachers, and if they do listen to teachers, it is because they are also witnesses."[1] Young people want teachers who witness with their lives the truths they teach. Then the teacher becomes a mentor, which is something that youth are searching for. This is why there is a new moment in adolescent catechesis; the supply of the Church's renewal of catechesis over the last 40 years has now encountered a heightened demand. This book is a small voice saying, "Seize the moment."

The moment will surely be missed, however, if, instead of action, we substitute reaction. Most seasoned Religion teachers would concur with Bishop Blair of Toledo, Ohio, who said, "With time it became clear that many of those being catechized were no longer learning the content of the faith in a way that they could or would remember," and that there has been "widespread erosion of specific instruction of Christian doctrine in much of religious education over the previous 30 years."[2]

This erosion must be halted and the banks of our students' religious knowledge shored up, but not at the expense of losing the insights we have gained in methodology – the way we have learned to engage the present generation in the ministry of Religious Education. Religion teachers have come to realize what youth ministers in parishes discovered some years ago – we need comprehensive, *total* Religious Education in our schools. This methodology is aptly described in what the *National Directory for Catechesis* in the US calls "the most effective catechetical program for adolescents." It describes the new moment in a nutshell:

> … a comprehensive program of pastoral ministry for youth that includes catechesis, community life, evangelization, justice and peace, leadership development, pastoral care, and prayer and worship.[3]

Catholic high schools are at the core of the Church's ministry to youth. Catholic high schools are the most attended and most funded youth ministry effort, and the one that puts Catholic adults and youth together for the longest period of time. Catholic high schools may also be, however, the most neglected youth ministry in the Church. There are over 700,000 youth in the care of our Catholic high schools in Canada and the United States, yet we often take this situation for granted, squandering the opportunity to engage our students with the full spiritual treasures of our faith community. We have, in Catholic high schools, what has often been called "a captive audience." But do we captivate our captive audience? Teens have to come to school, but do they want to? They have to take Religion class, but do they like it?

This book is not calling for a renewal of the Catholic high school Religion class. This renewal has been happening over the past 40 years, since Vatican II. The master chefs have been working hard in the kitchen. The guests have arrived. They are hungry and expectant. It's time to take the full course out of the kitchen and into the dining room. It's time to eat – that's the new moment.

Teaching Teens Religion: How to Make It a Favourite Class is written for the Religion teacher, in Canada or the US, new or experienced, young or old, reluctant or gung-ho. School administrators, parish youth workers, Directors of Religious Education, clergy, religious, and parents of teens will also find it useful. In the tradition of St. Augustine's long letter to a "perplexed" Religion teacher seventeen centuries ago, my hope is to offer some guidance and inspiration for the Religion teacher today who is at times bewildered, at times unsure and too often disheartened. My goal is to help "Build Bethlehem" in the Catholic high school Religion class.

In Chapter 1, I define some terms so you can decode the mysterious lexicon of Religious Education. In Chapter 2, I explore eight reasons why teaching Religion to teens is difficult, which will make you feel either emboldened, like a survivor, or fearful and depressed. In chapters 3, 4 and 5, I offer helpful guidelines and practical ideas that will diminish your fear and turn your despondency into hope. In Chapter 6, I draw some lessons from students I have taught. Chapter 7 is about parents and the teachers who represent them in the classroom. In chapters 8, 9 and 10, I offer thoughts on teaching three salient topics (I call them the three S's) of youth catechesis: Sin, Sex, and Social Justice. I end, in Chapter 11, with a pep talk.

Some years ago, a student gave me this note at the end of the school year:

To Mr. Brock:
I have learned so much from you in grade 8 and 10.
You have changed me into the person I looked up to when I was younger.
You are a very special person to me.

My heart is touched, even now, as I read that note. But I'm not bragging. This should be standard fare for Religion teachers. You should get these notes at the end of every year. Put them in your scrapbook; you'll need them to remind you why you do what you do.

Yes, they should erect a statue to the dauntless Religion teacher. They should have a stamp in our honour. They should have National Religion Teacher Appreciation Day … but maybe not. Ours is not a televangelist show. We don't smile into TV cameras; we smile before real teens who are, to paraphrase Mother Teresa, where Jesus is found in the often outlandish and exuberant disguise of the young.

The high school Religion teacher is not found in the lofty halls of the theological college. We are the ones in the trenches. We are the ones planting seeds in the field. We are the ones on patrol, walking the teen beat. Few adults see or understand what we do. Our work is hidden, like the grace of God – hidden now, but revealed in the all-revealing light to come.

When the final curtain rises, we'll be able to lean back and enjoy the laughter we provoked, the hope we fed, the love we fostered, the prayers we inspired, and the lives we shaped. We are God's ambassadors, intrepid missionaries to a teenage culture. When Jesus was looking for someone to teach teens Religion, we were the ones who dared to say, "Here I am, Lord!" And Jesus said, "Come!"

So say goodbye to terra firma and start walking … on water.

(Water-walking lessons to follow.)

1

A Practitioner's Pious Parlance

A Religion Teacher's "Terms to Know"

Student to professor in Philosophy class:
"I know the answer, but I just can't find the words to explain it."

Professor to student:
"Then you don't know the answer."

When I was a Philosophy major at the University of Dallas (a Catholic university with an undercover name), some of my teachers were Cistercian monks whose abbey was on campus. They all came, it seemed to me, from Eastern Europe, and their intellectual acuity was so intense that when they really got going, their whole head (often bald) would flush red from the cognitive workout.

Once, when I began to prattle on about some philosophical concept, my monk professor, standing in his cassock, began to rhythmically cut the air in front of him with hand movements as he interrupted me, saying, "Vat are you talking about? You must define your terms… define your terms!" Most of the philosophical content in that class went over my head, but I did gain some thinking skills, and the importance of "defining my terms" has stayed with me to this day.

Like any field of endeavour (think computers), Religious Education has developed its own lexicon. While my definitions will not, I suspect, pass the rigorous scrutiny of my Cistercian mentors, I believe they are functionally accurate and essential terms to know for the aspiring practitioner.

Thirty-one "terms to know" for Religion teachers

Revelation: God taking the initiative to communicate with us about truths we could never fully know otherwise – somewhat like a teenager receiving a note in class that says, "Guess what? Sarah likes you." Only this one reads,

> "I love you ... forever. Count on it."
> God

Revelation is an intimate sharing of God's inner life, and when received, feels more like a spiritual blood transfusion than just another idea about God.

Religion: A people's response to God's revelation. In Latin, *religare*, meaning to tie, fasten and bind. Hence, to bind us to God. If Religion were a letter, it would sound like this:

> Dear God,
>
> I believe.
> Help my unbelief.
>
> Love,
> Your pilgrim people

Covenant: More than a contract, it is a vow of love God makes to you. It binds you to God and you cannot get out of it, no matter how good your lawyer is.

Sin: Failure, on our part, to live up to the covenant. A freely chosen and deliberate act of turning from God's love. So don't blame not understanding the fine print of the covenant; there was no fine print, and no pre-nuptial agreement, either.

Free will: The Church's belief that, notwithstanding all the peer pressure, or all the dysfunction in our family, or all the bad things that have happened to us, there is still within us (weakened, but not eradicated), the ability to say "yes" and the ability to say "no." We may try to pass the buck, but it always comes back to us. "Christian," said the Church Father, "know your dignity."

Bible: God's love letter to us. Originally written by, for and to believers, it can be highly confusing, even unintelligible to non-believers. But that's often the case when you read someone else's mail.

Evangelization: From the Greek word *evangelion*, meaning "good messenger." For some, the word "evangelization" evokes images of soapbox orators, smiling televangelists, doorbell-ringing enthusiasts, or, for an older generation, Bible-thumping thunder sermons. In a book entitled *More Ready Than You Realize: Evangelism as Dance in the Postmodern Matrix*, author Brian D. McLaren offers the following mission statement for modern evangelizers. I believe he is also describing a good Religion teacher.

> Good evangelists … are people who engage others in good conversation about important and profound topics such as faith, values, hope, meaning, purpose, goodness, beauty, truth, life after death, life before death, and God … Evangelists are people with a mission from God and a passion to love and serve their neighbors. They want to change the world."[4]

Evangelization is a good message from a good messenger.

The Catholic high school Religion teacher is always evangelizing, but not proselytizing. The religious beliefs of all our students, of whatever faith background, should be respected and honoured – as shown in this letter:

Dear Mr. Brock,
I took the liberty to modify our project just a little bit. I am not Catholic (I'm sure you know that by now) and I don't feel comfortable writing about how I "met" God. From my reading and from listening

to you I can confidently say that God means Love. So that is how I have altered the project. Just changing the word "God" to the word "Love." If you feel that my project is unacceptable because of the alterations then I will gladly redo the project following your rules.

Sincerely,
Lisa

This student did not have to redo her project. *Ubi caritas et amor, Deus ibi est.* (Where there is love, there is God.)

Conversion: When a teenager goes to church on his or her own! In Greek, *metanoia*, meaning to turn around and see and move in a new direction. It is a reversal (con-version) of one's whole life. Grace is God loving you. Conversion is when you turn around and let God love you.

Teenage conversion usually happens when teens discover that their abandonment to the temporal trappings of teen culture suddenly leaves them spent, lost and short-changed. That's when they remember what their parents, pastor and Religion teacher taught, and make a decision to re-member themselves to the community (Church).

Religion teachers please note: Conversion is a free response and excludes any inquisitorial tactics.

New Evangelization: The realization that many of the baptized have not been converted, and many who have already heard the Good News don't find it that good or that new. The "new evangelization" is like sending the troops back to basic training. It was initiated by Pope Paul VI, given impetus and fervour by Pope John Paul II, and continues with Benedict XVI. Religion teachers are called to evangelize because "… catechesis is a work of evangelization in the context of the mission of the Church" (General Directory for Catechesis [GDC] #4).

Grace: Something that gets all the credit at the end of anything good. Grace is from God, and we are called to cooperate with what God is doing (that's the free will part). Grace is "amazing" because it enables us to share in God's life in order to become like God.

We used to have a big argument with the Lutherans over this point, but we agree now that it's all God, it's all good and "there, but for the grace of God, go I." "Man is born broken," wrote Eugene O'Neil, "he lives by mending, the grace of God is the glue."

Faith: When a person makes a free decision to accept God into their life, which they could not have done without God's help.

An intellectual assent to the truths that God has revealed that cannot be proved or disproved intellectually.

Faith is a verb and a noun, a point and a process, both a human and divine act within a person.

And you thought quantum physics was confusing.

You, as a Religion teacher, are asking teens to make a "leap of faith," when they tremble at the thought of venturing beyond the peer group. You are asking them to reach out for something they can't see, when there is so much they can see (a licence to drive) that is finally within their grasp. You are asking them to commit their life in an act of love, when they haven't yet "got a life" and are still trying to figure out what love is.

If this is the situation, is it even possible to teach teens Religion?

Yes, but it takes faith.

Catechesis: Teaching a person Religion when they *really want to learn* Religion. Technically, catechesis is religious education to the converted, but the term has been expanded to include "pre-catechesis" (GDC #62) and "initiatory catechesis" (GDC #64).

So, yes, we high school Religion teachers are catechists who catechize with our catechetics, unless it is to the catechumenate of the RCIA. Got it?

Catechism: A manual of instruction in Christian doctrine. Martin Luther started the "catechism movement" in 1529 by publishing, with the help of Gutenberg's printing press, his *Small Catechism* for children and youth. Catholics responded after the Council of Trent with the publication in 1569 of *The Roman Catechism*, on which *The*

Penny Catechism in Britain and *The Baltimore Catechism* in the US were based.

In 1985, on the 20th anniversary of the close of Vatican Council II, the Synod of Bishops asked the Pope for a new catechism; in 1992, *The Catechism of the Catholic Church* was published. This bestseller should be on your desk, because, as Pope John Paul II said, it is "a sure norm for teaching the faith."

Baltimore Catechism: Based on the Roman Catechism of 1569, this was the basic catechetical text in the US and Canada from 1885 until the late 1960s. Its formal name was *The Catechism of the Third Plenary Council of Baltimore*, and it was comprised of 421 questions and answers. Your students' grandparents still have it memorized. Test them!

Q. Who made us?
A. God made us.

Q. Who is God?
A. God is the Supreme Being who made all things.

Q. Why did God make us?
A. God made us to know, love and serve Him in this world and to be happy with Him in the next.

Faith Development: Something God does, using any and every means available. Some of God's primary tools are parents, parishes, Popes, girlfriends, getting married, having a baby, mountain vistas, close calls with death and … oh yeah, Religion teachers.

Some theorists have tried to map faith development and see if there are predictable stages people go through along the way. Can faith be "staged"? (More on this in Chapter 3.)

Religious Education: Everything the Religion teacher does to encourage students to cooperate with what God is trying to do. This generic term covers everything you do in class: catechesis, pre-catechesis, evangelization, pre-evangelization – everything from teaching inspiring

Christian truths to trying to get the students to raise their hands, take notes and get their homework in on time.

When people ask me what I do, this is the term I use. But if I were to coin a new word, I would call what I do "evangechesis." Catchy, eh?

Doctrine/Dogma: A concise statement of Christian belief. This is the bouillon cube in the Church's "Chicken Soup for the Soul." It is an essential ingredient in Religious Education, but don't eat it by itself. When we add water to the bouillon cube, we are not watering down the dogma; we are just making it more palatable.

Indoctrination: This is what people are talking about when they say, "Religion was shoved down my throat." Some people say the Church used to do this; others say that everything in those days was "shoved down your throat." Warning: teens choke on this method.

Vatican Council II: A series of meetings in the early 1960s called by Good Pope John XXIII and attended by over 2,500 of the world's bishops. The Pope wanted to usher in a "new dawn" for the Church and to initiate a dialogue with the world in order to share the joy and love of Christ.

The summoning of an ecumenical council by Pope John came as a great surprise to many. The Church at the time seemed stable and placid, and there were no thorny issues to resolve. "Why call all these bishops to Rome?" the curia asked.

"What do we intend to do?" said Pope John as he threw open a window. "We intend to let in a little fresh air."

Once the process was started, it was impossible for mere humans to control. The result is 600 pages of Holy Spirit–inspired vision.

For young people today, the post–Vatican II Church is the only one they have ever known. So to them "the miracle of Vatican II" is just normal – one of the many things that young people take for granted. And there are many who have never even heard of Vatican II. In a

2005 *Catholic Update* article, theology teacher Edward P. Hahrenberg writes, "I once mentioned Vatican II in class and a student in the back raised his hand to ask: 'Why don't they call it Vatican One, like Air Force One?' This sincere undergraduate thought I was talking about the Pope's airplane."[5]

Ecumenism and Interreligious Dialogue: Technically, ecumenism is the search for Christian unity, something we had better keep doing because it was one of Jesus' final "prayers of intention" at the Last Supper (John 17:11). My biggest ecumenical breakthrough came at the dawn of Vatican II when I slow danced with a Protestant redhead at the local neighbourhood dance – such things we never forget.

Interreligious dialogue means talking to, listening to and praying with Aboriginal peoples, Jews, Muslims, Hindus, Buddhists, Sikhs, and people of other faiths ad infinitum.

Ecumenism and interreligious dialogue come down to this: Just because we can't always agree with each other doesn't mean we can't dance together.

School secretary: The person who knows more than anyone else about what is going on in the school. If you need something, see this person (ditto for parish secretary).

Campus Ministry Coordinator/Chaplain: Religion class and campus ministry/chaplaincy are the interlacing threads of fabric – the warp and woof of the high school faith formation ministry to young people. Campus ministry involves the coordination of events outside the classroom that support what you are trying to do in the classroom. This may include retreats, youth conferences, mission trips, guest speakers, prayer services and liturgy.

Holy Cross Father James Mulligan, author of *Catholic Education: The Future is Now*, underlines the importance of campus ministry/chaplaincy: "the commitment of a high school to the Catholic vision of education can be measured by the resources, time and energy the school puts into chaplaincy."[6]

In my high school, Religious Education and campus ministry/ chaplaincy are the same department. Where they are not, they need to work closely together. After all, what can a woof do without a warp?

Youth Retreat: Spiritual immersion for young people, a primary experience of evangelization. 24 hours x 2.5 days = 0E, but worth every minute.

Youth Conference: A spiritual family reunion. World Youth Day on a local level. A must-go for teens because of its evangelizing influence. Check the closest diocesan youth conference near you and take your students.

For over 10 years, our high school has taken senior students across the US/Canada border to attend the annual Seattle Archdiocesan Youth Conference. This conference changes our students, our high school and our Religion classes. It is truly a holy (wholly) experience, engaging the mind, body, emotions and spirit. This is how one student expressed it.

It was truly an amazing experience. It was the greatest feeling of walking into the gym on the first day. It was like all of a sudden I was hit with this gust of positive energy, it just made me want to dance … all those youth didn't care what anyone thought of them, they were just there doing what they wanted and what God wanted.

Christian camp: Can almost rival a faith-based school in its ability to engage youth in the faith. Non-Catholic Christians are way ahead of Catholics in this area, mostly because Catholics have put their youth ministry efforts into schools. It doesn't have to be either/or. One student told me that "Summer camp keeps my faith life alive."

Director of Religious Education (DRE): This is the person in the chancery office/pastoral centre who wants to know what you are doing. As soon as you figure that out, you should let this person know. The DRE can provide a wealth of information, contacts, resources, coffee and donuts.

Diocesan Youth Ministry Director: This person oversees youth ministry in the diocese. She coordinates parish youth ministers, runs an annual diocesan youth conference, provides training for ministry to youth, and much more. So, guess what? You are under this person's umbrella because the Catholic high school is primarily youth ministry with an educational mandate. In other words, the Catholic high school is not an island off the coast of the diocese; it is part of the mainland. Get to know this person: you are in the same business.

RCIA: The Rite of Christian Initiation of Adults is the process (both experiential and instructional) by which adults come into the Church. The process is a restoration of that used in the early Church, when adults were the main recipients of catechesis and the community was the initiator. RCIA is based on the principle that conversion proceeds gradually, in stages, and involves inquiry, catechesis, service, prayer, liturgy, support and celebration. The candidate is assisted by a sponsor whose own faith is deepened by sharing it with the candidate.

The process of RCIA is a suitable model for teaching high school Religion. Consider yourself the sponsor of your class, their mentor, guiding their faith formation and undergoing formation yourself in the process. RCIA, like teaching teens Religion, is a win-win situation and "… has proved especially useful for catechetical renewal" (GDC #3).

Pedagogy: The art of teaching. The method, process and strategy that guides you in your efforts to inform, inspire and effect a spiritual change in youth. From a Greek word meaning "to lead the child."

The pedagogy of adolescent Religious Education has changed over the years. This should be no surprise, for as youth culture changes, so must the method used to "enculturate" the faith. Think of yourself as an undercover agent – Detective Pedagogy – trying to track the peregrinations of youth. Once you study them, it is easier to discover ways to get them to study. See chapters 4 and 5 of this book for details.

General Directory for Catechesis (GDC): In 1965, the Vatican Council called for a directory "for the catechetical instruction of the Christian people in which the fundamental principles of this instruction … will be dealt with." The directory was published in 1971 and revised in 1997. It encouraged national directories as well; in 1978, the US bishops obliged with the *National Directory for Catechesis* (NDC). It was revised in 2005.

High school: A bubble. A make-believe world with social rules that simply disintegrate at graduation. A trance you awake from and wonder, "How could I have done that? How could I have been so insecure, unsure, unaware, afraid and oblivious?" Something you want to survive so you can begin a real life. Faith will help you do this – even before you graduate. (For further information, see your Religion teacher.)

Now a few bonus definitions, courtesy of Dean Sullivan, author of *Papal Bull*.[7]

Sinner: Someone who cannot cast the first stone, but would be more than happy to hurl the next five or six.

Christians: People who follow Jesus, although they disagree on which way He went.

Original sin: What teenagers are always trying to come up with.

Justice: When your kids have kids of their own.

And finally, from my own file:

Spirituality: Something everyone has: a certain madness, desire, eros, longing – a fire in our belly. According to Fr. Ron Rolheiser, author of *The Holy Longing*, spirituality is what you do with this desire, this longing, this fire.[8]

High school Religion teacher: One who builds a fireplace for the wild holy fire of youth.

2

Mission Impossible?

Eight Reasons Why Teaching Religion to Teens Is Difficult

It seems to me more urgent than ever
to foster in the present generation
a spiritual philosophy and imagination
that shall keep the morning dew in their souls
when an age arrives
that know not the muses.

—Helen Keller

And Jesus said,
Blessed are the ... (*pause ... stare*)
Blessed are the ... (*pause, clear throat*)
Hey! Listen up!
We can be on this mountain for a long time.
I'm sleeping on this mountain, so I have all the time in the world.

It's up to you ... if ... you ... want ... to ... go ... home ... on ... time
you better listen up ... (*pause*)
There will be a test on this tomorrow.

Okay! Now focus in.

Blessed are the poor in spirit, for theirs is the kingdom of heaven ...
(*Whisper*) Pssst ... Peter, go tell those girls to stop giggling.

Blessed are the ...

s this the way it was when Jesus taught? I don't think so. So why is it that way in my class?

In this chapter, I want to explore why teaching Religion to teens is a difficult and challenging endeavour. I have eight reasons.

We go through life, said media theorist Marshall McLuhan, looking through the rear-view mirror. We assess what's up ahead according to what we are already familiar with. When I first started teaching Religion, I used the model I knew – the model in my rear-view mirror, the model I used for teaching Social Studies. It was like having three cylinders working in a six-cylinder engine. I puttered along, but it was not a smooth ride. Teaching Religion was unfamiliar territory to me. It is difficult to find your way in new territory when you are looking through the rear-view mirror. The road of Religious Education has some unique features. Knowing what they are will prepare you for the journey. Here's what you will see.

1. We want to do a good job

One reason why teaching Religion is difficult is this: we really want to do a good job. All teachers want to do a good job, but when Religion class fails, it cuts deeper.

When a student finds math boring and doesn't like Math class, we can at least use the excuse that "He doesn't have a natural ability in math." Try using the same reason to explain a bored Religion student. "Her problem is that she is not a spiritual person." Ouch! I don't want to make those judgments. We want our students to value Religion class, to see its importance in their lives, to enjoy it. When teens don't like Religion class, not only is our professional pride hurt, but our conscience starts bothering us as well. Have I turned that kid off God? We can even have nightmares.

I was in this cathedral during Mass,
but the priest wouldn't give me communion.
Instead, he pointed to the congregation.
A horde of teenagers, seeing me,

began screaming and scrambling over pews
and out the rear door.
The door slammed and the cathedral began to collapse all around me.
That's when I woke up.

If this is happening to you, don't worry. You can always pray to St. Dymphna, the Patron Saint of Nervous Disorders.

Your desire to do a good job teaching Religion is a healthy sign. Motivation is key, and the bulk of this book will provide ways to help you do just that – a good job.

2. Religion is not an "important" subject like Math or Science

"Why do I have to take Religion, anyway?" say some teens.

"Don't worry about it," responds another. "It's an easy class, a nice break in the day."

Some students even try to do their Math, Science or English homework during Religion because … "Well, it's due after lunch."

"How can you grade me in Religion class?" asked one of my students, insinuating that there are no "facts" to test him on.

It's a problem. Teens don't take Religion seriously.

Or do they?

Is there a silver lining to this cloud of indifference?

Can the stone rejected by the students become the cornerstone?

Religion class is different. And it is not just the content that is different; the approach, the methodology, and the environment in which it is taught are different, too.

Novice Religion teachers might complain, "Teens don't take this course seriously; they don't view it as a real course, as important as other courses in high school." But that is the point of Religion – to challenge the kids' definition of "important," "real" and "serious." Teaching Religion is difficult *because* it is different. The experienced Religion teacher knows that the "difference" in Religion is where all the blessings, joys and moments of grace come from. That's why they teach Religion: *because it is different.*

Religious Education is about formation, not just information. Religious Education is not just education about Religion. Education about Religion could, and should, be taught in public schools. Knowing what the world religions believe is essential to becoming culturally and historically literate. A class on the world's religions will also go a long way to dispel religious prejudice and bias.

Religious Education, however, is more than education about Religion. All theology has one purpose: to help us find union with God. Most of the time, good theology is just clearing away the rubble that separates us from God – rubble we have usually put there ourselves.

In a letter to a friend on the topic of prayer, C.S. Lewis once wrote, "The command, after all, was 'take, eat,' not 'take, understand.'"[9] Jesus did not say, "Take, think about this, add it to your collection of miscellaneous facts. It's part of the curriculum and you'll be tested on it next week."

What Jesus gave us was spiritual food, nourishment for daily life. Jesus wants to use Religion class to fill the immense hunger and thirst teens have today.

Religious Education is about

- *Curriculum* in the service of *conversion*;
- *Information* in the service of *formation*;
- *Ideation* in the service of *indwelling*.

Religion class is different, but it is different in a way that can make all the difference.

Have you ever witnessed a student cry in Math class? Okay, maybe when they receive the results of their Math test. A third of the students in my Grade 8 class shed a tear or two this year, touched by a lesson on God's felicitous care during hard times (a lesson that required the help of "Psalm 151", an episode from *Touched by an Angel*, the show that makes you – nay, lets you – cry).

Have you ever seen students in a Science class publicly thank one another for imparting Science wisdom in class discussions? Students in my class did that this year, in prayer at the end of the semester and at other times during the year. Many students were both surprised and affirmed when others saw gifts in them that they had overlooked (as teens often do) in themselves. Religion class is different.

Our school has one of the best Math teachers in the province. The kids love her, and she loves them. She is exceedingly smart and just as patient, and she'd probably get voted "most spiritual teacher" in the school. She is surely doing the work of the Lord. I'm just making the point that I'll bet we laugh more, cry more and pray more in our class (except before the provincial Math exam), because she's on a tight schedule to complete the curriculum for the Ministry of Education. Our curriculum comes from the Ministry of Celestial Affairs, and the Minister keeps reminding us that our real curricula are the children of God seated before us.

Students may start by seeing Religion class as "not that important," by which they mean "can't get me a scholarship, into university, or a big paying job." Then, gradually, they will be drawn to this class for its mysterious power to engage something else in them – their hearts. At the end of the year, or maybe years later, they will look back and say, "You know what? That was my favourite class."

The great 20th-century theologian Karl Rahner once explained that Christian faith is more than an idea about Jesus; rather, it is like throwing your arms around him – something you can still do today. Teens throwing their arms around Jesus – now that's a good description of Religious Education.

3. Everything else is more important

A student wrote an essay in Grade 10 entitled *God in My Life*. "My parents have brought me up in a Catholic environment … I have attended Catholic schools … thus God has always been a part of my life …." She describes her religious experience in elementary school.

"When I was younger and I learned about God, I couldn't really grasp it …. When I was young, God was like something I learned and could recite prayers … yet I don't think I really fully knew what I was saying."

Then came adolescence. "When I grew older and entered my teens, I can truthfully say that God was virtually non-existent in my life. While it is true that He was there for me, I never chose to take notice of Him. *Everything else was more important.*" (Italics mine.)

So what was more important for this student? What's "everything else"? Here's a partial list:

- My looks
- Friends
- Boyfriends
- Popularity
- Fashion
- The latest movie
- Sports
- Fitting in
- Becoming "somebody"
- Being cool
- What others think of me

Before we admonish this girl for being a secular humanist, let's consider what's important to adults:

- My looks
- Mortgage
- Job promotion
- Renovating the kitchen
- Cholesterol level
- High blood pressure
- RRSPs
- Mid-life crisis
- The Super Bowl

Let's take another look at the "everything list."

Friendship: Is God not concerned about it? Does God not want to give you enriching friendships through which you can learn to love, to have fun, and even to have conflict and learn to forgive?

Sports: Is God not concerned that you develop your talents, and does God not delight in your abilities and enjoy watching your games?

Fitting in / Popularity: Is God not concerned that you have a sense of personal value and feel okay, even "normal," even though God may have other ideas about how to achieve this, other than through "popularity"?

I believe so.

I also believe it is the task of the Religion teacher to teach Religion in a way that shows this student that – guess what? – God happens to be in the "everything else," too. There is nothing God is *not* in, except sin.

On closer observation, and from the teen's perspective, the parish, Catholic school, or Religion class may be leaving the teen behind, because when the teen heads for "everything else," the Church does not follow. It needs to follow.

It is true that the "everything else" list does suddenly explode onto centre stage in the emerging adolescent mind. Fitting in, being liked by peers, and having the right friends are paramount in a young teen's life. Teens are more interested in who is in their class than what is in the curriculum. Much acting out in class is a lure to catch other students' approval and admiration. The central point for religious educators is not to ignore or sidestep these adolescent concerns, but to make sure they are in the curriculum and in our consciousness as we try to enlighten student experience with faith.

Toward the end of her essay, the insightful student quoted above writes, "I feel that in order to have faith in God, one must become personally involved and develop some kind of relationship with Him. As of yet, I have not been completely successful in this task."

In Jesus' closing discourse in John's Gospel, Jesus says to his best friends, "Have I been with you all this time and you still do not know me?" (John 14:9). I want to say to that Grade 10 student, "Yes, it's a personal relationship, and I'm working on that myself. Let's work together."

She concludes with, "Finally, I hope that my faith in God will continue to grow in positive ways and that my relationship with Him will strengthen. However, I hope to always realize His presence, because I feel my life is more complete now that I have asked Him to share it with me."

Amen to that!

4. Religion is a lightning rod

Have you ever noticed that when teens have a conflict at home, with their friends, with their sense of self, they sometimes take it out in Religion class? Teens may shout out in Religion class, "There is no God!" but in English class will not make a corresponding outburst, such as "Shakespeare was illiterate!"

Religion is personal – very personal. Most atheists I have taught proved to have a serious rupture in parental bonding once the source of their atheism was revealed. Atheists are different from students who say, "I'm not religious," meaning that they don't go to church on Sunday, synagogue on Saturday, or mosque on Friday.

Religion is personal for the same reason politics is personal, but contrary to the oft-repeated warning, it *is* something we need to discuss. In our pluralistic-multicultural-blended-mixed-intact-extended-alternative-nuclear-family-global village, it is likely that anything you say could touch an exposed nerve and evoke an unanticipated reaction. "Religion is a dangerous thing," said Mark Twain, "if you get it wrong." The kind of pastoral wisdom needed in Religion class is not a common requirement in other subjects.

If Religion evokes expressions of emotion, you are doing your job. This is the way it should be. But it is scary, too; teenage emotions can be volatile. Consider it a compliment. Teens don't usually show you this side of themselves unless they trust you.

A devotee of the alleged apparitions of Mary in the town of Medjugorje visited the Catholic school I taught at some years ago. She gave a fervent presentation on the reality of evil, God's grace, and the need for religious discipline. She told the students to shake off their spiritual sloth and to be like the bridesmaids with their oil lamps filled, or risk missing the boat (the fishing boat with Jesus in it). Back in Religion class, I asked my students what they thought of the presentation. One girl immediately raised her hand. With perplexity mixed with indignation, she protested, "That woman made me feel like a sinner!"

Only in Religion class! Can you imagine a comparable statement in Geology class: "That guy made me feel like I had rocks in my head!"

5. Religion, where everyone's a critic

I must say that in teaching Religion and organizing teen retreats for over 20 years, I have had many parents give me kudos in superlative terms that I accept as gracious gifts. Most parents are thankful that someone is assisting them in the arduous task of raising their teen. Although they may not know all that you do or understand how you do it, they are, nonetheless, appreciative.

Teachers need always to understand that they are not only serving young people but are in service to parents as well. God gave parents the task of raising their children spiritually; you, the Religion teacher, are in locus parentis, taking their place in the classroom. Parents have a right and duty to ask questions and to participate in their child's formal religious education. In my experience, however, most parents are quietly appreciative.

Other parents, hypercritical and anxious about what they perceive as their son or daughter's flagging spiritual growth, may blame the school, or Religion class, or you, the Religion teacher. For the most part, they want faith implanted like a pacemaker in their child's soul. Knowing little or nothing of the stages of adolescent spiritual development, they want their child to have a mature adult faith ASAP – A Spiritual

Adolescent Perfectionist. These parents seem to believe that the right amount of Religious facts can provide a suspension bridge over which their child can traverse the canyon of adolescent struggles and doubts. These parents think you fool around too much in class, discuss too much, do too many projects, and want you to give them the "real stuff" because these teens are not getting "the basics."

These parents are filled with fervour, and will be the first to offer a helping hand when and if you need it for field trips, retreats or an upcoming youth conference. Work with these parents as best you can, assuring them that you are there to further their son's or daughter's religious faith – and the faith of everyone else in the class who might not have so thorough a religious upbringing as their child. From your knowledge and experience with youth, you have much to give this parent, if he or she will listen.

This parent might come to see that growth in faith is not as simple as being taught the correct religious facts, essential and important as that is. Tell them that St. Augustine had a different view. He believed that the mind does not direct the soul; the soul directs the mind. What the soul seeks, the mind will discover. We have to do Religion with teens primarily in their souls. Explain that when we begin with soul, we begin with context, not content. The context is the world of the 16-year-old – her emotions, perceptions and the cultural background of her individual life. When we begin with soul, we draw forth before we give forth, and we raise the questions before we give the answers. When we do religion in a teen's soul, we encounter messiness and mysteries, and it will never be as neat and tidy as the curriculum is on paper. Faith has its crises, questions, deaths and rebirths, false starts and dark nights. Work with these parents and their children, because they are already connected to the Great Tradition and are in a good position to understand the daunting task before you.

Still, some critics will discredit what you do, and undermine your efforts by sowing seeds of suspicion in their child's heart or by complaining about your lack of spiritual rigour to the bishop or other Church authorities. If the shoe fits, wear it – then start walking in a new direction. But if this parent has never walked a mile in your moccasins or in the moccasins of their teenager, then the religious education this parent should be mostly concerned about is his or her own.

Be prepared; you will meet other adults in the Church who still believe teens should be seen and not heard: seen stacking chairs in the church hall, but not heard expressing their own adolescent struggles with faith. May all those Church or school board personnel who are reluctant to open the school or church hall for a teen event, or have forbidden the use of candles at a youth retreat because they spill wax on the linoleum floor, or think that "fun" is not spiritual enough to be included in Religious Education programs – may all these adults receive as their punishment in purgatory the task of single-handedly putting 58 teens to sleep on a gym floor at a youth retreat every night of their sentence.

That'll teach them to respect the Religion teacher.

6. It's a competition for prime time

Then Jesus went out of the city
and a multitude gathered around Him
and He taught them.

And when He had finished
the people said:
"He looks good in a beard,
but he needs to style his hair,
and the colour of his robe does not suit him;
but I like those sandals;
I wonder if they come in black.
They should make a movie about him.
I'd like to see that."

And Jesus, hearing the crowd,
went alone into the hill country
to be with His Father.

I'll admit, I sometimes grieve this generation. I grieve how enamoured it is with technology, particularly visual technology. I asked a student what she did during the week of spring break. She told me, "Three movies a day for five days."

I remarked to another young adolescent, "You're pretty smart. You have a good sense of what's going on."

"I watch *Oprah*," she beamed.

Religion is difficult to teach because the competition is fierce. Teens belong to the Religion of Hollywood.

It wasn't always so. When I was a kid, I didn't belong to that religion. When I was a kid growing up in 19 ... uh, some time ago, we did not have PlayStations, Nintendo, Xboxes, 99 channels on cable (yes, we had TV!), DVDs, surround sound (excluding the air raid siren), cellphones, iPhones, iPods, MP3 players, YouTube, instant messaging, Facebook, MySpace, Internet or Internet chat rooms .... *We had friends*, and we went outside to play with them until the streetlights came on.[10]

I use the term "Religion of Hollywood" because I believe people are inherently spiritual and everyone has a religion, whether organized (like the Mormons) or disorganized (like the Catholics). Everyone believes in something. Religion is what gives your life meaning, focus, motivation and energy. Religion is what gets you up in the morning. ("You mean my alarm clock," said one literalist in my class.) Some people pray to the God of orthodox Christianity. Some pray in the name of the father, son and holy marijuana. Drugs are the virtual, mystical experiences of a secular culture, and casinos are a pseudo form of grace – a promise of something for nothing. It does not say in the book of Exodus, "Thou shall not have no gods"; it says, "Thou shall not have strange gods." There are many strange gods around.

If a galactic hitchhiker were to do a doctoral thesis on "The Religion of Earthlings," and landed on the northern part of the Western Hemisphere, he/she/it might conclude that

- Talk-show hosts are the priests of the Earthling religion.
- Movie stars are the saints.

- Oscars are canonization liturgies.
- Motion picture theatres (Silver Cities) are the cathedrals (I know of an elderly man who, momentarily disoriented, entered a movie theatre and genuflected before going to his seat).
- Hollywood, California, is the holy city and Graceland, which attracts over 10,000 people annually, is the USA's most famous pilgrimage site, a shrine to Saint Elvis (who is still alive).
- And finally, sex is the sacrament of the Earthling religion.

In *Saints and Madmen*, author Russell Shorto quotes a psychotherapist as saying, "My interest in religious issues in psychotherapy has been spurred on by a series of patients who have told me spontaneously, without prompting but after considered thought, that their impaired search for love was floundering because they were seeking religion through sexual intimacy."[11] For Catholics, as for Hollywood, sex *is* religious and *is* sacramental, but unlike for Hollywood, sex is religious for Catholics because it images the love of the triune God. We don't seek religion through sex; we express the religion we have already found. The finger pointing at the moon is not the moon (more on this in Chapter 9).

Our galactic religious researcher might conclude the report by saying that, despite some claims about low church attendance, Earth people still go to church on Sunday morning. It's a church called Starbucks.

What effect does a media-saturated culture have on our efforts as religious educators of teens today? An international student from Germany, attending our school for a year, gave a talk at an all-school retreat day. "In Germany," she said, "we don't talk about movies all the time like you do in Canada." Perhaps she was trying to say that in Germany, we have a life, and we talk about *our* life.

It is hard to have a real life when you live in TV land. TV land is a different place than Planet Reality. When teens think that success comes before work, they are living in TV land. When they think they should "inherit" their parents' standard of living without the antecedent years of thrift and hard work, they are living in TV land. When they think that love is a feeling that binds two very special people together in a very special relationship, and is unlike every other feeling because it lasts forever, they are living in TV land. When they think they can have sex with their boyfriend/girlfriend with absolutely no negative consequences to their body, soul and future marriage, they are living in TV land. When they think their image, outward appearance and style will substitute for character, integrity and moral living, they are living in TV land. And when they think that a more expensive pair of basketball runners will substitute for practice, practice and more practice, they are living in TV land. It's not easy teaching Religion to teens today. It often involves trying to convince them to leave their own land and go to a new land. That's what God convinced Abraham and Moses to do.

The big difference between adult and adolescent exposure to visual media is that adults have, for the most part, developed a core identity of values, beliefs and principles they are committed to while adolescents are in the process of formulating such a commitment. When adults watch a movie, they can contrast their own belief systems with that of the film. They can initiate an internal dialogue and a dialogue with others about the film's portrayal of life. Teens are less able to do this, and are less inclined to try. They just "move on." But the movie has left its mark. Underneath the storyline or the content of the film, teens pick up the message the movie can't help but deliver: this is what you should wear, this is what you should do, this is how you should look, this is the attitude you should have, this is what is cool.

Media is powerful – but only, as media educators have been saying for years, to the degree we don't reflect on what we watched or dialogue about the dialogue we heard. In youth culture today, this reflection is not taking place to the extent it should. The sheer volume of films being produced and the inclination to engage in the lazy man's date – "Let's watch a movie" – has resulted in a mass of incoming messages that are unprocessed, undiscerned, unreflected. Socrates' famous statement that "the unexamined life is not worth living" is prophetic, because not to reflect on media results in living a virtual life created by the media, a life that is not real at all. An unreal life is not worth living. Media-saturated teens can't help confusing virtual life with real life. Teens need to fast from media as much as they need to fast from fast food.

The real problem with overexposure to visual technology is not the technology itself – a gift from God and a powerful tool for the betterment of humanity. The problem comes when it becomes a substitute for life, rather than leading us to life. The right film or film clip at an opportune moment in Religion class can really bring a lesson home – or launch one. The goal of adolescence, discovering one's identity ("get a life"), can be facilitated by the religious educator who helps balance the external stimuli of the media with an internal process of personal reflection, dialogue and prayer.

When it comes to the culture of Hollywood, we need to follow Sitting Bull's advice to his fellow Sioux: "Whenever you walk on the white man's road and see something good, pick it up and take it with you. When you see something bad, leave it and walk on by."

The Catholic response to culture is to find where God is revealed and celebrate it, and confront culture where the ways of God are thwarted or opposed.

Anna Scally, the founder of Cornerstone Media, has been doing this for decades. Using contemporary youth music, she leads youth to reflect on the positive messages in many songs ("Psalm 151") and those that are counter to Christian values ("The Dirty Dozen"). Instead of banning the music or condemning the culture, she encourages youth to really listen to what they are hearing, and challenges them to consider whether the values the song promotes are the values they cherish. This is a more fruitful approach to youth culture, as the enthusiastic reception by youth across the continent to Anna's approach reveals. We are to critique the culture but never debunk it, and often teens critique it best.

When she was eleven, Ella Gunderson from Washington State wrote a letter to Nordstrom complaining that the jeans she was interested in purchasing were too tight and showed too much skin, and that many girls would wear more modest clothing if only they could find it. Ella's story was picked up by newspapers throughout the country. Her new-found fame made her uncomfortable, but she was happy the message was getting out. And the message *is* getting out. It is a message not just about jeans, but about being empowered to confront the sex-saturated commercialization rampant in our image-oriented culture. New Religion teachers are often surprised to discover how aware teens are of the cultural forces arrayed against them, and how they will welcome the teacher's assistance in interpreting and resisting these messages.

When you see that teens know more about the lives of the stars (whose pictures adorn their lockers) than they do about the lives of the saints, you can get discouraged and wonder whether this Gulliverian culture is too much for your Lilliputian faith. Shake off the discouragement, because you are a living, breathing, soul-spirited, embodied witness to the "Spirit of the truth … the world neither sees nor knows" (John 14:17). The images on the screen, if you look closely, are just a bunch of pixels in a liquid crystal display with increased lines of resolution. Nothing, really, to be intimidated by.

7. Students think it is all relative in Religion

Besides Saint Hollywood, another cultural phenomenon confronts the Religion teacher. It's been around for some time. In philosophy, it's called relativism, and is sometimes referred to as pluralism. You will encounter it in teens as an unconscious attitudinal perception articulated in this way: there is no objective truth; truth is always subjective. What you think is true is true for you; what others think is true is true for them. "The truth" does not exist. (The classic response is this: "Is what you just said about the non-existence of objective truth true?")

In class discussions, relativism looks like this: "If they believe it is okay for them, then it is okay. No one should be forced, but if that is what they want to do, they should be allowed to do it." Following this line of thought, one student concluded, "Slavery is wrong, but if a person wants to be a slave, that's okay."

And, if it doesn't come out directly, you will notice in class discussions the undergirding challenge of relativism: *Who are you to tell me what to think and do*? This query reveals that, when the search for truth is stifled, willpower (what I want) and force (who is gonna make me?) replace the claims of truth alone.

And the truth, when experienced, makes claims. The experience of truth is always one of being captured by truth, not of snaring your own. The truth does not belong to me; I belong to the truth. We don't determine what is true; we discover what is true. We don't tell things what they are; we ask them. Distinguished religious educator Fr. William O'Malley, SJ, uses this example. A man is seen swaying and stumbling outside a bar. What's the reality? He's drunk? No, he's diabetic and having a reaction. How do you discover this? You don't tell him; you ask him.

You don't tell marriage what it is; you ask it. You don't tell the fetus what it is; you ask it. You don't tell a poem what it means; you ask it. A sincere search for the truth of the reality before us entails a humble waiting for the reality to speak. Relativism involves a rude interruption by our own answer, because we assume reality is mute. St. Thomas Aquinas said truth is conformity of the mind to the real. Young people are swimming in a sea of relativism that demands that reality conform to their mind. The Religion teacher can show them another way by introducing them to the search for truth. Chesterton said that having an open mind is like having an open mouth. You should close it when you have something solid in it.

In my experience, tackling relativism with youth is a tough go. In one respect, the struggle is understandable. Young people equate a belief in objective truth with intolerance and diminishing human rights. Unfortunately, yet undeniably, the Church's historical record yields many examples of intolerance and human rights abuse: the Inquisition, the excess of the Crusades, the massacres in "religious wars," "Christian" anti-Semitism, and the list goes on. Pope John Paul II officially apologized 94 times for the sins of the Church – Luigi Acccatoli wrote an entire book, entitled *When a Pope Asks Forgiveness*, on the subject.[12] In light of these historical blemishes, many people believe that when religion comes in, tolerance and respect go out. The Religion teacher should be a living testimony that this is not so.

I have stood on my desk in class in an effort to explain the errors of relativism. Using the scientific law as an analogy for the moral law, I declare to my students, "Imagine this is a 20-storey building. I'm standing on the edge of the roof. What will happen when I step out?"

"You will fall and die," they say.

"Do it!" says the class clown.

"I won't die if I step out," I say. "I don't believe in the law of gravity. If you believe it, then it is true for you; but I don't and therefore it has no effect on me." They strain to make the comparison.

Moral relativism has robbed teens of a defence when faced with serious moral dilemmas. Young people facing moral decisions ("Should I or should I not?") are hardly helped by the current creed, which says whatever you are comfortable with doing is the thing to do; or the only thing that matters is what you really intend, or whether those involved are mutually consenting. When they have to make a moral decision – whether to pop ecstasy; smoke dope; ridicule and torment someone from a different race, religion or sexual orientation than them; spread slander; shoplift; have sex; lie to their parents, teachers, coach, boss, or girlfriend; throw a party when their parents are out of town; or despoil the environment – moral relativism tells them that there are no objective rights or wrongs, no objective truth. In the swirling storm of hormones, moral confusion, the desire to fit in and the example of media models, youth need a stake in the ground to hold on to. They need to hear about truth.

And in this effort, God has given us a great mentor in Pope Benedict XVI, who has often articulated a critique of relativism, which he calls the gravest problem of our time.

In this media-saturated culture, young people are bombarded with a plethora of points of view. It is no wonder they experience a semi-paralysis of the mind, stuck in a malaise of slogans, sound bites and movie quotes. Truth, for this generation, must be something more than an intellectual witticism, or it will not move them out of the fog of relativism. Teens today, as in past generations, are still looking for truth. Truth, for teens today, comes down to this – it must be:

- Relational – Bonding them to a mentor whose life is living truth
- Reasonable – Answers that make sense to the questions they ask
- Experiential – Moves them in a deep and heartfelt way.

This search for truth has created in youth today an interest in Religious Education. They sense, somehow, that what we are offering in Religion class is what they are looking for.

Relativism is on the wane, because it is boring. Youth today have a heightened spiritual longing, and the Religion teacher is poised to offer them an experience of the One who said, "I [relational] am the Truth [reasonable], and the Truth will set you free [experiential]." (John 8:32)

8. Swoosh – where's my brain?

Finally, there is one more reason why teaching teens Religion is so difficult. Technically speaking, teenagers are crazy.

This old adage attributed to the Jesuits – "Give me a child until he is seven and the world can have him thereafter" – needs updating. According to neurologists, while we used to think the brain was fully developed by age seven (the so-called age of reason), we have now discovered that only 95 per cent of the brain is developed at the onset of adolescence. The remaining 5 per cent often does not fully develop until the latter part of high school or after. Ninety-five per cent developed sounds pretty good, until we find out that the remaining 5 per cent is the part that interprets experiences, projects an action into the future, and imagines what consequences will flow from it. This is the part of the brain that makes complex decisions and enhances impulse control – in short, the most advanced part of the brain, the part parents (and Religion teachers) want so badly to be developed in their kids. Deficiency in this part of the brain, the pre-frontal cortex, makes the teenager comparable to the toddler, according to Michael J. Bradley, author of *Yes, Your Teen is Crazy.*

> Both that toddler and adolescent brain are at times unstable, dysfunctional, and completely unpredictable. They both have just developed a bunch of brain circuits that may fire off unexpectedly. Also, they both have neurologically deficient controls to moderate these impulses and to understand the likely outcome of their actions. In the science of mental health, we have a word for that. We call it crazy.[13]

In the great paradox of life, we have to work hard to help our kids, but we have to wait it out, too. We have to be vigilant and creative in finding ways to spiritually engage them, while exercising the patience of Job as we let the adolescent brain development phase run its course. The old bumper sticker was true (neurologically as well as theologically): "Be patient; God isn't finished with me yet."

I can see some teen getting hold of this book and using this information at home. "Hey, Mom, don't blame me; my pre-frontal cortex is broken." Teens are always in need of new and more creative excuses.

What does this information mean for Religion teachers? It means teens are changing rapidly as you read this. It means what you taught them last year might be lost in the rewiring taking place this year. It means when school starts in September, they are not only anxious about seeing you, they are anxious about seeing each other. They know they are changing daily; two months in the summer can shift a multitude of paradigms. They are wondering what their classmates have morphed into. It's scary enough in an earthquake zone to feel the ground move beneath your feet; imagine what it's like to feel your ground move within you.

On the first day of my classes, I have a plastic spider fall from the ceiling onto a student's head, a battery-operated rat comes alive when someone sits down at their desk, and a bogus lighter squirts water into the face of the student lighting a candle for opening class "prayer." If teens are going to be crazy, I want them to know they have competition.

Being crazier than them takes the wind out of their sails. It works, but I'm not advocating it in this book. It's my own insane and idiosyncratic way. You find yours.

I'll let Dr. Bradley have the last word on this subject.

The good part is that these behaviors are not character flaws or signs of an evil nature. In adolescent children, the maddening behavior is just the result of mixed-up wiring that will straighten out in time if, if, and only if, we adults respond not with raging, hurtful punishments, but with carefully crafted responses intended to calmly but firmly teach brain-challenged children to become functional adults.[14]

Mission (im)possible

Pope John XXIII was sinking into despondency one evening, considering all the problems in the Church. He caught himself falling and said to God, "Wait a minute, this isn't my church, it's your church. You have to take care of it ... good night!"

This is why our Impossible Mission is possible – it's not ours alone. We have all heard of Murphy's Law: If something can go wrong, it will. Religion teachers are protected by O'Malley's Law: Things are going much better than you think. That's because God is using you to "write straight with crooked lines." The student who seemed incurably bored and oblivious will tell you how much they learned and enjoyed your class. With God working within us and through us, the eight reasons why teaching Religion is difficult become the eight reasons why teaching Religion is a super-human endeavour ("super" is the God part). You may already know this, but I bet your colleagues don't. So when they say to you, "Oh, you've got it easy teaching Religion," just let them read this chapter. They'll think twice about stealing your coffee cup in the staff room.

Now that you see the obstacles in your way, the next three chapters are an attempt to help you thrive, not just survive, in the mission of adolescent Religious Education.

3

Mapping the Mission

Faith Development Theory

When the student is ready,
the teacher will appear.

—Chinese Proverb

As far as I know, William Glasser, author of *The Quality School*, has never written anything specifically on teaching Religion. His recipe for quality education, however, is very much applicable and entirely amenable to Religious Education.

Glasser's passion is to help schools become, in the promotional words of my own diocese, places "where students love to learn and learn to love." If Religion class is to be a favourite class for youth, they need to include it in what Glasser calls their "quality world." Simply put, the "quality world" is that part of a student's brain where all the things they like are stored.

Every parent has experienced the immediate reaction of their teenager when a certain thing, event, place or person is mentioned.

"Do you want to play soccer this season?" a parent asks.

"No!"

"Why not?"

"I don't like soccer!"

"Since when do you not like soccer?"

"I don't know."

"Do you want to visit Grandma this weekend?"

"Sounds good!"

"Are you going to the school dance, church youth group, Mass, summer camp? Would you like to work at your uncle's shop, play golf with your cousin, visit the museum, enroll in theatre class, take guitar lessons, go on the youth retreat …?"

When teens are asked these questions, what will always register first is an emotion, pleasant or painful. Parents will try to get reasons for why a teen feels a certain way, but will often encounter resistance with the classic teen response: "I don't know!" For the most part, this is true. There may be multiple reasons why they do or do not want to do something, and often they do not know what these reasons actually are. What they do know is *how they feel*. According to Glasser, the reason you like something is because over time you have consistently experienced this event or activity meeting your basic human needs. When this happens, a student moves this event into a part of their memory called "my quality world." The thought of that activity automatically evokes a pleasant emotional response.

According to Glasser, a young person's needs include

- *Belonging* – feeling connected and accepted in community
- *Empowerment* – being significant and needed
- *Fun* – joy, laughter, humour
- *Love* – positive affirmation and respect
- *Freedom* – respect for expression of thoughts and ideas.

Many Religion teachers get caught up with such goals as completing the curriculum, keeping up with the other Religion teacher, satisfying the expectations of the department head, or making sure the students are prepared for the upcoming Religion test. What they need to put at the forefront of all these concerns is making sure that Religion class is in the students' quality world.

This will happen only if the students' needs are being met in Religion class. What good is any other goal if the students do not actually *like* Religion class?

It might be argued that teens can still learn in a class they dislike. This is true in university, and it may be true in other subjects in high school, but it is not true in the high school Religion class. Or, put another way, students learn to dislike Religion in a Religion class they dislike.

Glasser has a striking way of communicating this concept to adults. When speaking to an adult audience, he calls a number of high school students to the stage and asks them this question: "Where in high school do you feel important?"

> This question always seems to the students to come from outer space; they look at me as if I had asked something ridiculous. Even for the very good students, who are the group usually selected to be interviewed, feeling important (powerful) in school is an experience that few seem to think relates to them.

> However, when I persist, most students tell me that they feel important in their extracurricular activities: sports, music and drama are most frequently mentioned …When asked why this is so, they say that in the extracurricular situation, where they *work together* as a group or on a team, they work harder and accomplish more because they *help each other* and have more *fun*. They also emphasize that they are both *more comfortable* and *less bored* in these situations because it is accepted that they *socialize* while they work ….[15] (italics mine)

Look at the words that stand out in the students' "quality world" and how they relate to the students' need for belonging, empowerment, fun, love and freedom. Teens feel important when they feel needed. They see more meaning in the class when they discover that the class is more meaningful because they are in it. When they feel the freedom to explore who they are and who others are, they not only find it fun but their laughter reflects a deep sense of belonging, joy and a sense of being loved. Then, not only will Religion class be in their "quality world," but you, the teacher, will also be.

How do students describe a "good teacher"? Glasser writes:

Students tell me that a good teacher is deeply interested in the students and in the material being taught. They also say that such a teacher frequently conducts class discussions and does not lecture very much. Almost all of them say that a good teacher relates to them on their level; the teacher does not place herself above them, and they are comfortable talking to her …. Students also tell me that they appreciate teachers who make an effort to be entertaining.[16]

Glasser may not know it, but what he advocates is the winning formula for teaching teens Religion. My own list, compiled from student evaluations, both oral and written, confirms Glasser's observations. This is what students say about why they like Religion class, why it is part of their quality world:

- I learned so much about myself in Religion class.
- You always believed in me, you gave me hope.
- Your classes were fun.
- You made me feel like a person.
- I loved the discussions.
- You were always welcoming.
- Your classes were different from other classes.
- You make Religion make sense.

And the mother of all compliments, the ultimate teacher gratification:

- Thank you for putting up with us.

This should be our mission statement: *Adulescentias toleramus* (We put up with teens).

The unique opportunity we have in Religion class to attend to the deeper needs of teens is appreciated far more than we realize. Sometimes we receive confirmation that we are on the right track – as in the following letter from a parent:

Dear Mr. Brock,

We thought you would like to know how much Tracy enjoyed her Religion class. She's usually quiet at the supper table except for the days she had your class. She always wanted to discuss that day's lesson with us. We asked her why she enjoyed the class so much and she said it was the only class that she could discuss her thoughts, opinions, concerns, etc. Thanks so much for all your hard work, care and concern. Have an awesome summer.

Mr. and Mrs. R.

Some teachers may balk at the above, protesting that life is not a bowl of cherries and it takes hard work and serious effort to grasp the theological concepts in Religion class that will protect a student's faith life in the years to come. I believe in quality work, hard work, work that students take pride in. I believe, however, that quality work is best achieved in a Religion class that is at the core of a student's quality world. Students work harder and value the work they do when Religion is a class they value.

In all the years I have taught Religion, the pedagogical tools that have helped me the most in making Religion a favourite class (meeting students' needs) are what religious educators call Faith Development Theory and Learning Process Theory. In this chapter, I will explain the four stages of faith development. In chapters 4 and 5, I will explain the learning process and what it looks like in your day-to-day lesson plan. Simply put, an understanding of faith development and the learning process helps teachers develop a teaching strategy that takes its cue from the way teens learn and is directed at meeting their needs. This way, Religion class will be in a student's quality world – a favourite class.

The four stages of faith development

Mark Twain said, "When I was thirteen I couldn't believe how ignorant my father was. When I turned 20 I was amazed to see how much he had learned in seven years." When the student is ready, teachers and fathers and mothers appear. The proactive teacher knows what the student is ready for, and then appears. One helpful tool for discerning the faith readiness of adolescents is faith development theory.

The researcher most associated with stages-of-faith theory is James Fowler, but I have found the four stages described by John Westerhoff helpful for situating teen catechesis in a useful context. Westerhoff uses the rings of a tree as a metaphor for faith development. A tree acquires one ring at a time in a slow and gradual process. The addition of each ring of a tree does not eliminate the previous rings.

Each stage is roughly associated with the following age group:

- Pre-born, newborn and primary school.......................................
  Experienced Faith
  (Childhood nurturing)

- Elementary school..
  Affiliative Faith
  (The need to belong)

- Adolescence: teen and young adult ....
  Searching Faith
  (The search for meaning)

- Adulthood...
  Owned Faith
  (My own faith story)[17]

Experienced Faith: Stage 1

… a universal image of trust in painting and sculpture is a child nursing at its mother's breast. Not only will the child decide that it can trust the world, but it will also decide that it can trust itself, because it sees that its needs (and therefore its being) bring a good response. It's as if the child says, "Something good happens when I express my needs. My needs must be good. I must be good."[18]

We don't think of ourselves teaching faith to newborns, but in fact we are involved in Religious Education even before that. Religious Education begins in the womb. Albert Einstein's celebrated profession of faith, "The universe is friendly," is "picked up" by the unborn child in the voices and sounds she hears, and in myriad ways we may never fully understand. We learn that the "universe is friendly" in the smiling, adoring eyes of our parents, in their secure embrace and in the nurturing we receive. We learn that life is good, I'm good, God is good – or we learn otherwise. The father you see in the mall throwing his little child in the air and catching her, to the child's great delight: that is "experienced faith."

In his book *Scattered Minds*, Dr. Gabor Maté includes a section about his own early childhood. Born in Budapest, Hungary, in 1944, during the time of the Nazi occupation, Gabi was the first child of Jewish parents. He writes:

> Two days after the German occupation, my mother called the pediatrician. "Would you come to see Gabi?" she requested. "He has been crying almost without stop since yesterday morning."

> "I'll come, of course," the doctor replied, "but I should tell you: all my Jewish babies are crying."

> Now, what did Jewish infants know of Nazis, World War II, racism, genocide? What they knew – or rather, absorbed – was their parent's anxiety. They drank it in with their mother's milk, heard it in their father's voices, felt it in the tense arms and bodies that held them close. They inhaled fear, ingested sorrow. Yet were they not loved? No less than children anywhere. If in the photograph the love may be seen in my mother's face, her fear and worry are reflected in mine.[19]

Years later, as an accomplished physician and author, Dr. Maté was looking at the diagnosis for Attention Deficit Disorder when he suddenly realized – that's me! His book *Scattered Minds* is subtitled *A New Look at the Origin and Healing of Attention Deficit Disorder.* What makes it especially engaging, besides the obvious scholarship, is that it is written by an "insider." In technical language, Dr. Maté reveals how the wiring of the brain is influenced by the emotional environment in which the child is conceived.

Experienced Faith reminds us that the spiritual journey began long before our students entered our classroom, whether they consider themselves "religious" or not. A striking illustration of the influence of child rearing on spiritual development is cited by Sheila Fabricant, co-author with Dennis and Matthew Linn of *Healing the Eight Stages of Life*. In the book, Sheila tells the story of how, as a theology student in Europe, she was reading a number of books by East European theologians, all born in the early 1900s. In each of the books, she sensed an image of God as remote and unapproachable. Human life seemed to be a long search to find God. The theologians seemed to be saying that only rarely would we actually feel God near us. Mostly we were to just walk in darkness and summon the will to believe that God is out there – somewhere, hearing our cry.

This approach disturbed Sheila, because it was not her experience. She had always experienced God as warm and approachable, rather like her grandfather. Searching for an answer, she eventually asked a woman friend who was married to a German scripture scholar. The friend told Sheila that, at the time these theologians were raised in that part of Europe, parents did not pick up or hold their babies when they cried. The parents believed this was the best way to develop self-discipline in their children. As Sheila reflected on this point she thought, "I wonder if these theologians who are crying out to a distant God are really crying out to a mother and father who never picked them up or held them."[20] Their faith life patterned their earliest experience of being parented. Particularly in early childhood, our sense of God is synonymous with the sense we have of our parents. I say "sense" because it cannot yet be articulated or formulated; it is just "experienced faith." The point is this: in order for people to grow in the love of God, they must have a God-like experience upon which their love of God grows. The natural place for this to happen is in the family.

In practical terms, this means that the student in your class who has a close bond with his or her parents will be more receptive to Religious Education. (More on this in Chapter 7.) The student who has a broken or damaged bond may have some issues with religion. It may be protested that "faith is a gift of God, and God cannot be curtailed." True, the grace of faith is a free gift, but grace acts on a person according to that person's nature. A damaged parental bond must eventually be grieved, and grieving is not a process many people readily enter. Most adolescents are not anywhere near the point of honestly assessing the pain a strained parental bond has caused. Instead, and unfortunately, their pain often comes out as projection in the form of anger and rejection of a particular peer (someone to pick on and bully), or a rejection of authority (including God and the "business of God" – Religion class). In time, when the adolescent identity is stronger, the real pain can be faced, the grieving begun and the healing commenced. A Religion teacher who understands this process will not be so ready to dismiss a student as the agnostic nuisance in the class.

Affiliative Faith: Stage 2

> To force a strong spirituality on children before they are ready is unnatural and can kill a child's interest in religion and even in God .... So many of my friends in their excessive zeal to arouse their children's spiritual lives saturated them with religious activities. When the children became adolescents, they couldn't stand religion and went to church only after horrendous fights.[21]

I grew up in the north Bronx. One Saturday in mid-March when I was of mid-elementary school age, I heard the sound of bagpipes close to the schoolyard where I was playing. Exploring, I soon discovered a parade forming on Riverdale Avenue. It must have been on or near St. Patrick's Day. Although the parade was just a miniature version of the one in downtown Manhattan, it was big to me. I joined the parade and marched to the drone of bagpipes, feeling a sense of connection to something bigger than my family – a sense of being Irish (the Patrick part), and Catholic (the Saint part). I was Irish-Catholic, and where the Irish left off and the Catholic started, or the Catholic ended and the Irish began, I could never tell you. It didn't matter – *I belonged.*

Why does this event stand out in my memory? Why are the emotions experienced that day so easily recalled? No friend accompanied me in that parade; my brothers and sisters were not present. I marched alone, but not lonely – I felt affiliated.

Affiliative Faith is about belonging, more than believing. It is about being socialized into a religious group and community. We're Catholic, Pentecostal, Hindu, Jewish, Sikh, Presbyterian, Anglican, Mormon, Muslim. If asked why you are a Catholic, you might respond, because we go to St. Mary's Church. We are Catholic because we do Catholic things. We go to church on Sunday, say grace before meals, have a crucifix on our wall, we even had Father Flynn over for dinner – that's why we're Catholic.

After every youth retreat, the students fill out an evaluation form. When they evaluate the part of the retreat when we celebrate Reconciliation and Eucharist, I sometimes hear a clear Affiliative Faith response: "We have to have Mass, because we are a Catholic school." This is true, but not the deeper truth. We don't have Mass because we are Catholic; we are Catholic because we have Mass. This would make little sense to someone in the Affiliative Faith stage.

Affiliation is bonding with the tribe, the group, the community and the great tradition and story of our Church. Routine (ritual) is important. "We always do it that way. We say Ah-men not Ay-men."

Students who have the Affiliative Faith ring in their tree connect more easily with what you are doing in Religion class. Teens who don't have Affiliative Faith sometimes let you know that "I'm not religious." I sometimes say, "Do you believe in Love?"

"Yes!"

"Well, then, you are religious because the Bible says God *is* Love."

What they really mean when they say "I'm not religious" is "I'm not marching in the same parade as you."

On the positive side, Affiliative Faith is natural; faith always inculturates itself for a people. The body of faith dresses itself in the songs, traditions, rituals and expressions of the ethnic community. Attend a Portuguese, Polish, Filipino or Italian religious festival, and you will see affiliation celebrated.

On the negative side, Affiliative Faith can become empty if it is just an auxiliary attribute of my ethnic group (cultural Catholics). It can even become hypocritical if the next ring in the tree of faith is not eventually formed. In the movie *The Godfather*, the director intersperses scenes from an Italian baptism with the criminal activities of the mafia. One is left wondering, what kind of faith is this?

Affiliative Faith also entails a "first naïveté," a concept developed by theologian Paul Ricoeur (the "second naïveté" occurrs in Stage 4). Belief in the faith story, handed on by significant adults, is unhampered by doubt and dissension. The questions of Affiliative Faith are attempts to put the pieces of the faith story puzzle together, not questions about the relevance or reliability of the puzzle itself. Knowing the story – what happens next and how it all fits together – is the primary need in Affiliative Faith. Children love stories.

Respecting the nature and limitations of each faith stage is critical. Attempting to accelerate a child's religious education can derail the process. Teaching Religion in a manner that exceeds a student's ability to engage hampers their natural religious imagination and sense of wonder. You can't force-feed Religion, just as you can't induce a plant to grow by pulling on its stem. You will uproot the person's genuine and natural interest in things spiritual. Running, playing, feeling the wind on your face, smelling the grass beneath your feet and having a sense of timelessness – this is spiritual. Childhood is spiritual immersion. Deprived of this immersion, we sever or strain the roots that will nourish our faith life in the years to come. Religion teachers can strain this faith development when, instead of working with the nature of the child, they try to advance them by exposure to "higher" expressions of religious life. As Conrad Baars has written,

> Since the principle of spoiling is not limited to material objects, but extends also to the spiritual realm, excessive and premature exposure to things religious and spiritual will interfere with the development of his sense of wonder and faith.[22]

The following story by Danny Dutton, a grade 3 student in Chula Vista, California, was sent to me through cyberspace. It is a fun and informative example of Affiliative Faith. Notice how Danny is putting the pieces of his faith story together. He wrote it for the homework question "Explain God."

Explanation of God

One of God's main jobs is making people. He makes them to replace the ones that die, so there will be enough people to take care of things on earth. He doesn't make grownups, just babies. I think because they are smaller and easier to make. That way he doesn't have to take up his valuable time teaching them to talk and walk. He can just leave that to mothers and fathers.

God's second most important job is listening to prayers. An awful lot of this goes on, since some people, like preachers and things, pray at times besides bedtime. God doesn't have time to listen to the radio or TV. Because he hears everything, there must be a terrible lot of noise in his ears, unless he has thought of a way to turn it off.

God sees everything and hears everything and is everywhere which keeps him pretty busy. So you shouldn't go wasting his time by going over your mom and dad's head asking for something they said you couldn't have.

Atheists are people who don't believe in God. I don't think there are any in Chula Vista. At least there aren't any who come to our church.

Jesus is God's son. He used to do all the hard work, like walking on water and performing miracles and trying to teach the people who didn't want to learn about God. They finally got tired of him preaching to them and they crucified him, but he was good and kind, like his father, and he told his father that they didn't know what they were doing and to forgive them and God said, OK.

His dad (God) appreciated everything that he had done and all his hard work on Earth so he told him he didn't have to go out on the road anymore. He could stay up in Heaven, so he did.

You should always go to Church on Sunday because it makes God happy, and if there's anybody you want to make happy, it's God! Don't skip Church to do something you think will be more fun like going to the beach. This is wrong and besides the sun doesn't come out at the beach until noon anyway.

If you don't believe in God, besides being an atheist, you will be very lonely, because your parents can't go everywhere with you, like to camp, but God can. It is good to know He's around you when you're scared, in the dark or when you can't swim and you get thrown into real deep water by big kids.

But you shouldn't just always think of what God can do for you. I figure God put me here and he can take me back anytime he pleases.

And … that's why I believe in God.[23]

Searching Faith: Stage 3

There are two urgent needs for the young person … The first is someone who understands and accepts him with all of his vacillation and ambivalence … The second need is for a model … he needs very badly to see someone who has passed through this wilderness, who has passed out of the darkness into the light … He needs a model of faith.[24]

A very loving and pious couple spoke with me during parent–teacher interviews. Their daughter, a very articulate and spiritually sensitive student, was in my Religion class. The parents said, "We don't know what is happening; we used to always read her parts of the Bible when she went to bed. Now she doesn't want us to do this. We don't know what is happening to her faith."

The Many Faith Faces of the Searching Teenager: Searching Faith – Choosing for Oneself

I assured them that her faith was not diminishing, just changing. Parents and teachers who have nurtured an Experienced and Affiliative Faith must now learn a new way to nurture. There is a saying that "God has no grandchildren." Our parents chose our faith for us when we were young; now we must choose it for ourselves. We must choose to be daughters and sons of God in our own right. The birth of Owned Faith (the fourth stage) begins with the labour pains of Searching Faith (the third stage). In order to choose something that has already been given, you must place it at a psychic distance. From there you can begin to really see it, question it and eventually choose it for yourself. Searching Faith is not rejecting faith or rebelling against faith (though sometimes it will look like this). Searching Faith coincides with the adolescent ability to think in ideals, to think abstractly, to imagine, for instance, what "perfect" is – as in "perfect love." Hence, Searching Faith can be hypercritical of Church, which, alas, is not perfect. The old invitation is still valid. For those who refuse to join the Church because there are too many hypocrites in it, come and join anyway. We always have room for one more.

Searching Faith – Deconstruction Before Reconstruction

During the Affiliative Faith stage, children experience an increased sense of well-being and belonging as they put together the puzzle pieces of their life in the family and the Church. In the Affiliative stage, faith and family are the same, joined at the hip. The angst of the teenager, in Searching Faith, is the experience of having to take everything apart – faith and family – and then put it back together, in a new way. Taking things apart (deconstruction) is painful to youth. It's like a series of mini-deaths – naïveté dies, unquestioned obedience dies, unself-consciousness dies. Ask your young adolescents, "Be honest: how many of you sometimes want to go back to childhood?" They will all raise their hand. They miss it. This is where the Religion teacher becomes a grief counsellor. The death of unself-consciousness allows self-consciousness to emerge, with its attending insecurity. The death of naïveté and unquestioned docility allows a unique and personally confirmed faith and identity to emerge (construction). Now the Religion teacher becomes a midwife. Through it all, teenagers are searching for something that can make sense of all these changes – wisdom – and something that can keep them going – hope. For the teen, that "something" they are looking for is a "someone" – a model of faith, a mentor, a believer on the road ahead, a Religion teacher: you.

Searching Faith – A Necessary Stage

Those who study the stages (passages) of life note that we skip passages at our peril. Searching Faith is a necessary life process. The older adult who, by all appearances, has been a pillar of the Church and then suddenly abandons the faith completely is often testimony to a skipped stage. "Happily married" mother of three, a fixture at the church on Sunday, leaves a note for her stunned (soon to be ex-) husband revealing her six-month affair with a younger man. She's breaking out and rejecting what has been, up to now, a smooth, unruffled, model life. What should have occurred in adolescence went underground, only to emerge in later life in an extreme and malevolent form. Religion is not a way to escape life; religion is a way to enter into life more fully and to experience it abundantly, even the confusing, questioning, painful parts – the adolescent searching part.

A spiritual principle is at work here: nothing changes until it becomes what it is. Some adults see adolescence as a phase they would like to wish away. Yet it is spiritually unhealthy to bypass any stage of life. It has a way of returning to haunt you. All "hauntings" have to do with unfinished business. We need, in Stage 3, to help teenagers enter into the business of adolescence. If we don't, there is the possibility that, like the woman above, they will take their adolescence out on their spouse and children years later.

Adolescents need to be adolescents. It is not a disease to eradicate or a cold to wait out. Adolescence is not a phase to get through; it is a life stage to get into. It is not only a problem to be solved, it is a treasure to be unlocked. Helping adolescents to be what they are is the only sure step in helping them become what they will one day be.

High school Religion teachers should not just like teenagers, but delight in them. Their idealism, with all its naïveté, can be a balm for your spirit. Their openness can rub off a few layers of your cynicism. Their humour can subvert your tendency to take things too seriously as you get older. And, most delightful of all, their gratitude for what you teach them can warm your wintry soul. In this dollar-focused, image-obsessed, frenetic culture, the summer breeze of adolescence can be a holy wind.

Searching Faith – Positive Questioning/Negative Questioning

Searching Faith entails questioning your faith. Questioning one's faith can be either a positive or negative endeavour. Positive questioning involves a sincere attempt to understand faith with the newly acquired cognitive abilities of adolescence. The dramatic growth and changes of adolescence are brought, as it were, to the altar of faith. Coming to God without our newly conceived questions is not coming to God as we are. Not questioning, in this sense, would entail a lack of faith. Teenagers need to chew on faith before they swallow it, because if they swallow it whole, not only will they be wondering what it is they ate, they will have a feeling of being force-fed. Questioning faith is the only way teens can make faith come alive within them. Their questions are much more than intellectual arguments, as Eva Frances Santos, age 15, explains: "When people say not to question God 'cause it's wrong, they're wrong. It never hurts to question something we don't know. All you are doing is wanting to know God in your heart."[25] Questioning faith is the way teens nourish their faith, and it is the job of the Religion teacher to make sure the faith of our youth does not die of starvation or malnutrition.

If a student is an honest doubter, then faith cannot permeate his or her heart until the doubts are given expression. The wise teacher facilitates that expression. When students articulate their dilemma as best they can, they are, in this very process, preparing themselves for the gift of faith. Being authentically oneself is the necessary precondition for the grace that awakens faith. St. Augustine said, "You would not be searching for God if you had not already found God."

When students say something in class that they know goes against the teaching of the Church, all their sensors are activated to detect one thing – your reaction. Depending on your reaction, these students will either put up more defences to the claims of faith, or begin dismantling the defences already in place. If we are going to influence teenagers with our Catholic faith, we must love them into it, not argue them into it. As Bishop Fulton Sheen once said, "Win an argument, lose a soul." At the core of faith development is a radical acceptance of the person with all his or her doubts, questions and protests. People must come before faith as they are, or they can't come to faith at all. The Religion teacher must be, first and foremost, a minister of hospitality – come, just as you are.

Negative questioning, on the other hand, is questioning to prove the faith wrong. Students whose behaviour contravenes Church teaching are caught in a dilemma. They either question their behaviour in the light of faith, or they question the faith in the light of their behaviour. A student with a guilty conscience may engage in negative questioning.

It is sometimes difficult to know when a student is involved in positive questioning or negative questioning. The move from elementary school (Affiliative Faith) to high school (Searching Faith) is also the move from a mostly supportive playground community to the jungle of teenage cliques, popularity wars and stinging put-downs. A student's religious affiliation in elementary school garnered support, recognition and acceptance by others; now, in high school, it may prove a social liability. The siren sound of peer acceptance is very tempting, and some teenagers may begin to question their faith as a way of ditching it. Allegiance is now given to a new religion, a religion called Popularity. As the familiar religious maxim goes, if God seems far away, guess who moved?

Questioning is also a teen's way of saying, "Do you believe this, Mr. Brock?" They are testing you because it is their way of learning from you. We discover what teens learn by testing them. Teens discover what we believe by testing us. Their tests are harder.

This is where the adult critic mentioned earlier can raise a false alarm. The faith that has been so carefully cultivated and received with docility is now, seemingly, under attack. What are they doing in that Religion class? What we should be doing! Giving youth a place to search and question – a place to be real. Even saints went through it. Parts of St. Therese's *Story of a Soul* were edited by her superiors – probably some of the dramatic Searching Faith parts. The world-revered Mother Teresa kept her faith alive, as a recent book and newspaper headlines attest, by expressing to her spiritual counsellor her painful sense of the distance of the God she longed for. It is necessary to express the struggles we have with faith in order to "keep the faith."

Searching Faith – Evangechesis

Students in the Searching Faith stage appreciate teachers who guide them in the search. Teachers do this best not by showing students what they are looking for, but by helping them find it for themselves. The Latin word *educere,* the root of "education," means to *draw forth,* not *put into* – as in "put this religious knowledge into their heads." Teachers who do not understand the difference, though they have the best intentions, will be perceived by the students as close-minded. What teens really mean by this is "you did not validate and value my adolescent need to search myself." It feels like this: they show up for an Easter egg hunt only to find you handing the eggs to them as they arrive at the door. They feel slighted, pre-empted. "Didn't you believe that I could find the eggs? Thanks for taking the joy out of searching (the joy out of Religion class)."

The bewildered teacher will wonder, "Why do they not accept what I have to say?" The resentful teenager will silently fume, "Why don't you respect me and like me?" The teacher will present what he thinks are reasonable explanations for his belief, to no avail. The student experiences this approach as preaching instead of teaching. Reasonableness is less valued than the feeling of personal worth, which the student has lost in Religion class. His friends and peers will soon join his cause. Anything the teacher says will be met with stubborn resistance. This class is quickly moving in the wrong direction. Up ahead looms a cliff.

The despondent teacher wonders, "How did this happen? I was just teaching the correct religious answers." It happened because you were teaching teenagers, not adults. Being immersed in your own adulthood, you forgot what being adolescent is all about. You did what we are all tempted to do on a daily basis: you assumed other people think and feel like you do. They don't – especially teens. Adults and adolescents appear similar because they are both on a faith search. Understanding the crucial difference between the adult and adolescent faith search will help the aspiring teacher avoid a Religion class meltdown.

Adults search to deepen their faith.

Adolescents search to find faith.

Adults have discovered a measure of significance in their life, and are motivated by the values, principles and beliefs they have committed to.

Adolescents are searching for personal significance in their life and are often "on stage," performing for the acclaim of those around them.

Experiencing one's own significance is the first fruit of evangelization. "I am loved by God. I have a mission on this planet. God will be with me always on this mission – my life."

Catechesis always follows evangelization, because the evangelized are seeking greater understanding of this faith they have accepted. The teacher who gives only religious answers in class is trying to catechize those who have not been evangelized. That is why these teachers experience resistance. The successful teacher has found the answer to this dilemma: "evangechesis." When students experience their significance in the eyes of the teacher, they are not only empowered to ask religious questions, but become more open to receiving religious answers. The Religion teacher who can enable students to experience their own significance (evangelization) will also be lighting a fire of faith interest within them (catechesis). In short, the success of your Religion class will depend on whether the students feel significant in your class. They will feel this way if

- their contribution is solicited by you,
- their contribution is valued by you,
- they are taken seriously and respected, and
- they feel needed and wanted in the classroom.

It looks like this.

Adults have walked through the door of the house of faith, and are interested in exploring the many rooms "in my Father's house." Adolescents stand outside the house wondering why they should go in at all. The adult opens the window and shouts to the teen, "God loves you!" The teen still stands outside wondering, "Who is God, what is love, and who am I?" This is when the adult must make a decision. "Do I keep shouting out the window about the religious faith I found, or do I leave the house and go to where that young person is standing? Do I wait for them to come to me, or do I go to them?" The answer is found in both Christian theology and sound pedagogy. God did not wait for us to come, but sent his Son to where we were. The religious educator leaves the house to go to where the youth are.

This is what evangechesis means: we do not use teens to teach theology; we use theology to teach teens. We do not use teens to teach the curriculum; we use the curriculum to teach teens. Touching the hearts of young people must be our first priority, for until you touch their hearts, your lesson will be just another class the student has to get through, pass and forget. William O'Malley SJ said it succinctly in his insightful endorsement of Mitch Finley's book *Let's Begin with Prayer*. "Mitch Finley understands young people's needs. He knows we have to go for their hearts (as Jesus did), not their heads, because their heads are just starting to work, while their hearts have been working overtime for a very long while."[26] This is what I mean by evangechesis. We have to direct what we do in the classroom to their hearts while we engage their emerging intellect. *Evange* (heart) + *chesis* (head) = Evangechesis!

Searching Faith – Religion on the Bench

Becoming a "somebody" and achieving social success is the all-pervasive concern for teens. Teens themselves hardly notice how they have pushed faith, as they have previously known it, to the periphery of their lives. As one 16-year-old boy wrote,

God always plays a big role in my life because I try to base a lot of my decisions on his word. Right now, though, it doesn't seem God is as important as he was when I was younger. The most important things to me are sports and my friends.

Bringing new adolescent questions to God will help this student regain a sense of God's importance in his life. Failure to do so could put faith on the bench for the whole season.

Also, during the Affiliative Faith stage, the young person may have incorporated ideas about God that are simply not true – the most common being that if people have faith, they are spared trouble in life. For faith to grow, it will need to crack the shell of our delusions that we mistake for God's truth.

Searching Faith – "Give me faith, Lord, but not yet!"

Searching Faith is experienced by the adolescent as a smorgasbord, with Christianity being one of the dishes served. The adolescent thinks, "It looks good, I'll probably take it … but let me see what else is being offered." How can you commit to something unless you know, to some degree, what it is you are committing to? Every yes involves a no; yes to this means no to that. "More is gained," said Helen Keller, "by the mistakes of those who honestly try to think for themselves than by the correct opinions of those who hold them simply because they have not heard the other side."

A group of four young seminarians came to my Grade 10 Religion class one day. It was a Pentecost experience. It felt like a great wind had blown the door open, and four zealous apostles came sizzling in, all on fire for the Lord. My students were taken by storm; if it had been a platoon of US Marines, they would have felt no difference. These four guys were what my wife calls IYM – Intense Young Men. I thought they might be the Four Horsemen of the Apocalypse.

They stood before my Grade 10 class, and, one by one, gave a telling witness to the power of God, the truth of the Catholic Church and the life we should be living. It was fast paced, airtight and concluded with a rousing call to commitment.

Then one of the IYM said, "Any questions?"

It sounded more like a challenge than an invitation. Silence and blank stares ensued. No one even moved. I think my students were afraid of doing anything that might make them appear a target for recruitment.

Finally, a boy in the last desk of the middle row slowly raised his hand and said, "What you guys are saying sounds really convincing … But – uh, you forgot one thing."

"What's that?" said the seminarian.

"What if you are wrong?"

The class erupted in laughter. Searching Faith strikes again.

For high school youth, faith is like one of the many channels on TV. They may like what they see, but they want to know what else is on. Watch teens with a remote (especially boys): they keep surfing for fear they might be missing something better. Teens want to know what is around the corner. It's not that the grass is greener, it's just that it might be "new" grass, grass they haven't seen before, maybe purple grass – who knows, let's go see. To youth, every new idea is a revelation freshly minted; every new person is an interesting alien awaiting immigration into their world.

At the end of a school year, one of my students told me she was leaving the school.

"Why?" I asked.

"My mother wants me to go to public school," she said, "so I can experience the real world."

At what point do they say, "I've seen enough; faith is the answer"? At what point do they say, "Faith makes sense. I will build my life on it"? At what point do they say, "*This* is the real world"?

Most youth in high school are still trying to sort out the big identity questions:

- Am I OK?
- Am I lovable?
- What am I good at?

- What makes me special?
- Who is my friend?
- Why do I feel the way I do?

Considering all this, we can understand why making a faith commitment in high school is often postponed. Youth will still see themselves as affiliated to their faith, but that is not the same as the deeper, personal conversion of choosing faith for oneself – the call of the "new evangelization." For most young people, this commitment happens after high school, in their 20s, at the time they are making commitments in other areas, such as career and relationships.

When kids come back to visit their old high school, two or three years after graduation, the difference is striking. They are more focused, assured, congenial and inquisitive. They have taken charge of their lives. Even more surprising is the way they shake their heads, incredulously, as they recall who they were only two or three years before, or bemoan the current high school students as being so different from "when I was their age." They have become young men and women. It happens.

This is why ministry to youth after high school should be a priority in the Church. A young adult College and Career group meets every Monday night in my parish. That's when they not only ask the bigger questions, but delve into them more deeply.

It is not that high school kids can't make a commitment to faith. They can. But the person they commit is still in the process of becoming a self, and the commitment often rests on a weak foundation – like a high school romance. Teens find themselves acting Christian when in a Christian setting, acting otherwise when elsewhere. The chameleon lack of congruity in their lives prods them to search and question. The result is the formation of a life stance, a choice and a commitment. Praise God! They have come to the threshold of Owned Faith.

I was in university when it happened to me. I was sitting in a Theology class when it hit me. This makes sense, I thought. Not just about me, but about the world – the big picture. I discovered a theological outlook for all the big questions in life. This can be *my* world view. I made this private commitment and the subsequent years have been a continual unpacking of the contents of that choice – that Catholic faith outlook. Some of our Grade 11 and 12 students might be ready for this commitment. We need always to call them to it. We cannot assume away the mysterious ways of the grace of God and the hidden readiness of young people.

Grace acts according to our nature. It may be in the nature of some youth to respond, and in the nature of others to be "not yet ready" during their high school years. This is something God knows, not the Religion teacher. You may have prepared the soil, or you may have planted the seed. It is no small task either way.

Owned Faith: Stage 4

Thomas Merton, the Trappist monk, wrote of an experience he had in downtown Louisville while on an errand for the monastery.

> In Louisville, at the corner of Fourth and Walnut, in the centre of the shopping district, I was suddenly overwhelmed with the realization that I loved all those people, that they were mine and I theirs, that we could not be alien to one another even though we were total strangers. It was like waking from a dream of separateness, of spurious self-isolation in a special world, the world of renunciation and supposed holiness …. There is no way of telling people that they are all walking around shining like the sun.[27]

If there are stages on the journey of faith, then Merton has described the homecoming. Waking from a dream of "separateness," he experiences being one with everyone, everything. This is Owned Faith, not so much that I have faith, but that faith has me. In pursuing God, we are suddenly caught.

Can the adolescent have this faith? Can the teen say, "Walking down the hall, I was suddenly overwhelmed in the realization that I loved all the students, the upper grades, the lower grades, the geeks and nerds and losers and the ones who look at me funny and the tough guys who scare me and the snobs who ignore me and the ones who think they are so cool and the jerks in Grade 9 and Jamie who has a big mouth and ....." That's pushing it. Most adolescents accord only their friends full rights as persons, with everyone else being second-class citizens.

The goal of adolescence is to shore up the banks of an eroding character. It is to navigate the whitewater of peer expectations, and to arrive on the other side with an identity on board. It is to develop a new set of courtesy norms to ensure some measure of domestic tranquillity at the base camp called home. And it is to reflect on one's emerging personhood in order to develop into a real person, not a role, copy or image of someone else. The progress made in developing one's own personhood is directly proportionate to the progress that can be made in developing one's relationship with God. Then, in the emerging reality of self and others, one's understanding of the reality of God can take a new and heightened dimension. "Lord, that I may know myself, in order to know Thee," wrote Saint Augustine. This is the challenge of adolescence and the necessary precursor to Owned Faith in adulthood (and I didn't even mention hormones). To celebrate every step teens make along this way is so much more encouraging and respectful than to expect them to be where the adult has predetermined they should be. Owned Faith, in contrast, presupposes a stable identity and firm character. If you are going to give yourself to God, you have to make sure you have a self to give.

The spiritual writer Henri Nouwen said,

> I know that I have to move from speaking about Jesus to letting him speak within me, from thinking about Jesus to letting him think within me, from acting for and with Jesus to letting him act through me. I know that the only way for me to see the world is to see it through his eyes.[28]

This is Owned Faith, the movement from knowing about Jesus, to knowing Jesus, to becoming "not I but Christ living within me" (Galatians 2:20). St. Francis of Assisi said, "What I once loved I now disdain, what I now love, I once disdained." Could he have been talking about being cool, being popular, wearing the right name brands and being a real player with the ladies – a rough description of his adolescent life?

Owned Faith is the integration of your whole life with a committed outlook and direction. It happens when conscious faith permeates your subconscious, when controlled behaviour becomes habitual, when first nature becomes second nature and when there is no discrepancy between how you want people to see you and how you really are.

Owned Faith is also about "second naïveté" – a deeper openness to the mystical and the beyond. It is about the Chestertonian paradox: being sure and sensing mystery; committed to one's own faith, but affirming the faith of the other; spiritually confident, yet relying on God's grace; one integral person, but, in St. Paul's words, being all things to all people.

What is Owned Faith? Look to the saints and the holy ones, for that is what Owned Faith looks like:

"I die the King's good servant, but God's first."
—St. Thomas More (last words before his execution)

"Like anybody, I would like to live a very long life … But I'm not concerned about that now. I just want to do God's will."
—Dr. Martin Luther King (the night before he was assassinated)

"Why should we refuse to support a just cause just because the Communists support it?"
—Dorothy Day (often accused by other Catholics of being a Communist)

"I would like to take the place of Sergeant Gajowniczek."
—St. Maximilian Kolbe (moments before being led to the starvation bunker)

"I make myself a leper with the lepers to gain all to Christ. That is why, in preaching, I say 'we lepers'; not 'my brethren.'"
—Fr. Damien De Veuster (who died of leprosy)

"To me, to find God is to find the whole human family. No one can be disconnected from us."
—Sr. Helen Prejean, CSJ (author of *Dead Man Walking*)

In our consideration of the lives of the saints, and in our own lives, we do a disservice to youth if we omit the shadow side. Owned Faith is not surprised to discover that vices, like weeds, keep springing up in the garden of our virtue. You come, in adulthood, to an acceptance of your weakness, fearfulness, pettiness, need to control, temper, impatience and ego-centeredness. Acceptance is not giving in. Acceptance is not surrendering to your weakness. Acceptance entails a greater and final surrender to God *in your weakness*. These are the weeds and wheat brought to God at the end. We become tolerant, in Owned Faith, of the weeds and wheat in others, because we accept them in ourselves. In the words of St. Therese,

> You are wrong, if you think your little Therese always marches along the way of virtue. She is weak, very weak; every day she experiences it afresh. But … Jesus delights to teach her as he taught St. Paul, the science of glorying in one's infirmities. That is a great grace, and I beg Jesus to teach it to you, for in it alone is found peace and rest for the soul.[29]

Faith development – A mystery

"A sower went out to sow his seed" is how Jesus began his teaching on faith development. The sower sows generously, never knowing where the seed is going to fall. Teachers of teens need enough patience to accept that some seeds may lie dormant for quite some time.

Catechetical and youth ministry educator Michael Warren offers the following vignette for those engaged in the ministry of adolescent faith development.

> A young man … shocked his parents by announcing at age seventeen that he had "lost" his faith. Knowing his depth of reflectiveness, his parents, hurt though they were, decided to respect his decision. It took eight years of patient waiting before their son came to them and told them that he had recently been converted to Christian faith. The words of this young man to his parents impress me greatly: "I can tell you now that if you had not shown the respect for my

liberty of judgment that you did, I don't know if I should have ever found the Faith again."[30]

St. Augustine should be the patron saint of faith development. His growth in faith was a reluctant letting go, a hesitant moving on. Looking back, he lamented the lateness of his love.

Yet it is the same with all of us.

We want to say, "Lord, you're finished with me, right?"

And the Lord keeps saying, "Not yet, not yet."

This is faith development: Christ has died, Christ is risen, Christ keeps coming again and again and again.

Faith development theory caused a rethinking of the question "How do teens learn Religion?" This chapter leads naturally to a discussion of the four stages of the learning process, the subject of the next two chapters.

4

Foundation for the Mission

Step 1 of the Learning Process

Meaningful learning is rooted in life experience. Students' personal experiences are the primary resources for understanding life issues and Church teaching. In designing this course, the authors researched the life experiences of today's young people: What concerns do they have? What questions are they asking? The Experience portion of each chapter is critical to the unfolding of the lesson.

—Stand by Me (Year 8 Teacher Manual, Canadian Conference of Catholic Bishops)

Preparing a lesson plan that works is a teacher's biggest brain stretcher. The hour that students are in your classroom will seem like a breezy summer drive or bumper-to-bumper traffic. A good lesson plan makes all the difference. What is a good lesson plan? Learning process theory provides an answer to this question. An engaging and exciting lesson is one wherein students are "with it."

When I was a young teacher in charge of the teaching of Religion, I thought it essential to give my students a well-ordered lesson following a logical plan, with well-defined divisions and precise definitions. I am not saying now that all that is useless, but I have ceased to believe it is of prime importance. I remember being stopped in my tracks by one young man's remark: "Your lesson is very fine, but we are not with it."[31]

How do you know when students are "with it," when students' needs are being met, when students are learning?

They tell you!

They tell you directly, "Good class!" or indirectly, "See ya later, Mr. B."

You know they have learned something, because you see it in their faces. The frown they came in with is turned upside down. They bounce out of the classroom, because there is more life in them. Your lesson has lifted them up – they even seem taller.

When students do not learn, they shuffle out of class like prisoners recently cut loose from a chain gang. They are bored, lethargic; you have sucked the wild fire out of them (don't worry, within minutes they'll be with their friends and they will fire each other up again). Understanding the learning process is the key to creating lesson plans that work.

There are four steps in the learning process. Although these four steps may be referred to with different names, here is what my teacher guide calls them:

1. Experience: Students explore their life experience.
2. Information: The wisdom of our faith is explained.
3. Application: Students apply the faith to their life experience.
4. Action: Students "walk the talk"; the lesson has changed their life.

In this chapter, I will devote what will seem to be an inordinate amount of space to the first step. I do this because Step 1 is the foundation upon which quality learning is built. I will also address some misunderstandings regarding Step 1 and its limited purpose in the overall learning process. In Chapter 5, I will explain Steps 2, 3 and 4, and give practical suggestions for each step.

Step 1: Experience

The bottom line is this:
We can lecture kids to our heart's content,
but if they don't care what we think,
or there is no relationship between us

that matters to them,
or they think we are ignorant
of the reality of their lives,
they will not listen.[32]

Step 1 is all about listening to teens so we are not "ignorant of the reality of their lives." Show a kid that you understand their world, and they will listen *to* you. Show a kid you don't understand their world, and they will listen *at* you.

The saintly Jean Vanier is a former Canadian naval officer and ex-philosophy professor from St. Michael's College in Toronto. When he began to live with two men who had developmental disabilities in 1964, they quickly rejected his professional tendency as an officer and teacher to tell others what to think. Instead, they forced him to answer a fundamental human question: "Do you like me?"[33]

This is the first question teens ask on the first day of Religion class, but they don't ask it with words. And words won't answer it, either. "Hey, I like you," from the teacher will be met with "Guy's weird!" from the students. "Do you like me?" is answered in your willingness and ability to learn "the reality of their lives." Teens do not initially care how much theology you know. They don't care how much you know until they know how much you care.

Jean Vanier is a great teacher. He reminds us that we don't just listen to others so we can help them. In listening to the struggles, questions and brokenness of others, I get in touch with the struggles, questions and brokenness in me. We must have compassion for our own wounds before we can be compassionate with others. Don't run, he reminds us, from our own poverty by running to the poverty of others. Know your own poverty, and then you will be in solidarity with the poverty of others. Step 1 builds a foundation of solidarity between you and your students.

The Religion teacher: Missionary to a teenage culture

Step 1 reveals the difference between the imperialist and the missionary. The analogy I am offering is useful, even if somewhat simplistic.

The missionary, who comes to serve, begins by assessing the needs of the people. The missionary learns their language and culture, and tries to speak in a way that can be understood. He knows that next to God, it is the people who are served who will evaluate the service. He is always aware – indeed, it is the motivation for the mission – that what is offered is the pearl of great price: the ineffable gift of God's love and truth.

The imperialist also believes he has something of great value to give. But his gift cannot be received by the heart, because it does not come from the heart; it comes from the ego. In the end, imperialists are either feared or resented, because they make others feel inferior. The imperialist attitude is picked up by the recipient: you are superior; you are the giver, you are significant, you are the one from God; I am not.

The big difference is that the imperialist never learns from the people he helps, whereas the missionary never stops learning from them. The imperialist says, "God is in heaven and I want to tell you about him." The missionary says, "God is here in this class. What is God saying and doing here?"

When Jesus sent the first missionaries out two by two, he sent them with no gold, no bag, not even sandals (Matthew 10:9-10). So we, too, go to youth in Step 1 with no gold nuggets of truth, no bag of clever ideas, not even sandals that help us feel firm and secure in their presence. Religion teachers are missionaries to a teenage culture. It is natural to feel a bit insecure. What will buoy you up is the realization that they long to be known by you (Step 1) and to learn from you (Step 2).

The turbulence of adolescence today comes not so much from rebellion as from the loss of communication between adult and kids, and from the lack of a realistic, honest understanding of what the kids' world really looks like … young adolescents do not want to be left to their own devices. In national surveys and focus groups, youth have given voice to serious longing. They want more regular contact with adults who care and respect them.[34]

When God became human, it was Step 1. We were not left to our own devices. God became one of us and fulfilled our serious longing to be known by God in a personal way. The Religion teacher, in Step 1, also initiates the incarnational process. The turbulence of adolescence can then be calmed by someone who is able to sympathize with them: "For we do not have a high priest who is unable to sympathize with our weakness" (Hebrews 4:15.)

Starting with adolescent experience has greatly enriched my Religion lessons. It has helped to accomplish a number of things:

- To enable youth to reflect on the reality of their lives. "The unexamined life," as Socrates said, "is not worth living." The age of journals and diaries is being crowded out by Facebook and MSN. The long, reflective sentences of the past are being replaced by sound bites, catch phrases, one-liners and computer shorthand. The teacher who can facilitate reflection is a teacher who nourishes a student's spiritual life.

- To assuage normal adolescent fears that "I am completely alone and no one will ever understand me."

- To show youth that we care for them and accept them. Acceptance is not condoning or agreeing with what a person says or does, but rather is the first step in a three-step process of love:

    1. I accept you as you are.
    2. I encourage you to be all that God is calling you to be.
    3. I confront you when you violate the principles you confess.

    Note: Confrontation works only when the student realizes you care for them. Support must always precede a challenge.

- To counteract passivity by motivating students to be involved in the lesson. "Catechesis encourages a climate of understanding, of thanksgiving, and of prayer. It looks to the free response of persons

and it promotes active participation among those to be catechized."
(GDC #145)

- To build class community where students feel comfortable, welcomed and connected to others in the class. Adolescents want a united class; they want to know their classmates, especially in Religion class. A warm class spirit takes root when the skilled teacher begins with Step 1 in the learning process.

The confusion around Step 1 arises from not understanding its limitations. Step 1 is *not* valuable for the following reasons:

- Because "personal experience" is the only valid basis for guidance in life.
- Because we are sinless beings capable of constructing our own criteria for judging what is true and what is good.
- Because we believe human nature is sufficient unto itself, without need of divine assistance.

This would be the doctrine of secular humanism, not Christianity. When we start with Step 1, we are turning the soil in order to plant the seed, not just continually turning the soil to see what interesting things we can find. "Human experience," explains Archbishop Wuerl, "is a significant factor in this process to the extent that it can offer a starting point for the seed of God's word to take hold, grow and bear fruit. It cannot, however, substitute for the seed or its flowering."[35]

Christianity professes a revelation from God to us. The interface of God and ourselves has provided much theological reflection over the centuries. "Grace builds on nature" is the Catholic synopsis of this mystery. It means, among other things, that you can't be a good Christian unless you deal with your baggage. It warns us to avoid the temptation, prevalent in Church history, to encounter divinity by discarding our humanity. The late Cardinal Suenens explains it this way in his book *Nature and Grace*:

Such an approach [starting with human experience] is of value in that, starting from man's aspirations it can awaken his need for the infinite and the absolute, thus guiding him toward God. But an introduction cannot claim to be the end of the search, even temporarily.

It is a "threshold" method in that it prepares the way for faith. Faith itself comes from elsewhere. Faith is born of a Word communicated by God and received by man. That Word summons each one of us. It is a call that demands an answer, an action of God who asks us to adhere to his Word. It is that Word which judges us and not my subjectivity, my lived experiences, my feeling, my preferences. God has opened his heart to us in his Word, and our Christian life consists in responding to that Love, that freely offered covenant …. Between nature and grace there is a relationship of reciprocity in unity, and we must never disregard it in the concrete circumstances of our everyday life.[36]

Religion teachers discover another reason to begin the learning process with Step 1 – the sheer delight of listening to the stories of youth. Delight is a word created from a mix of fun, joy, surprise and wonder. I have no doubt Jesus experienced this delight when he taught. Jesus' parables must have provoked many a response that Jesus was delighted to hear.

In Step 1, the Religion teacher asks the same question Jesus asks of the depressed disciples on the Emmaus road: "What are you talking about?" It was Jesus' way of getting the lesson started.

Your teacher manual will offer some ways to initiate Step 1 in the learning process to connect with students' personal experiences. But that shouldn't stop you from using your own ideas. Over the years, I've put together many ways to elicit student experience.

Provoking a response

When attempting to get teens to reflect on their thoughts, feelings and experiences on a given topic or issue, it is best to resist what most people would consider the obvious thing to do, such as simply asking your class what they think about the following:

- angels
- playing the lottery

- consumerism
- violent video games
- pollution
- lying to parents
- prayer
- life after death
- friendship
- sex

"So, what do you think?"

"Say what?" would be the spoken or unspoken response.

If you did it this way, a few students would respond – the ones who always respond. But even they would be 50 per cent conscious about answering you, and 50 per cent conscious of what others might be thinking about their answer to you. The discussion would be like a dying battery in a portable radio. There would be an initial surge of chatter, quickly dropping to a murmur, then silence.

"Thank you … anyone else?" … (blank stares)

And you will end up saying (to yourself), well, that didn't work (and to the students), "Well, the Universal Catholic Catechism of the Church says …."

You can't just throw a question out there. It's like throwing a piece of string into a lake and expecting to catch a fish. The Religion teacher has to bait the hook. You have to put teens into a corner that they can't get out of … without thinking.

I call it "Provoking a Response."

Provoking a response is not new. In the 1970s, it was called Values Clarification, a learning experience designed to clarify the values motivating one's behaviour. Dialogue with others in a supportive, non-threatening, non-judging group was the method. Provoking a response includes this aspect of Values Clarification, but sees it as *only one part of a four-part process*.

In my role as facilitator of discussion, I sometimes play the devil's advocate by arguing against my own beliefs, as St. Thomas Aquinas did before proceeding to answer his own objection. I also use the Socratic method of asking questions to foster thinking and awaken interest in the topic. I intervene when needed, but most of the time I just do active listening. What encourages me in the use of this method in Religious Education is that it works. The topic is opened up and the students are engaged. The proof is in the pedagogical pudding.

Why do I provoke a response rather than just invite dialogue? I find I have to prod, provoke and pester teens to put their cards on the table. Is it because our media-mesmerized culture encourages a passive posture in our students? Is it just ideological option shock in a pleni-pluralistic culture that stuns students into passivity? Whatever it is, I want my lessons to launch, not sputter. Hence, I provoke their response. "I want your opinion," my approach implies, "and I will beat it out of you."

Here are seven ways to Provoke a Response:
1. True or False
2. Agree or Disagree
3. Choose the Answer Closest to Your Own Thoughts
4. Put in Order of Importance
5. Complete the Sentence
6. "Survey Says," Anonymously
7. Voting with Your Feet

The following examples I wrote myself. You can create your own "provocations" for practically any lesson. Here is a lesson launcher called "Christ and the Consumer Society."

1. True or False

1. Kids age 11 to 14 are mind controlled and manipulated into "needing" name-brand clothing sold at exorbitant prices.
2. I should own my own car by the age of 18.
3. Most people with credit cards misuse them.
4. Shoplifting in our society is caused by the advertisers who suggest we "must" have certain things.

5. Most really fun things to do cost money.

6. Let's face it; the more money you have, the more respect you get.

7. If all people in the world had the lifestyle of those in North America, it would be an ecological nightmare.

These statements will raise all kinds of issues in discussion, such as personal responsibility to resist media pressure; creativity and imagination in finding no-cost fun things to do; what determines the worth of a person; global inequity regarding the use of natural resources; and the lure of materialism and consumerism.

2. Agree / Disagree

This will introduce a unit on the sanctity of life.

1. Video games and computer games are far too violent.

2. The government has the right to execute criminals who commit murder.

3. People with a terminal illness should be able to end their life of pain by choosing death (euthanasia).

4. Countries have the right to have nuclear weapons to defend themselves against their enemies.

5. The sport of boxing should be banned.

6. Certain kinds of popular music encourage violence.

7. Guys are more violent than girls.

3. Choosing the Closest Answer

The best way to engage an issue is to take a position and try to defend it or fight your way out of it. When students are asked to choose the statement that is closest to their belief, they are invested in the outcome of the discussion. This is for a lesson on transcendent reality.

1. On the existence of angels, I believe …

   a. Angels are real.

   b. Angels are real and sometimes you can experience them.

c. I have no idea.

d. Angels are like Santa Claus, fairies, and Easter bunnies.

2. On life after death …

a. I believe in life after death. I remain myself, in a new way.

b. I believe in reincarnation; we come back to earth in another form.

c. I believe we are assimilated into the great cosmic force.

d. I believe death is the complete end of my existence.

3. About prayer …

a. God really hears my prayers; I'm not sure if God answers.

b. God hears and answers.

c. I'm not sure if God hears prayer.

d. Prayer is wishful thinking.

4. Put in Order

This method has been around since Values Clarification was first introduced over 40 years ago. One need not endorse the ideology of relativism that some claim is implicit in Values Clarification in order to use a method that helps generate critical thinking. Here are two examples from different lesson plans.

1. Put the following in order of "who is most responsible" for the drug problem in our country, with "1" being most responsible, and "4" being least responsible.

a. The poor farmer in Latin America who grows it.

b. The organized crime syndicate that buys it.

c. The middle man on the street who sells it.

d. The person who uses it.

2. Put in order of importance the following criteria for a good friendship, with "1" being most important, and "4" being least important.

a. We like to do the same activities.

b. We are in the same class together.

c. We can trust each other with secrets.

d. We have the same moral values.

5. Complete the Sentence

Students will surprise even themselves when discovering how they complete an open-ended sentence. Writing, as diary and journal keepers testify, is not only recording your ideas, but also creating them. This is for a lesson on honesty.

1. A time I was lied to was …

2. When I was lied to, I felt …

3. The worst thing about lying is …

4. People lie in our society today in order to …

5. Telling the truth at all times is difficult because …

6. Anonymous Survey

Certain topics are too close to home to discuss openly. An anonymous survey method can help raise them. The anonymous survey is written out on a small sheet of paper (all the sheets are identical), which I distribute and preface with the following instructions:

1. Do not put your name or anyone else's name on your paper.

2. I will read the responses out loud.

3. Do not write anything you do not want me to read out loud.

4. When I read these out loud, do not ask who wrote it or look around. Respect people's right to express their thoughts.

5. Write your honest ideas. If you really have nothing to say, write, "I have nothing to say," for that would be honest. But I would appreciate hearing your ideas, and I think others will, too.

Here is a sample survey:

1. My opinion about the way people in our school are made fun of is …

2. The biggest problem with friendships in high school is …

3. What I see going on in my high school regarding sex and guy-girl relationships is …

Shuffle the papers before you read them. When reading them out, you may want to break the tension with a joke. For instance, on the subject of sex and guy-girl relationships, pretend someone's paper reads, "I'm a really good-looking guy, and I want a date. Call 963 …." Many times, a student's response (intentionally or unintentionally) will provide laughter enough. Thank the class for being open and honest. You may spark some discussion with questions like these:

- What common responses did you notice in this survey?
- What surprised you the most?
- What response made you think?
- Why was this survey worth doing?

7. Voting with Your Feet

Here is another way to provoke a response. Present an issue with a duality statement, such as, "Would you rather have no friends or unhealthy friends?" On one side of the classroom post a page saying "NO FRIENDS"; on the other side post a page saying "UNHEALTHY FRIENDS."[37]

Do not define the term "unhealthy"; that will emerge in the discussion. Instruct the students to "vote with your feet." A few of the boys will raise their feet in the air. "No, no, no … when I say go, stand up and walk to the sign on the board that represents your belief. Don't say anything out loud; don't follow the crowd; don't just go where your friend goes; think for yourself. Now … Go … Vote with your feet."

When they have taken their "stand," go around with a simulated microphone (or a real one), and interview random teens like a talk-show host.

Good evening, Ladies and Gentlemen. Here we are on *Teen Talk*, your weekly reality Teen Talk TV show. This week the topic is … Friendship. Let's get the word on the street. Why would you rather have no friends? Tell me, Jonathan, why do you want to be a loner?

That will get them going! Here are some other "Vote with Your Feet" dilemmas, taken from a book entitled *Would You Rather ...?* by Doug Fields.[38]

Would You Rather ...

- Be rich and alone   *or*   poor with lots of friends
- Know all there is to know   *or*   experience love in the universe
- Have no values   *or*   no friends
- Be gossiped about   *or*   lied to

Discussion Time

During the group discussions we can express our true feelings, help each other with their problems, and can further understand what's going on in our lives. Through this, we become more compassionate toward each other.

—Michelle

Now that the students have begun to consider their own thoughts and feelings on a given topic, the next step is to generate discussion. My usual method is twofold: small-group discussions followed by a large, all-class discussion. Very rarely do I say to students, "Get into groups of three or four." Most teachers know what might happen next. Student A looks across the aisle. Eye contact is made with the person sitting in the next row, Student B. At this point, Student A quickly looks away and walks two rows over to join a group of "friends." Student B thinks, "She hates me." Student A said nothing; her body language said it all. Young teens especially can be insensitive and unaware of the feelings of others. A simple request from a teacher – "get into small groups" – can create hard feelings that may last for years. To avoid this situation, I organize the small groups.

At the beginning of the school year, I give every student a permanent class number. Every time a small group-discussion is to be formed in class, I put a different overhead on the screen. The student finds her number and the group she is assigned to, indicated by the letter in the column on the left.

✓					
A	10	2	5	20	
B	14	1	15	17	
C	6	9	4	8	
D	13	3	12	21	
E	7	19	11	25	
F	16	22	18	23	

In different parts of the classroom, a letter is attached to the wall indicating the area for that group to meet. Sometimes I strategically put the class numbers on the chart when I want to keep certain students together, to balance the number of guys and girls, to ensure that they will be with different people for each small group, or to separate certain students. Mostly, I randomly place the numbers on the chart. Students like this system. They wonder which group they will be in this time, and with whom. There is no stress about who to be with, and randomness is a fun surprise. I make up about a dozen small-group configurations at the beginning of the year, checking them off in the blank boxes at the top of the overhead sheet as I use them.

Once they are placed in a group, the students follow the rules below.

Rules for Small Group

1. Sit close together (if the chairs are not connected to the desks).

2. One person speaks at a time.

3. Listen to each other.

4. No inter-group communication. (No using sign language to communicate with your friend in a different group.)

5. Stay with the topic and task.

The following directions are also given when applicable:

1. The first number for each group on the overhead is the recorder. Recorders gather the group's answers.

2. Try to come up with an all-group answer.

3. After everyone gives his or her answer, always ask the magic question "Why do you think that?"

4. Write your answer on the board.

Every once in a while, I remind the students of the following motivation principles for effective thinking:

- "I may not agree with what you say, but I'll fight with my life for your right to say it."
- "Friends are not clones."
- "Before I know if I agree or disagree, I want to understand, so keep talking."
- "I like you; I just don't agree with what you said."
- "I don't want you to think so you are like me; I want you to think so you find the truth."
- "Great minds think alike? No! Great minds think for themselves."

All teenagers love group discussions on topics of interest. Senior students are more adept at discussion than younger students, and will be engaged in the discussion for a longer period of time. During this time, I go around the classroom troubleshooting: "Stick to the topic; argue your point but listen to the other person; challenge when you disagree."

Survey the class. How is it going? You can tell right away when the lesson is working. A continual buzz of chatter permeates the room. Laughter over here; a friendly debate over there – the lesson is catching on. You will also sense when the small-group discussion should be concluded. Or a student will let you know: "What do we do now?"

Surveying the responses of the small group as indicated on the chalkboard, or even without written feedback from the group, you can decide that the issue warrants a "Stop Pillow Discussion," the large group, all-class discussion.

The "Stop Pillow" Discussion

Before the class, write the student numbers on separate index cards. Desks are moved out of the way. Students form one big class circle of chairs facing inward. Shuffle the index cards and place a card face up on each chair in the circle. Students sit where their card is placed. This way, they will sit next to different people in the class rather than with their close friends, with whom they might be tempted to carry on a private conversation. Collect the cards when all are seated.

In the "Stop Pillow" Discussion, only one person talks at a time; and they talk to the whole group. Use the pillow to facilitate this process. I call it the "Stop Pillow" because my original pillow had a stop sign picture on it, which for our purposes meant "everyone must stop and listen to the person with the pillow." I follow this rule, too, unless I am forced to intervene for disciplinary reasons.

Anyone talking without the pillow gets a penalty from the teacher. The penalty consists of turning the participant's chair to face outward – like being sent to the penalty box in hockey. After a minute or two or three, the penalty is over, and he can turn his chair to face inward again. In rare cases, the teacher may have to exclude someone who repeatedly can't or won't wait for the Stop Pillow before speaking. This hardly ever happens, because teens respect the Stop Pillow exercise. Sometimes when an exclamation is uttered because some student is astonished over what was just said, or when someone overcome with righteous indignation utters a spontaneous outburst, I might just give a warning (yellow card).

The pillow is tossed around to students who, by raising their hand, indicate they have something to say. I join in on this, and sometimes try to incite some response: "The only reason girls talk to guys is to flirt with them. They will deny it, but it's true." About a dozen girls shoot their hands into the air to respond to that one – and the beat goes on.

Over the years, I have developed my skills in asking questions that help teens get to the heart of the issues under discussion. Listening to teens has enabled me to do this. After a Stop Pillow Discussion, I find myself rethinking the next day's lesson. The things teens say, their reactions and assumptions and questions, show me the direction my lesson needs to take.

Here is a sample of comments made in a Stop Pillow Discussion. Can you spot the religious issues and questions being raised?

A Stop Pillow Discussion:
Is the Bible True?

Of course the Bible is true. It doesn't say "fiction" on the back. It's the Holy Bible, not the Holy Make Believe.

Some parts are true; some are not. Like when God drowned all the Egyptians in the Red Sea. I don't think God would kill people.

Well, he warned them. He told them, "Let my people go."

If they did something really bad they deserved it.

How many times do your parents warn you?

Three.

Then what happens?

I get grounded.

Why didn't God just ground the Egyptians?

Ground them, drowned them, what's the difference?

The Bible is a book to teach people how to be good. It's not whether it is true or not, it's whether it makes you a better person.

It's just a story written by a man. Men make mistakes; it could be true or false.

Why would someone just make up stories like that? People have been reading these stories for thousands of years. It must be true even if we don't understand how it happened.

Yeah, like Jesus walking on water.

Chris Angel walks on water.

Who's Chris Angel?

If you believe the Bible is true, then it's true for you. It's what you believe.

I believe I can fly, I believe I can touch the sky ...

We believe the Bible is true because that is what we were taught. We are being loyal to what we were taught. But we can't really say it is true because we haven't experienced it.

(*I read chapters 1 and 2 of Genesis out loud as the students follow in their Bibles*)

There, that's what happened and it is a fact.

A talking snake is a fact?

If God wants to make a snake talk, God can do it. Besides, that's the problem with women. They want to talk so much, they end up talking to a snake.

The woman talked to the snake because Adam wasn't talking to her. He was probably being a typical duhhh guy.

Snakes talk in *The Jungle Book*.

Aaarghh!

After a good Stop Pillow Discussion on the Bible, the students are ready for the next step in the lesson plan. They raised the questions, so they are more open to receiving the answers.

The Bible is not a book of scientific truth; it is a book of religious truth. We discover what the Bible is saying when we get close to the truth the author is trying to teach. The Bible is God's message in human words, and it is a message we still hunger for today.

The student who said the Bible teaches us how to be good is close to understanding the purpose of the scriptures – transformation. The student who admitted that her belief in the Bible is based on loyalty has articulated a clear Affiliative Faith posture, seeking something more to base her belief in the Bible on – personal experience. Both students are now ready to learn about the Bible in a new way. The goal is to help adolescents connect the word of the Bible with their own life, so that they experience God speaking to their heart. Then they will be able to say with conviction, "Yes, the Bible is true."

There will be some students who will participate not by talking, but by listening. Some students are quiet observers by personality; every personality or temperament is to be respected and accepted. Now and again, a very quiet student will raise her hand and offer some gem of wisdom that is very beautiful to hear. Often I am inspired and impressed, thinking to myself, "I never had those insights when I was in Grade 9." (Come to think of it, I can't even remember Grade 9.)

In a Stop Pillow Discussion, youth will learn from you and from each other, and you will learn from them. You will learn that teenagers are not all cut from the same cloth. They are all dealing with the tasks of adolescence (belonging, self-worth, competence), but they approach these tasks with their individual outlooks, temperaments and personal baggage.

You will learn about the real-life joys and struggles of the individual students in your class. You will learn that they are all on a unique spiritual journey, and you will notice, when it comes to teaching boys and girls, that girls are much farther along the journey.

Okay, this is a generalization, but one worth commenting on. Are teenage girls more spiritual than teenage boys?

The Gender Difference

Solicit volunteers for a retreat leadership team. Fourteen girls will sign up and four guys (actually two: one guy just signed his friend's name as a joke and another joined because his girlfriend did). You end up beating the linoleum, recruiting guys in the hallways.

"Listen, John, you're a spiritual guy; you have good values; come join our retreat team."

"Okay … I'll think about it … I don't have to do anything, do I?"

"No – just be a guy; that's all."

A poll conducted by *Reader's Digest* revealed that women are more "definite believers in God" than men. Women envision a more loving

God; pray more frequently; draw greater meaning from their faith; and claim to have had first-hand experience of the supernatural to a greater degree than men.[39]

Ask guys why God created the earth and they will tell you – to play paintball. When Jesus was experiencing his agony in the garden and reached out for support, his male friends fell asleep. Every guy understands why they fell asleep. After all, they had just finished a big meal and a tall flask of wine. Food and drink: that's what's important to men. Besides, it must have been while drinking wine that the argument over who is the greatest took place (Luke 22:24). That takes a lot of energy. It's the last night of Jesus' life; and his male friends are arguing over who gets first place – waz up wit dat!

This was the same night Judas betrayed him. Judas didn't initially want to betray Jesus; he wanted to manage him. But Jesus would not be managed by men. When Judas tried his last management ploy – forcing Jesus to miracle work before the Sanhedrin – and it failed, the great empty failure space in his life opened up, and he fell in: he killed himself. Men dread being a failure the most. Being a failure – a loser – is not cool. When it comes to the "mystery of faith," many men stumble on the "Christ has died" part that precedes "Christ is risen; Christ will come again."

In the economy of salvation, "Let it be done to me according to your word" (Mary), wins out over "Let me be your right-hand man" (James and John). Spirituality is all about receiving and being open to God's grace. Spirituality begins with "Let it be," not "Let me do." Even older women manage to maintain spiritual superiority over men. Case in point: the members of the Red Hat Society. The overall purpose of this society is to … that's just it, it has no purpose. The point is that there is no point. It just is. You can't get more spiritual than that – pure being.

Jesuit priest Peter G. Van Breemen maintains that Jesus was the only person in history who never did anything; his Father did everything *through* him. Men want to do things, run things, raise money, and build an extension on the Church. It needs an extension, too! But Mary has chosen the better part: just sitting at the feet of the Lord. If men were seated at the feet of the Lord, they would be checking out the linoleum and planning to replace it with hardwood.

Girls are innately spiritual, but they aren't angels all the time. Guys stand perplexed on the sidelines when queen bees and wannabes fight it out in girl-land. Guys can't even begin to understand girl fights. Girls sometimes say, "My guy friends are just so much better to talk to than my girl friends because guys just really listen and don't judge." That's because guys don't understand what you are saying. Girls say, "Guys are so much more forgiving." That's because guys can't remember what you did.

Younger teenage boys can't stand highly intellectual, overly pious Religion teachers. They like semi-macho, pseudo-sergeant-major-redeemed-goofball types. If you teach guys Religion, you have to either crack a lot of jokes, or come across as some theological ultimate fighting competitor, with a gym bag of wit and wisdom. I prefer the joker, but you still have to be tough because a lot of guys only respect power. A winning combination is a cross between Jim Carrey and General George Patton.

If you teach girls, you have more options. You can be a witty wonder woman like Oprah, a lyrical literate woman like Helen Steiner Rice (the Hallmark lady), or better yet, be like Rebecca St. James – young, beautiful and Christian, with an Australian accent as a bonus. Actually, you can be almost anything, because most girls aim to please.

The difference between guys and girls in Religion class will be poignantly revealed during a Stop Pillow Discussion. A guy will put his hand up first. It's the class clown. You can tell by the suppressed grin on his face. He'll get a laugh from the class and a moment of glory. All the girls will have myriad relevant thoughts circulating in their brains, but very few girls will initially offer an insightful observation.

The women's movement notwithstanding, many girls are still intimidated by guys in the classroom. That is one reason why some girls will not speak out in class discussion, why other girls will take their cue from what guys say, and will avoid putting their own ideas out on the table first. Too many girls wait to see what the guys think, and react to it.

This is especially futile when a guy is not talking about the topic per se, but rather *uses* the topic to get a reaction from others – laughter, shock or admiration. While most girls are interested in having a conversation, many guys are interested in establishing or maintaining status. Guys will throw out something to see what happens. Girls will offer something to get a response. Guys will argue over issues abstractly, as though it had little to do with them. Girls will argue something very personally, having everything to do with them. And some girls will say nothing publicly, but everything privately, with their friends after class. "I can't believe what Matt said; he is such a …." Still, too often, the guys are calling the shots and girls are reluctant to contradict them. Ignoring or suppressing her deep inner voice is a girl's biggest spiritual weakness.

There are, however, a number of girls who will take a stand, and, in an act of heroism, express the sum total of their real thoughts in contrast to what a cocksure guy has just said. What girls don't understand is that the guy is secretly admiring the girl for her wise counsel, but saving face in this public competition (as he sees it) is far more important to him than discovering truth "from a girl." Girls are more confident (precocious?) in Grade 8, but their confidence level begins to drop for the next few years. It recovers by grades 11 and 12, leaving the girl bewildered as to why "I was so insecure back then!"

You, the teacher, can do something to shake up the gender discussion dysfunction. You can argue on the side of the wise girl. You can say something half-brained yourself and humbly take a shot from one of the girls to show the guys by example how humility is a small price to pay for even a morsel of wisdom. You can confront the guys' inconsistent reasoning or affirm a guy's genuine attempt to think at all. You can even say something mildly offensive to provoke the ladies in the back bench to speak out.

What's going on inside the teenage boy? Are guys spiritual?

The reason why guys don't appear as spiritual as girls is because we misread guy behaviour (see Thomas Newkirk's *Misreading Masculinity: Boys, Literacy, and Popular Culture*). When guys wrestle, jostle, tease and make everything into a competition, some mistake this behaviour for aggression, lack of compassion, or even bullying. But guys know what's going on: they're connecting, communicating, relating – it's a male-bonding experience.

When guys have a spiritual moment, they need to jump around, run wild or wrestle each other. I've seen this! It may not look very spiritual, but it is – it's called "spiritestosterality." Guys are physical. I can say to a male student, "Sit down before I knock you down," and they get it – "it" being the wit of it, the humour of it, and the connection to the "guy-world" it displays. Girls would see it as being mean and rude. One of the most popular boys in Grade 12 made the following spontaneous announcement at a retreat: "I can do this forever." The "this" was Grade 12 guys sharing with each other what was really going on in their lives and in their hearts. Sharing their fears, joys, hopes, hurts, and what they love most is something guys crave as much as girls.

So why do they walk around acting so cool, so immature, so insensitive? "Boys learn to mask their inner world with bravado or with clowning behaviour," writes Barry MacDonald, author of *Boy Smarts: Mentoring Boys for Success at School*. "While their masks can obscure, they are not impenetrable."[40]

Why do adolescent boys wear a mask? Their mask is both to hide and to protect. With a mask, they can hide the painful emotions they feel and often can't name. Too many boys subscribe to the boy code as summed up by MacDonald: "1.) Be tough and strong; 2.) Don't show your emotions; and 3.) Don't be a girl."[41] A mask also protects them from the taunts and put-downs of others, and the threat of being excluded by their peers.

The key to diminishing the boy code and helping boys remove their mask has always been the same – significant older males who show them a different way. Boys need male mentors. "Although mothers and female teachers can model healthy female behaviour," notes the author of *Boy Smarts*, "they cannot provide boys with models of masculinity."[42] "When boys feel accepted by men, they can relax into their passage of manhood."[43]

The teenage boy is also beset by the pervasive, explosive, unpredictable flow of sexual energy that has suddenly begun to surge through his body, mind and emotions. He simply and frankly doesn't know what to do with it, and it scares him. Fear produces insecurity; insecurity produces stress; and stress is too unbearable to admit; so he covers it up by acting cool.

If he only knew what was really happening to him, he wouldn't panic as much – the force is with him. All this sexual chutzpah within is simply a spiritual force compelling him to become a *man* someday. The early adolescent can't even conceive of this idea, so he spends the day on his PlayStation instead. That's a good place to hide!

Why do guys lie on their bed for hours listening to music, spend eons staring into a computer screen, endlessly practise skateboard tricks or play killer hacky sack? And why do they walk around with baseball caps sideways and low riders looking like hip-hoppers from LA, when they have never been to LA? Because not knowing what to do with the pulsating mass of male energy inside them, they put on an "I'm so cool and in control" exterior image. It's a façade.

Facades are not really that bad. If I showed my confusion, my fears and my messiness, all sorts of people would be running to me (especially my mother), wanting to help me, fix me, heal me, shape me.

They'd say, "What's the matter with you?"

And I'd say, "I have no idea. It's happening too fast; it's too close; it's in my face and my loins; and I can't step back and get a good look at it; so when I find the right question I'll ask it; but in the meantime, will you please leave me alone?"

Most guys don't really know how to say all that, so they just put up a sign on the door of their outer image that says, "I'm cool – go away!" It's as if they are standing on the porch of their own house, hands on their hips, wearing the coolest cool clothing, hair gelled perfectly and a look of cocky confidence on their face – while the inside of the house is occupied by invisible aliens that scare the living jeebies out of them. *They're afraid to go inside.*

Guys are spiritual, too. They just need a trusted mentor to lead them into the house, and help them discover that there are no aliens after all, just a vibrant Holy Spirit seeking to bring out the holy wildness of their manly nature. If there are boys in your school, there should be male Religion teachers. I'd say the same for women and girls, but I'd be wasting my words. I'll bet the Religion departments in schools across the continent are chock full of women. E-mail me if I'm wrong.

If all this gender reflection sounds simplistic, and if what I have written resembles caricature more than calligraphy, I agree. When we attempt to understand the sexes, we enter into mystery; even jokes about the mysterious are a way in. Pondering the other sex provides a lifetime of wonder.

Back to the Pillow

The journey to authentic living, to discovering your own voice, to becoming a real person, is not a weekend road trip. It is the journey of life. In a Stop Pillow Discussion, it is sheer delight to observe a young person's cautious, faltering, yet sincere steps along the path. It is inspiring to see a girl forsake a misplaced loyalty to others by choosing to speak with integrity, and to see a guy forsake ego and surrender to Truth – who is God. For guys, that usually takes something dramatic, like falling off a horse (St. Paul), being thrown into jail (St. Francis), or being bedridden with a broken leg (St. Ignatius). The spiritual shifts that take place in the classroom discussion might not be high on the Richter scale, but the little rumblings you do notice are portents of greater conversions to come.

The initial individual exercise, the small-group discussion, and the Stop Pillow Discussion that followed could occupy the entire class – sometimes two or three classes. It is worth whatever time is needed, because, as my teacher's manual says, "It is critical to the unfolding of the lesson."

Teens find the Stop Pillow Discussion insightful, challenging and a lot of fun. They also find it reassuring that others experience things the way they do. A recurring feeling for many young people is "no one understands the way I think and feel." It is heartening to know we are not alone.

In a Stop Pillow Discussion, youth get a chance to cut their theological baby teeth in their attempt to give actual reasons to support their ideas. "I think it is true, because that is the way I feel" just won't do it. You can do some prompting: "What is your reason?" You will be able to introduce to students a number of philosophical principles for rational discourse, such as

- Two wrongs don't make a right.
- Find out if your principle holds up when applied to other similar situations.
- Your opinion is only as valid as the evidence you present to support it.

Picture the scene: a group of teenagers sitting in a circle. They outnumber the teacher 26 to 1. When the teacher sits in the circle, he is on an equal level with the students, physically and psychically. The teacher obeys the Stop Pillow rules. At times, he may have to jump-start the discussion, offer some challenging comment, keep the discussion on topic, or periodically impose a "penalty." Mostly, however, he just listens – a window into a teen's inner world.

Consider what is happening here. You have been accepted, albeit temporarily, into the fellowship: The Benevolent Order of Adolescent Wildlife. This is a rare privilege, like an explorer being initiated into the quixotic rituals of the Xavante tribe in the jungles of Brazil. And the strange thing is, the students thank *you* after a class like this. "Good class, Mr. Brock." Most just say it with a smile. And I know why they thank me. Because I gave them a gift: the gift of my attention. Before I begin to teach them, I learn from them, and that is a teaching in itself.

I anticipate that a Religion teacher reading this might protest: "I'm not going to sit in a circle with my students throwing a pillow around." My response is, "Don't, then!" I am no ideologue. I wouldn't want a practical idea turned into an "ism" – as in "Stop Pillowism Belief." Every teacher has his or her own gifts, skills and personality that will shape his or her teaching of Religion. I will, however, stand by the principle: listen and begin with student experience. How one actually does so will vary. However, if someone were to say, "I'm not interested in pop culture and other trivial things youth are dealing with; I want to teach them higher theological concepts that will help them in the future," he or she has just made three big mistakes. Teens will conclude that

1. Faith is an adult thing, and I'm not an adult.

2. If what I'm dealing with as a teen is not important, then I'm not important.

3. My real life and my faith life are different and distinct (a scary concept and one that Jesus often railed against).

In the end, some teens will say without words, "Just tell me what I have to do to get an A in this course; I need it for my GPA and a scholarship. If it means pretending I'm religious, then that is what I'll do!"

Let Your Students Do the Talking

Here is another big mistake: thinking that youth don't already know some of these higher theological and ethical principles we wish to impart, or assuming that a discussion of youth experience can't reveal these lofty ideas. Consider first a few glimpses of the dark side of popular culture. The following are all taken from a recent book by Jim Taylor entitled *Your Children Are Under Attack: How Popular Culture Is Destroying Your Kids' Values, and How You Can Protect Them.*

- 80% of the most popular video games have violent themes.
- 70% of M-rated games (for mature audiences, over 17 years old) were targeted to children under 17. For example, advertisements for *Resident Evil 2* appeared in *Sports Illustrated for Kids*.

- An ad for *Carmageddon*, rated M, reads "as easy as killing babies with axes."
- The *Grand Theft Auto* series allows you to hijack cars, shoot cops, kill women with baseball bats, have sex with prostitutes (and then kill them too) .... In this game, you don't kill the bad guy; you *are* the bad guy. (*Grand Theft 4* added drunk driving and lap dances to its repertoire.)
- 69% of girls surveyed said that magazine content influenced their view of an ideal body type; 47% said the content caused them to want to go on a diet to lose weight.
- Over two-thirds of television programming has sexual content, yet only 10% mentions the potential consequences of sexual activity.
- The Internet has become a significant source of exposure to sexual content. For example, 25% of children aged 10 to 17 unintentionally encountered sexual content while on the Web.[44]

All this makes you want to stand in front of your class and denounce the deceits, the malfeasance, the wickedness, the brutality, the banality, the greed and the depravity of our culture.

Resist the temptation. Let your students do it for you.

"Kids themselves," writes Taylor, "recognize how destructive American popular culture is … most children aren't fooled … They know how bad it is. They know that all American pop culture cares about is making money … children have good values deep down."[45]

And this is what I find in the circle discussion. Students critique their own culture and they challenge each other.

Sometimes girls will say, "Why do you guys love violent video games so much?"

The guys might say, "What's with all the dieting?"

One girl said, "Advertisements and other media influence girls to always compare their looks to some perfect ideal – but there is no perfect ideal."

Do teens have a sense of what it is like out there?

Yes.

Do they need help to decode and resist?

Yes.

Addressing the second question, Taylor writes, "They lack the experience and tools to resist its messages on their own … children have good values deep down … but they lose touch with them because the contradictory messages are so intense, invasive, and persistent." He describes the siren song of popular culture: "its bells and whistles, its bright lights and loud music, its beautiful people, its short attention span."[46]

Students appreciate it when you help them look at what they are looking at. When you help students question their everyday reality, you help to dethrone the omnipotent culture (as youth experience it), and put it on the witness stand for questioning. In the process, you are empowering them.

Here are some student comments evaluating Religion class:

• The Stop Pillow conversations were fun.
• Sometimes I was having so much fun I didn't realize I was learning.
• Most adults treat us as lesser people, but you treated us as equals.
• Thank you for the deep class discussions.
• Thank you for making me feel comfortable enough to speak my mind.

And you wondered whether that last kid had a mind. They do; they all do. Teens are not stupid. They know more than we often give them credit for; and they know when to reach out for a helping hand when they need it. You are the helping hand they reach for, to raise them up from the empty promises of pop culture. Peter said, "I have no silver or gold, but what I have I give you … and he took him by the right hand and *raised him up* … and he entered the temple … praising God" (Acts 3:6).

Teaching teens Religion is not easy. At times it is plain scary. Twenty-four students tumble into your classroom to learn about … God. You stand before them all alone. Forty-eight eyes looking at you. How do I pull this off? What do I do?

Easy!

Pull a fast one on them.

Surprise the hormones out of them.

Don't start with God (that's what they expect you to do). Start with them.

This will shock them. "I thought this was Religion class?"

It is. "Come and see."

And as the lesson continues, they will come to discover that, when we start in Step 1 with student experience, we are standing on holy ground.

5

Completing the Mission

Steps 2, 3 and 4 of the Learning Process

To reach a child's mind
a teacher must capture his heart.
Only if a child feels right
can he think right.

—Haim G. Ginott

Lesson plans. It's like planning a military operation. Or, if you prefer a more pacific analogy, it's like cooking spaghetti.

That's what renowned religious educator Fr. James J. DiGiacomo, SJ, said in his keynote to the National Catholic Educational Association.[47] And he should know, he's Italiano.

Cooking Spaghetti	*Cooking Religion*
First: Boil the water	Evoke, arouse, induce, awaken, prompt and otherwise provoke student interest and curiosity. Fr. DiGiacomo (henceforth referred to as "the chef") offers the following ways to do this (add these to your collection of provocations from Chapter 4):

- a news item
- an open-ended film clip
- a song
- a poem
- a photograph
- a story
- an excerpt from an article
- a survey

"Motivate before teaching," says the chef. "To effectively reach students in a Religion class, the teacher must get the water boiling."

Second: Put in the spaghetti

Communicate the content. "A teacher can become so skilled at arousing curiosity and stimulating discussion that he or she could get lost in the process and forget to communicate the content." The Church is not a debating society, it is more like a restaurant. You come for content, for spaghetti.

Third: Sauce and seasoning

I once ordered spaghetti in Ireland. That was a mistake. There was no seasoning in the sauce (that was years ago, before they joined the EU). I remember thinking: I'm full, but I'll never eat here again. Students might get some content (spaghetti) from your class, but will they really like it, enjoy it, relish it – want seconds? Will they come back? Not unless the sauce is seasoned.

How do you season sauce? Easy: you put some spice into it. You add surprise, fun, humour, imagination, colour, activities, skits, stunts – be creative, flamboyant. As the chef says, "If students are bored, some of the fault may lie with their teachers, as well as with themselves. It certainly isn't due to the subject. Maybe we're serving spaghetti without sauce or seasoning."[48]

And then there are the other variables. What you can teach on a Friday morning is vastly different from what you can teach on a Friday afternoon. If the year were a day, students are morning people. They can learn more at the beginning of the year than at the end. After Easter, the batteries start running low.

Plan strategically. A successful lesson is like a successful joke: timing is critical. Watch how your students walk into your classroom for the first period of the day. Watch the way they walk (run, push, chase, fall) into your classroom immediately after lunch. How can your lesson plan be adjusted accordingly? I sometimes turn the lights off, put on soft instrumental music, and direct the students to put their heads on the desk and close their eyes for a few minutes. If I put some of them to sleep for this short siesta, I consider my plan a success. I met their need. The quantitative time I lost in siesta is made up by the qualitative time I gain in the instruction that follows.

Let's take a close look at Step 2 of the four-step learning process: content, or putting in the spaghetti.

Step 2: Information

After exploring their own experience in Step 1 of the learning process, students are now ready for Step 2: lessons from a 2,000-year wisdom tradition. In Step 2, we "interface" the students' reflections on their own individual experiences with the experience of the ecclesial community, the Church. Or, as religious educator Thomas Groome calls it, we bring their lives to the Faith and the Faith to their lives.

Students often say, "I can learn from my bad experience." I tell them, "It is better to learn from someone else's bad experience. That's why we study History." The truth, however, is this: experience teaches us nothing. It is not experience that gives us insight, but *reflection on experience* that can give us knowledge, wisdom and a whole new direction in life.

We reflect on experience, as the commonly used phrase "in the light of" indicates. We reflect on our experience in the light of a philosophy, a psychology, a political party, a book we have read, a family belief system or an ideology. In the light of some wisdom tradition, we try to "make sense" of our lives.

In Step 2, we reflect on our experience "in the light of the gospel." The wristband found in Christian bookstores engraved with "WWJD" offers the clearest and simplest description of Step 2: *What Would Jesus Do?* WWJD entails a look at who Jesus was, what he taught, how he acted and what relationship he had with the one he called Abba, Father. This reflection also involves the story of a people who, for 2,000 years, have sought to come close to Jesus and pattern their lives on his. A people Jesus promised to be with and to guide in the Spirit. A people called the Church.

In Step 2, the teacher says, "Come, I want you to meet someone; I think you will really like him." That "someone" is Jesus: Jesus, who can be known in the Church through the scriptures, authoritative teachings, sacramental ministry, and the lives of the prophets, teachers, and saints, the daughters and sons of the Church – teens included. Students will come to realize, in varying degrees, that when it comes to their spiritual journey, they are not alone; the Force, the Church, is with them.

Because of the respect and trust established in Step 1, students are willing to meet or re-meet this friend you talk about. In Step 2, the teacher is the primary presenter. I have always found that students are more willing to listen to what I have to say in Step 2 when I was willing to listen to what they had to say in Step 1. In the discussion of a moral issue, I have often heard students say, "I believe it is not right, but I don't know why." Step 2 explains why.

Your quest in Step 2 is this: How can I present the Church's ancient wisdom on this topic to these students in a way that they can grasp, in a way that *moves* them? Your teacher manual will provide a number of ways to do this. You might, however, discover ways for yourself, especially after listening to what students had to say in Step 1.

Example: Teaching the Sacredness of Life

During a Stop Pillow Discussion on the sanctity of life, I noticed that the big stumbling block for many students was the repeated refrain, prevalent in our culture, "It's your life; you have the right to do what you want with it." This point was particularly noted in the discussion on euthanasia. I asked myself, how best can I address this view? I came up with an idea.

The Art teacher had a box of discarded artwork, first drafts of a painting project. I gave one "artwork" to a senior student and instructed her to knock on my classroom door ten minutes into my class and say, "Mr. Brock, I made this in art class for you, because I really appreciated the retreat we had last week and I just wanted to say thanks."

I tell her how sweet she is, and thank her profusely. After she leaves, I continue my lesson, and proceed, in front of the class, to rip up and throw the artwork gift into the recycling bin. Acting oblivious, I keep delivering my lesson on the value and sanctity of life.

You should see the response. Students gasp and stare wide-eyed. Various inarticulate sounds of disapproval spontaneously erupt, and someone finally blurts out, "That's so mean!"

"What?" I say.

"You just ... you just ... that girl gave you her art project and you just ripped it up."

"So what?" I say. "Do you have a problem with that?" (This is the "Provoke a Response" technique I'm getting adept at.)

Students respond with all sorts of reasons why I was so mean and wrong and rude and … Now comes the clincher. I say, "Wait a minute; that girl gave me the picture, right? So that picture belongs to me, right? Well I didn't like it. If you didn't notice, it wasn't a very *good* picture. But it doesn't matter what you think; the picture belongs to me and therefore I have a right to do whatever I want with it." For a few students, the light goes on right away. Slowly, they all start getting it. They begin to see that the giver of Life is God (the girl at the door). My life is God's gift to me (the artwork). There are times I may not value my life (I didn't like the picture), but to take my own life (ripping up the picture) is an insult to the one who gave it to me.

This is the Church's teaching presented in a way that can move students emotionally. They begin to see the artwork of their life from the viewpoint of the Master Artist. This is new information: Step 2.

When presenting the teaching of the Church, try to put Church doctrine into words that teens can more readily understand, while maintaining the integrity of the doctrine. Try to find some tangible object or action that can serve as a symbol or analogy of a particular Church teaching – a show-and-tell methodology.

Example: Teaching Grace

Call for a student volunteer to come forward and face the class. Drape the sign "HUMAN NATURE" over his neck for the class to see. Instruct the student to keep his feet together and to lean to the side as far as he can without moving his feet or losing his balance and falling. Call for another volunteer. Give her the sign "SIN / EVIL." Instruct this student to push "HUMAN NATURE" in the shoulder in the direction he is leaning. "HUMAN NATURE" will lose his balance and fall (unless he catches himself or you catch him). Call for a final volunteer. Drape her with the sign called "GOD'S GRACE." Ask "HUMAN NATURE" to lean to the side again. This "GOD'S GRACE" person puts her arm on the shoulder of "HUMAN NATURE" that is on the opposite side of "SIN / EVIL." When "SIN / EVIL" pushes again, the firm hold of "GRACE" prevents "HUMAN NATURE" from falling. With the strong arm of God's grace, we are upheld and can stand firm against the power of "SIN / EVIL" to take us down. With its visual impact and student participation, this is a concept students can more easily remember.

Example: Teaching About Our God-Given Gifts

Here is another example of using a tangible object to reveal an intangible reality. In Chapter 12 of Paul's letter to the Romans, he reminds us that we are gifted persons, and our gifts are to be used for the good of the community.

> God has given each of us the ability to do certain things well. So if God has given you the ability to prophesy, then prophesy whenever you can – as often as your faith is strong enough to receive a message from God. If your gift is that of serving others, serve them well. If you are a teacher, do a good job teaching. If you are a preacher, see to it that your sermons are strong and helpful. If God has given you money, be generous in helping others with it. If God has given you administrative ability and put you in charge of the work of others, take the responsibility seriously. Those who offer comfort to the sorrowing should do so with Christian cheer. (Romans 12:5-8)

To demonstrate this point, I bring out a heart-shaped (Valentine candy) box with various things in it. I shake the box and ask the students, "What's in here?"

"How am I supposed to know?" they'll say.

This heart, I explain, represents your deepest self that God created you to be. In this box are gifts God has given you to become the person you were meant to be. What are these gifts? You say, "How am I supposed to know?" That is what I would have said if I had been asked this question when I was 16 years old. I didn't know I had any gifts; I really didn't see anything like that in me. Over the years, however, I've gradually discovered the gifts God has given to me.

I open the box and explain the symbolism of each article in the box.

A key   I took a Philosophy of Education elective course in my junior year of high school. I found this course difficult but intriguing. In university I was again attracted to philosophy, which ended up becoming my major. The key is a symbol of my quest for wisdom.

A pen   Somewhere during my high school years, I discovered I liked to read. I like to buy used books. This pen is a symbol of how I value the way the written word reveals beauty and truth.

A paintbrush Since I was small I have often made homemade greeting cards and posters. This paintbrush represents the way I enjoy making arts and crafts projects.

A hook   Growing up, I used to take upon myself the task of straightening out the chaos in the garage of our family home. I enjoyed putting things in their place on a shelf, in a box, on a hook. This hook is a symbol of my desire for order and harmony.

After explaining the other items in the box, I take out a smaller heart-shaped box that was within the bigger box. I explain that this is my heart of hearts. This is the gift I have that I may never know about until I meet God face to face. This is the mystery of me that I may never discover in my life. This is the deepest answer to the ultimate question: "What was God's point in making me?" The answer is hidden in this box. Ultimately, our lives are hidden in the mystery of God.

Thus continues a lesson on discovering the gifts of God's gifted students.

Divine Revelation

In Step 2, we present the teachings of the Church, the doctrine or dogma of our faith. The purpose of doctrine in the Catholic Church is to protect mystery. Great beyond all question, writes St. Paul to Timothy, is the mystery of our religion (1 Timothy 3:16). A mystery is not something we can't understand; a mystery is something we can't *fully* understand. A mystery, G.K. Chesterton said, is like the sun. You cannot look at the sun directly, but with the light of the sun you see everything else more clearly. "A mystery is not a wall against which you run your head, but an ocean into which you plunge," wrote Eugene Joly.

The traditional orthodox Catholic teaching on the nature of Jesus Christ is this: Jesus is both fully God and fully human. Is that perfectly clear? It is perfectly mysterious! Yet in the light of this mystery, we draw closer to understanding the nature of our humanity and God's divinity. The doctrine is a paradox, a creative tension that each generation is tempted to unravel. The ancient Nestorians denied Jesus' divinity; the Monophysites denied Jesus' humanity; and the fashion continues today. Doctrine is the security force that protects and defends the mystery.

When people complain that doctrines are too mind controlling, they miss the purpose of doctrine, which is to expand the mind into the mystery that is all expansive. A doctrine is like going down a very narrow alleyway. You feel hedged in; the light is subdued, blocked by the great walls that curtail you. You are tempted to turn back. This is too narrow, you think; yet you keep walking. Suddenly, and surprisingly, you come to a great courtyard that opens up into an expansive sunlit vista that stretches farther than the eye can see. This is doctrine.

A doctrine is a core belief of the Church that emanates from the revelation of Jesus and is, in essence, unchangeable (Christ yesterday, today, and forever). A doctrine is not to be confused (as, unfortunately, it has often been in Church history) with pastoral practices of the Church, which may be prudent at one time, but subject to change in different circumstances. Such directives or practices do not come from the revelation of Jesus, but from human discernment (e.g. the Church's original ban on cremation). Discerning the difference between divine revelation and human discernment is the ongoing story of the Church. It is the Holy Spirit, and not the spirit of the world, that guides the Church in this endeavour.

In Step 2 of the learning process, we do something that is literally extraordinary. We present to our students graced knowledge – truth given to us by God as pure gift. The Church calls it Divine Revelation – truths we would not otherwise know or know as clearly. Church authority is often misunderstood as a demand to cease thinking, when it is really a call to never cease thinking about that which was hidden, but now is revealed. The core of this revelation, states the *General Catechetical Directory*, is Jesus.

Coach Jesus

Apart from Christ we know neither what our life nor our death is;
we do not know what God is nor what we ourselves are.

—Blaise Pascal

The life and ministry of Jesus is the animating spirit of the Religion program and the core of the curriculum for each grade level. Religious educators who teach adolescents need to present the gospel story of Jesus in a way youth can connect with. At every stage of our life, the Jesus story will speak to us in new ways. How can we be successful facilitators of this story to teens today? The great task of adolescence is the search for meaning in one's life. This is why the Jesus story should be paramount in class: the meaning of my life is discovered in the life of Jesus; and the meaning of the life of Jesus is discovered in a sincere reflection on my own life. The temptations Jesus faced are our temptations; his encounter with the "spirit of this world" is our encounter as well. When we help young people to see that a pattern in their own life can also be seen in the life of Jesus, we have come a long way in fulfilling our mission.

Consider, for instance, one such pattern:

The Good News that Jesus came to announce was that holiness, bonding with God, was now available to all. Holiness is being scattered like seeds on a field. It's raining grace, and everyone, not just priests, popes, adults or Religion teachers, can stretch out their hands and receive it. The search for god substitutes is over; God has arrived.

Repent, said Jesus, and turn away from proving your worth by the things you own, the titles you bear, the people you dominate and the status you cling to. Your captivity to these false gods is over; your salvation is at hand. The good news is this: God is coming to you, to all of you. Do not shut the door in his face.

If you bear good news, you can't help but get caught up in the positive energy of the news you announce. The Good News was a fire inside Jesus, a fire he wished was "already blazing" in each of us. So Jesus travelled the countryside – transparent, open, in love and reaching out to the people, all the people, with the good news.

And then Jesus began to notice something. People were not going to accept the good news after all.

The status quo was too entrenched, the pecking order too heavily endorsed, the power structure too invested, and since the message of the good news was too appealing, the messenger had to go.

When Jesus read the signs of the times, the depth of his sadness was in direct proportion to the joy he felt in anticipation of the kingdom "on earth as it is in heaven." And in his grief, the tempter came again, as he always does when a crisis looms in our life and we are most vulnerable to his false promises and seductive solutions.

It didn't work, did it Jesus? Your little plan, your not-so-good-news, your so-called mission. But all is not lost. I can restore it all for you. You just have to change one little thing – yourself.

Learn to play the game, fight fire with fire, adapt. If you want to get ahead, you have to strike a deal with the powers. Lie – just a little. Be someone you're not – just a little. Put on a mask. Change your image. Do a makeover of your message. Drop the culturally incorrect stuff. Let us manage things from here. Believe me, we know how to avoid being a loser. We'll make this work – for both of us.

It was the tempter telling Jesus to change his true self, as he once told Jesus to change stones to bread. And then Peter, the one with foot-in-mouth disease, takes Jesus aside and endorses the adversary's proposal. "Don't go to Jerusalem," Peter says.

"Get behind me, Satan," says Jesus, rebuffing him, "for you speak the words of men, not God."

Jesus rejected the temptation to alter his true self, to divert his true mission and to compromise his true relationship with his Father. He went to Jerusalem, suffered, died and was buried – remaining, to the very end, faithful to his mission, his Father and himself.

The glory lay dormant for three days. Three minutes would have been enough for anyone to lose hope and place their bets on men, not God.

But when the glory did come, Jesus "rocked" the stone that enclosed him – and us – and a new day of freedom and grace broke forth like the sun on Easter morning.

"So what?" the faces of our students say.

So what?!

This is your story, too.

Every one of you, if you haven't already, will be faced with the same decision Jesus faced. You will be tempted to trade your best and true self for what's cool, what's popular and what the adolescent power system says is what you need to be. Many, perhaps all of you, will fall. That's why you need Coach Jesus. He made it through to the finals, and was the first to cross the finish line. His last words were "It is finished." There is glory on the other side of that line, and Coach Jesus can help you get there. He's been there, done that, and wants to do it again, in you.

Does It Work?

As one man said to me, "I care about whether or not it's true, but to be honest, right now in my life I care more about whether or not it will work."

—James Emery White, *A Search for the Spiritual: Exploring Real Christianity*

Teenagers are hungry not for theoretical abstractions, but for practical, how-to spiritual direction in their lives. Hence the popularity of books like Steven Covey's *Seven Habits of Highly Effective People*, and his son Sean's book for teenagers.[49]

Teens don't want just an explanation of the Beatitudes, but direction on how to live them. They don't just want to know what the theologians are saying about God; they want to know how to personally connect with God. They want what works.

They want to know how to handle their emotions, make friends, make decisions, stand up for their own dignity, and they want practical advice, such as "How do I say no and still keep my boyfriend?" They don't want to find the "meaning of life" unless it helps them find the meaning of *their* life. They want to know how to think in order to know how to live.

Teaching teens Religion is a pastoral ministry. The Religion teacher is a spiritual counsellor. "Feed my sheep, feed my lambs," said Jesus to Peter. Don't let your students leave your class hungry.

Divine Pedagogy

In Step 2, we encounter new information – so new it may seem impossible to believe. How could we have known that last is first, that losing is gaining, that weak is strong? How could we have known that the gentle will receive a blessing, that mourning (not revenge) will bring comfort, that a fully satisfied life is the fruit of doing good, and that the pure will see God? How could we have known this?

This is why the revelation of Jesus is the pattern by which we judge, evaluate and discover the meaning of life. "A stress on divine pedagogy," wrote Bishop Blair of Ohio, "serves to remind those involved in catechesis that what we do believe as Catholics does not originate from personal insights or personal experiences, but rather has its origin in God."[50]

Church authority, when not abused, serves revelation and protects the integrity of this divine message for the world. Without revelation, we take our nods and our winks from each other, not God. The wants and desires and myths of our group, our circle, our culture, our country take precedence over the wants, desires and ways of God. The memorable last words of St. Thomas More capture this principle for the ages: "I die the King's good servant, but God's first."

The Religion teacher has the sublime task of announcing the truth of the Gospel to young people. The Gospel is meant to unlock deep places in a teen's heart. From the film *Jesus of Nazareth,* I showed the scene of Jesus exorcising the demon from the possessed boy (Mark 1:23-27). Here is how one student responded.

> During the film, I met Jesus when he commanded the demon out of the possessed boy. Jesus had a lot of control and said, "Satan, leave," with so much confidence that it boosted my own confidence. It gave me courage and made me think that if Jesus is confident, then I can be, too. I got through the day easily and felt great about myself.

Who would have thought that the Word (heard and seen through the medium of film) would have this effect on this student? That's why we call it God's Word. It does things we can't imagine, but God can. "So faith comes from what is heard, and what is heard comes through the word of Christ" (Romans 10:17).

One day, as St. Paul says, every tongue will confess and every knee will bend, but what a great honour it is to be one of the first to help young people choose it now.

In a Catholic school, students have a right to know the Church's teaching, and teachers have a duty to present the authentic teaching of the Church in matters of faith and morals. You can't be doing God's work if you compromise God's word. You want to take your students to a sunlit vista.

Step 3: Application

Use fewer examinations, fewer quizzes, and more essay assignments. You don't know anything about a subject until you put your knowledge into some kind of expression.

—Wayne C. Booth

In Step 1, we explored life experience; in Step 2, we explored the Faith of the Church. Now we want to explore how this Faith teaching changed our students' understanding of the topic. In everyday conversation with our friends, we sometimes say, "Now that you've told me that, I see what happened in a whole new way." This is Step 3: thinking in a new way.

In the play *Twelve Angry Men* (made into a film twice), eleven jurors see things one way, while one juror sees things another way. The eleven are intolerant and impatient. To them, it is a matter of plain common sense. Step by step, the one lone juror sifts through the evidence, and gradually helps the other jurors to see in a new way.

You are that juror. You see what was not seen by students, or perhaps not as clearly seen. You try to win them over by presenting the evidence. You want them to see it for themselves; when they do so, they change their verdict, their "verdict on life."

We want students to apply what they learn in Religion class to their lives, not just a unit test. Some students mistakenly think the purpose of education is to get good grades. Wrong. The purpose of education is to discover the truth and to live according to it. Getting good grades may mean you can repeat what the teacher has taught. Real knowledge means being changed by the teaching you have learned. Learning begins when you know which road to take. Learning continues when you choose to walk down that road.

In Step 3 we ask, "How has this changed you? How are you a different person because of what you have learned? How do you see things now?" There are a number of ways to ask these questions, but one of the best methods I have found is the student essay.

The Essay

In other classes in high school, students learn to write essays. They learn to glean information from books, the Internet and other forms of media. They learn how to do a bibliography, how to introduce a subject and organize their points. In Religion class, students write a personal reflection on their own lives in the light of the topic explored in class. Our past is always being "re-visioned" by new discoveries in the present. We want our students to do a re-visioning of their lives.

With this essay, I'm more concerned with substance and depth than structure and diction. I give them lots of leeway – they can write a narrative poem if they wish – but I insist on quality work that reflects sincere effort and is a product they are proud of.

I tell the students that I alone will read it, and ask them not to write anything they do not want me to read. I will write comments at the end of the essay and return it. I tell them they will be graded according to the following guidelines:

- It must be on time.
- It must be neat.
- It must be on topic.
- It must be the required length.
- It must show obvious care and effort (e.g., correct spelling).

I explain that I will not grade the content. "I want your genuine thoughts, and I am very interested in learning how this unit has affected you." I give them additional rules and suggestions:

- Use "I" language: "I believe …", "For me …".
- Use stories, examples and illustrations from your life experience.
- Be honest; be real; be yourself.
- Seriously consider again the new information you learned in class.

I'm looking for something closer to St. Theresa's *Journal of a Soul* than Thomas Aquinas' *Summa Theologica.*

Some students are either unwilling or unable to write on a personal level, and will usually hand in a summary of what was taught taken from their class notes, plus a few ideas and definitions acquired from the Internet. This may or may not be their best effort, but I am in no position to judge. If they fulfilled the basic requirements of the essay, they will receive full marks.

Although homework is the bane of student life, most students enjoy writing this essay. Writing not only records their thoughts; it is also a method of discovering them. The Catholic author of *Black Like Me*, John Howard Griffin, once said, "I write not because I understand anything … I write to seek understanding."

Adolescence is a time of new cognitive abilities, searching faith, advancing self-consciousness, and a plethora of new experiences, all waiting and needing to be expressed and understood. Students realize that this is an "essay with a difference," and are just as interested in seeing their grade at the top of the paper as they are in reading your comments at the bottom of the page. Your comments give you, the Religion teacher, an opportunity to encourage and affirm each student. You will have no trouble doing this because the essay itself will touch and inspire you. You will learn more about who your students are, and they will appreciate being known by you.

In Patricia Hersch's book on adolescence, *A Tribe Apart*, the desire of youth seeking to be heard and understood is a continuous theme.

> There was a plea to be heard and to be understood that led to the great unfolding of stories. Their stories reflect an unspoken yearning for a congruence most have never known – not because they come from parents who don't care, schools that don't care, or a community that doesn't value them; but rather because there hasn't been time for adults to lead them through the process of growing up.

> The influence of a single adult reaching a youngster at the right moment cannot be underestimated.

> There is so little time for adults to know and embrace the younger generation, to guide them with understanding and to share the moments of their lives.

Kids need adults who bear witness to the details of their lives and count them as something.

Every adolescent needs a mentor, not just the "deprived" children of the inner city. Kids need adults to listen to them and serve as role models.[51]

Over the years, I have found "the essay" an invaluable tool for being an adult confidant and guide to young people. Here are some student essay topics I have used over the years:

- Me and My Conscience
- Dealing with Tough Times
- God in My Life
- My Virtues
- Love and Infatuation
- My Adolescent Journey
- My Experience of Forgiveness
- Honesty in My Life
- My Struggle with Self-Worth
- Friendship and Me
- My Manifesto to the World (How to Make it a Better Place)

I always delineate the essay topic by listing a series of suggestions, starters, hints, and helpful recommendations. Students are reminded that these are only suggestions. How to approach the topic is entirely up to them. Here are a few examples:

- Essay Title: *God in My Life*
  - How my understanding of God has changed over the years (elementary to high school)
  - Questions and difficulties I have had in my relationship with God
  - My prayer life
  - What I have learned on this topic in Religion class
  - About my relationship to God, I hope …

- Essay Title: *Friendship and Me*
  - The qualities I look for in friends are …
  - My best quality as a friend is …
  - Mistakes I have made with friends are …
  - Things I will not do to make or keep a friend
  - My worst and best experience of friendship
  - My friendship with God
  - What I have learned in this class that has helped me

- Essay Title: *My Virtues*
  - Virtues I try to live by
  - Examples of how I live out my virtues
  - Times I struggled with living out my virtues
  - Choosing and living virtues is hard because …
  - The merits of a virtuous life
  - The people who have influenced me in my virtues and how they have helped me

Sometimes I ask students if I can read parts of their essay (without giving their name) to another class or to a parent group I may be talking to about Religious Education. Youth are often taken aback by the thought that their words merit such value. But they always say yes.

Here is a medley of different student writings gleaned from a number of essays. The first five excerpts are from girls; the last three from guys. The titles are mine.

My Perfectly Imperfect Parents

by Dora

All you ever hear is "nobody's perfect," but it's not true. In my eyes it's my parents' imperfections that make them perfect. They are everything I could ever ask for and are so incredibly close to portraying the perfect image of God. Of course God doesn't make mistakes; He doesn't make wrong decisions; and He sure hasn't walked down the wrong path of life; but people who make those mistakes and are able to correct them or turn their lives around are truly people of God. People who have used their sense of right and wrong and listened to it – people who feel God's presence and can pass it on to others; these are people that allow me to see and get to know God – these are my parents.

My Confirmation Dress – a Sacramental Sign

by Kimberly

If I'm at home and I bring up the topic [of having more freedom], Mom usually says "school night," which means no T.V., no friends over late, no going to a friend's after 8, no going out. Then I usually scream about how all my friends get to do this and that, and then I run to my room and slam the door – loud enough for the whole block to hear. Once inside my room, I will either cry until I'm calmed down or then start wandering around my room, which eventually leads me to my closet. I am sure that everything I own has been in that closet at least once and half the population of my stuff is in there right now. I will go to the back of my closet and find the white silky hanger; and on that is my confirmation dress. It is a long dress that goes past my knees and short sleeves that are puffy. It is completely covered in flowers – pink, red, purple, green, and blue. After I put on the dress I feel wonderful – all my bad thoughts are gone.

Society Says – God Says

by Bridget

Society tells us we should do things that we feel like doing. It tells us that without money we are nothing; and that if you buy this you get attention. Society doesn't care who they are hurting when they send these kinds of messages. Whereas Christian teachings tell us the opposite. It doesn't matter if we don't have one thing because money or wealth means nothing when you don't have love from family members. It tells us we are all worth something no matter how we look or our physical ability or our mental ability, because no matter who we are, God still loves us.

God, Why Did You Take My Grandpa?

by Jeri

Over the years, my faith has grown a great deal. Up until grade 6, I believed in and cared a great deal about God. But something happened; my grandfather died. I was so destroyed. He was everything to me. I guess he was more of a father figure than anything; and I really needed that at the time. I was so full of anger and hurt. I had no one to blame; so I blamed God. I know this is bad to say, but I hated him and I totally forgot about him. I kept this hate in me for a long time, right up until grade 9 almost. I went to my Religion class, wrote my essays but didn't believe what I wrote. At this time, I was going through a very hard time and I only had one person to talk to. She helped me a lot and made me realize that I had two people to rely on, her and God. When I prayed to say sorry for all the years of hate, I felt a lot better and all my problems seemed so small. I could also, finally, come to terms with my grandfather. I could finally let him go and accept the fact that his death was no one's fault. Now I pray and talk to my grandpa and I'm so thankful to God for this.

Sex in the Hallway

by Catherine

About everyone I know makes jokes about sex, sexuality, and body types. All boys my age, from what I see (and I see a lot), tend to check out girls in a disrespectful way, whether it's a thought or a comment. I absolutely hate it! For example, there might be an innocent girl walking down the hallway and a group of guys whistle and say, "I'd do her." It's like they don't see past the physical aspect; they're not interested if her dog just died or if she's a good writer; if she's smart or funny. They don't even care if the comment hurts her, which is the last thing on their minds. However, there are some girls who like the attention because they may feel lonely for whatever reason. Then these girls go out with these boys and this adds on the pressure.

Being Adolescent – Harder Than It Seems

by Francis

Now that I'm a teenager and in adolescence there are more difficult struggles that I have to deal with. Sports are still a big part of my life and a lot of the people I look up to are good at sports. When I think back to the way life was when I was a child, I often wish I could be there again. I had no big worries; fitting in wasn't as big a deal; my mom and dad did most things for me. Now I have a job and I have to pay for things myself. Now that school becomes so important it puts on more pressure. School used to be, in early grades, more for fun. Now, it is still fun with sports and stuff like that, but work is much harder and more important. As a child, nobody cared who your friends were as long as you are having fun. Now you are stereotyped by the people you hang around.

Little Boys Are Desperate

by Aaron

One day, as I was going out with my friends, we met up with some girls and they were looking for a good time and so were my friends. So we went to my friend's house and some girl took me to a room and shut off the light and we were sitting on the bed and she said, "Do you always wait to make the first move?" I said, "No." Then she said, "You are a little boy." And I said, "No, little boys are desperate." Then I got up and left the room. After a few weeks, she apologized to me and we are now friends; and I told her why I didn't do it, and she said she was totally not thinking, and she hasn't done anything since. Then all my friends were bragging about what they did and I said, "Does that make you feel macho; does it make you feel any cooler knowing maybe you have AIDS or an STD or made her pregnant?" And they totally shut up.

Getting By – With a Little Help from Above

by Scott

I have a tendency to fight with a friend. Mostly because they sometimes, not very often, put me down. I never was very popular in my old school. I was put down every half hour, and it drove me

COMPLETING THE MISSION

crazy, until I finally told a counsellor my parents wanted to send me to. She showed me that I was a special person, and that suicide was not a good thing to do. When I finally came to this school, I made many new good friends. The role God has played in my life has helped me through the tough times and has guided me on the straight and good path. He helped boost my morale in times of trouble, and for that I thank Him.

For two decades, I have been assigning "the essay" to my students in Religion class. I'm sure there are other ways to do Step 3 in the learning process, but for me, the student essay has become an essential part of my ministry. If the temptation of the Religion teacher is to pontificate, the student essay will keep you humble. I tell my students that I am privileged, honoured and grateful for the gift they give me in their essays.

Step 4: Action

Teachers in Catholic schools may not be preaching from pulpits, but they certainly can minister from the sacred place of the classroom. The teacher's spiritual life and the student's fundamental hunger for God make the classroom sacred.

—Fr. James Mulligan

Some years ago, when I was the Religious Department Chair at a Catholic high school in northern British Columbia, I would climb the hill behind the school, which led to the chancery office. I was off to see Sister Rose Marie, the Director of Religious Education for the diocese.

Inevitably, in the course of our discussion on teaching teens Religion, she would ask, "Do you pray with your students?"

"Yes," I replied, "we say a prayer before every class."

"Yes, that is good [sweet Sister smile], but do you pray with your students … at other times, in other ways?"

"Well … not really."

Sr. Rose Marie would then give me some suggestions on ways to pray with my students. I took these gifts of her insight and faith, but

I kept them in a mental box for over two years. It is true of adults, not just teens, that we often know which way to go long before we actually set foot in that direction. Since then, I have led my students in guided meditation, imaginative prayer, prayer journalling, the rosary, and other ways of prayer.

In Christian tradition, all action begins with prayer, is animated by prayer, and ends in prayer. Pray always, says St. Paul. In our self-help culture, prayer and action seem like opposites. When we think of self-help, we think of things to do and steps to take. We want to improve, to be more in charge, less dependent, more successful. "What can I do?" we ask; and much healthy practical advice is offered. Over the years, I have noticed that therapists, counsellors and psychologists who write books on these topics have also discovered the power of prayer – or have noticed, in counselling, the need for prayer. The final chapter in many self-help books is a reaching out for God via meditation, mantra repetition, visual imaging – practices Catholics have been doing for centuries. In what many claim to be the most successful spiritual movement in modern times – A.A. (Alcoholics Anonymous) – the first two steps of the Twelve-Step program are these:

Step 1: We admitted we were powerless over alcohol – that our lives had become unmanageable.

Step 2: We came to believe that a Power greater than ourselves could restore us to sanity.

More things are wrought by prayer, said Byron, than we can dream of.

When Sister Rose Marie gently prodded me into prayer, ignorance of "how to" (how do I do it?) and fear of "what if" (what if the students don't respond?) held me back. Yet, there is no authentic prayer without risk. Risk involves the uncertainty of knowing where the Lord is taking us.

Since then, a prayer service has evolved in my classroom that I think is an answer to Sister Rose Marie's patient prodding. The prayer service I explain below is only one example of many prayer experiences you can facilitate in your classroom. It incorporates some of the key elements that make prayer come alive for teens. The effectiveness of prayer is not judged by the cleverness of the way the words and readings reflect a theme, or even the beauty of the words we read. The effectiveness of prayer is judged by how our prayer enables us to become aware of the presence of God, and opens us to the influence of God.

How else will you know prayer has occurred? You will know. Students will seem unusually serene. The all-pervading adolescent self-consciousness momentarily recedes. A spirit of calmness is noticed – the classroom even smells different! Classes that go well smell swell. This is true for all classes in high school, except phys ed. But the telltale sign is this: you, the teacher, are able to actually pray as well, rather than monitor, troubleshoot and discipline. This happens because you are not needed anymore. God has taken direct control. Even the usual attention-seekers in the classroom have found what they are seeking – what we are all seeking.

This is how we pray.

Getting Ready

As in the Stop Pillow Discussion, chairs are placed in a circle facing inward. Index cards with student numbers are randomly placed on the chairs, and students sit in the chair indicated with their number. The lights are turned off. Where I presently teach, I was assigned a classroom with no windows. This is considered a liability to most teachers; to me it is an asset. With the flick of a switch, you have a blackout (though I keep a small lamp lit in the corner). Praying by candlelight helps teens enter into prayer. Darkness dispels exterior distraction and directs one's thoughts inward. Darkness brings mystery to the fore; and in darkness we feel less in control and acquire a more humble spirit. Darkness also diminishes normal teenage self-consciousness; teens feel less "on stage." Candlelight symbolizes Christ, the light in the darkness. I tell the students to respect the candles; they are a sacred symbol of the presence of God.

I suggest taking whatever measures are necessary to enable your classroom to descend into darkness. I once built lightweight wooden frames covered in black tar paper that stood against the windows. In another classroom, I requested approval to put up thick black curtains.

At the beginning of the year, I appoint two students to be the cross and candle set-up people. Once everyone is seated, I announce that when the lights go out, our prayer begins.

1. Beginning

Lights are turned off and a song is played on the CD player. I often use the Praise and Worship song "Open My Eyes" at this time. While the song is playing, the two candle-bearers light the candles and set a crucifix on a cloth in the middle of the circle on the floor. I instruct the two students to do all this gently, slowly and sequentially – cloth, crucifix, candles, Bible, in a reverent and prayerful way. All these articles are on my desk, so the two students move back and forth between my desk in the corner and the middle of the circle. I instruct them to light the candles at my desk, as the spectacle of striking matches in the circle is distracting – particularly to adolescent boys. This may seem a little thing, but ritual is mostly about little things done well and inconspicuously.

The crucifix I use is a transparent cross with the corpus of Christ encased within. It picks up the candlelight and enables everyone in the circle to see the form of Jesus. Recall the essay assignment I explained earlier in this chapter. This prayer service always takes place on the day the essay is due. Students bring the essay to the prayer circle and put it on the floor by their feet (so they don't rattle the pages in their hands – another detail worth noting).

The song is now complete, and the students are seated in a circle with their focus naturally and effortlessly on the crucifix and candles before them. I begin with the sign of the cross and some words of introduction.

We've come to the end of our topic "Dealing with Hard Times." We've looked at some hard times young people experience: loss, loneliness, always feeling compared to others, competition, etc. We have also reflected on the promise that God's love is with us, in good times and in bad times ....

At this point, I will usually play a song that is current and popular with teens and that reinforces the theme of the topic. You may choose the song, or ask a student advisor for suggestions, or invite students to bring in songs that relate to the topic and are appropriate to share with the class. When a song speaks about life's problems and hurts, joys and hopes, or expresses our universal longing for love, that song can evoke in youth a sincere reflection on these themes, perhaps like nothing else.

At the conclusion of the song, I usually have a reading from scripture as well as an inspirational poem, reflection or short story. When scripture is read, indicate the sacred words with a simple "The word of the Lord." "Thanks be to God" is the student response. Readings are done by volunteers and take place wherever the student is sitting. The person beside them takes a candle from the middle and holds it to assist the reader.

2. Student Sharing

Before we began the prayer service, I have asked the students to read through their essay and to get in touch with what was most important for them during the unit. I tell them that, during the prayer service, I would like everyone to share at least one thing. I explain that when you share, you help others. "There are 23 teachers during this prayer service, and what you say is valuable to the group. The candle will be passed around during the prayer, and that is when you can share."

With younger teens (particularly grades 8 and 9), I ask them to say "something." With the older grades, I encourage and invite, but leave the option to just pass the candle without sharing. For the younger grades it is too tempting to "opt out" and just observe. Mental laziness is also a factor. So I mandate saying something, but give them a virtual out as well: "Just say, 'I agree with what Matthew said,' and pass the candle." Encouragement can go so far and should never be experienced by the student as duress or being put on the spot. Freedom and dignity are inviolable in the classroom. When a relationship of care and trust has been established (as I have advocated before), the teacher can gauge the proper degree of encouraging student sharing.

This is a beautiful moment during the prayer service. Over the last two or three weeks, you have led the students through the four steps of the learning process. You have provoked gently, listened carefully, confronted occasionally, guided continually and instructed clearly. Now you see the fruits of your labour. It is beautiful to hear what teens have to say. When the candle comes back to you, share something as well, then place the candle back in the middle of the circle.

3. Group Dialogue

At this point, I want to animate group dialogue. The right questions will prompt such a dialogue.

You have just heard what others have said; I invite anyone to affirm someone by saying what you liked and found helpful in what they said. For example, I like what Tyler said because …

I'll start them off. Hand raising is not necessary; students speak spontaneously. Positive feedback from your own peers for something you have said is a heart-warming experience for youth. Adolescents often doubt they have anything worthwhile to offer. It comes as a unique epiphany when the reaction and responses of others reveal otherwise. This is true for adults as well, but more so for youth. Other questions can also prompt discussion:

- Do you think this issue was harder for you last year or this year? Why?
- Do adults understand what is going on with teens in this area?
- Can someone explain how they have been helped in this area by friends, family or other people in their life?

4. Beefs and Bouquets

Now begins the closure of this prayer service with a ritual that never fails – the acknowledgment of beefs and the offering of bouquets. I introduce the activity.

Okay, before we close this prayer service, I want you to look around this circle and recognize anybody who has helped you in any way; or in whom you see a gift or talent that you would like to mention. Perhaps they contribute to class discussions; or have helped you see things in a new way; maybe it's just their warm smile or their friendship. Whatever it is, you can now give them a "bouquet" by saying "I want to give you, (name the person), a bouquet for (name the reason)." You may also give them a "beef" if they have bothered you, irritated you, or bugged you in any way. If you give someone a beef, you must also give them a bouquet, too.

Note: Having only a bouquet can work, too; but my experience is that teens cannot go through a day without enduring some pestering annoyance, some over-the-line put-down, or some other school-day misdemeanor perpetrated upon them or by them. By the time this prayer service is invoked, the beefs have accumulated, and may even be festering. It's time to clear the air. In the prayerful, positive, even fun-loving atmosphere of the prayer circle, such petty annoyances are named and released. Teens will do this in the right (often humorous) spirit; and when they follow it with the prescribed bouquet, the message is received without the customary sting. "Beefs" and "Bouquets" are the frosting on the prayer cake.

5. Conclusion

It is now time to bring the prayer to a conclusion. You may offer a spontaneous prayer of thanks to God and a petition for God's continual guidance. Then say,

The essay you wrote expressed an honest and sincere reflection on your life. God wants us to come just as we are, and to offer all that we are to God. In a few moments, you will place your essay on the floor around the prayer cloth as a sign that you offer yourself to God, and that you invite God to help you in your life.

The closing song begins as students place their essays around the cross and candles. This ritual transforms what the students previously thought was "just homework" into a prayer. Perhaps students will begin to sense that if their words matter, if their essay is a word to God, perhaps their lives can be a word to God as well – a word of thanks, a word of praise, a word of love. I ask students to listen during the final song (or instrumental) to what God is saying to them. Halfway through the song, I pick up all the essays on the floor. I accept them as a minister to youth in God's holy Church. Then the two students begin removing the Bibles, candles, crucifix, cloth. When the song ends, we conclude with the sign of the cross.

I mentioned earlier that this prayer service contains certain characteristics for effective youth prayer. These include

- preparing students beforehand,
- a prayerful setting,
- scripture,
- teen-sensitive music,
- student sharing,
- an opportunity to affirm and thank one another, and
- quiet reflection time.

Praying Our Experiences

In 1980, Joseph F. Schmidt, FSC, wrote a book entitled *Praying Our Experiences*. This book has been reprinted a number of times; the *Twentieth Anniversary Expanded Edition* has a preface by Father Richard Rohr. Fr. Rohr describes the result of being "addressed" by God in prayer. In prayer, God addresses us as one known and loved intimately by God. The result, Rohr wrote, is this.

My God, this is not a game! It is for real. God is treating me as if I matter, as if God hears me and cares about me! Maybe I do matter. Maybe this whole thing called life is for real! Maybe I am for real ....[52]

This describes well the goal of the learning process. When students come to see that their life matters, and that a faith walk with God is not an act on a stage, but something real, then the learning has a life of its own. Where do we learn that life is real? We learn it in prayer.

The beauty of *Praying Our Experiences* is how Schmidt explains that coming to know God and coming to know ourselves advance along the same path.

> This means that in prayer we are neither on the one hand dialoguing with an outside source who utters messages from without nor are we simply talking to ourselves. We are reaching deeply into ourselves and sensing more clearly that we are in God's knowledge and love. We are discovering the Divine within us. We are experiencing ourselves and our lives as uttered by God, and we listen.[53]

By nature, teenagers are on a search for self; by grace they search for God. Religion teachers discover it is the same search.

Thus you come to the end of the four-step learning process. To experience deep prayer with a class of young teenagers is something many adults would consider improbable, if not impossible. Adults leading prayer with a few teens playing preordained, rehearsed roles – that is not unusual. "Teenagers need to be active, need to be kept busy, need to be on the move," they will say. "You can't expect them to sit and pray for an hour."

"Come and see" is the biblical response. We fail as adults when we interpret a teenager's vivacious physical and often erratic energy as a lack of depth and spiritual longing. It is more often an expression of a desire for the soul-mindedness they are seeking and the prayer that can lead them to it. "There is so much love in this room," said one student at the conclusion of the prayer service.

It is reassuring to close down a lesson with a prayer service where I can pray to God to take my efforts of the last three weeks and transform them into something beautiful in the lives of my students. In the subdued candlelight, I look around the circle and see all these young faces with so much life before them, so much yearning within them and so unaware that they are all sitting there "shining like the sun."

In a few moments, they will be jostling out the door on their way to Math or English or Science, and bracing themselves for whatever teen culture may throw at them today. Still, they are taking something with them; something serene, something reassuring. Something different – something from Religion class.

I want to say, "Lord, stop the bell from ringing; I want to stay up here with my students on this mountain of prayer. I'll build three tents, one for you, one for me, and a big one for all these kids. The kids are quiet, Lord; they are still and they are praying. This is good; this is the teachable moment. Let us stay."

But the Lord bids me go down the mountain as the inevitable bell rings and the students depart. The next day we will start all over again with Step 1 – Student Experience.

And once again, I will be delightfully surprised to hear what they have to say on yet another topic in Religion class.

6

Students I Have Known

And the Lessons They Have Taught Me

You don't have to suffer to be a poet.
Adolescence is enough suffering for anyone.

—John Ciardi

Over 30 years ago, Merton P. Strommen, a Lutheran pastor, religious researcher, and founder of the renowned Search Institute, wrote a youth ministry classic entitled *Five Cries of Youth*. The five cries are the cry of self-hatred (low self-regard); the cry of psychological orphans (family pressure and disunity); the cry of social concern (societal injustices); the cry of the prejudiced (stereotyping and exclusiveness); and the cry of the joyous (discovery of a sense of identity in God with others).[54]

What, I wonder, are the cries of youth today?

In this chapter, I have chosen five stories from youth I have taught over the years. For each, I asked myself what cry was being expressed. What struck me most, however, was not the cry itself, but the intensity and depth of its expression.

Meg: The cry for acceptance

Meg was short, pretty and athletic. She played softball in a city league, but she never joined the school basketball team, because "I'm awful at basketball." Joining the school basketball team might have helped her in the area that she struggled with the most – friendship. Some of the nastiness she experienced in elementary school – exclusion, rumours, derisive little notes left on her desk – followed her to high school. Meagre evidence is enough in high school to be branded an outcast.

Academically, Meg was smart. "Being smart," said Meg, "is something hard to deal with when you're young, being a square. I could read the most books in the school read-a-thon, mainly because I turned to books for entertainment instead of friends." Lonely in the hallways, reading books at lunch, going home at the end of the day with no one to talk to on the bus, Meg's feeling of being a misfit got worse and worse. "Then I finally snapped. It got so bad that I felt suicide was a serious option to consider. Nobody would miss me, and I would be happy."

But Meg didn't kill herself. Someone intervened. Someone reached out a hand of welcome, a hand of friendship, a hand with a cigarette between two fingers. There was a small group of teens in the high school who met in a little concrete enclave and smoked at lunch. "The smokers' group," they were called. One of the girls befriended Meg, and she was accepted as part of the group.

When Meg's mom found a pack of cigarettes in her bedroom, she "yelled and cried." "The thing about that," said Meg, "is that she didn't know how much being a part of the smokers' group helped me. Even though it was bad for my health, it probably saved my life." And so I propose to the Surgeon General that, on every pack of cigarettes, right under all the health warnings, it should read, "But in rare cases, smoking may actually save your life."

Meg's story sounds like one of Jesus' parables, where the ending turns your assumptions upside down. The smokers are God's agents, ministers of hospitality taking in the stranger. The mom, who cries and yells, thinks her daughter is heading for the abyss, when she has just been rescued from it. We adults seem to know as much about the ways of teens as we do about the ways of God – often very little. A 16-year-old girl states,

After a while you get sick of trying to fit in. But I have learned to adapt. I just know that I shouldn't have to change and I won't. And it is hard for an adult to understand that exactly. I mean, teachers don't know half of what actually goes on with the students at school.[55]

In his book on adolescence, *Get Out of My Life – But First Could You Drive Me and Cheryl to the Mall?* psychologist Anthony E. Wolf says the following:

> Newly adolescent girls, forced by their adolescence to separate from their parents, are not confident ... the young teenage girl feels the ever-present threat that she could lose it all. This underdog insecurity gives rise to much cruelty. At the same time, teenage girls make strong, almost loving attachments to girls they admire, which often creates intense jealousy. The result of this combination of insecurity and strong attachment to girls they admire is an unparalleled nastiness.[56]

This insecurity breeds the formation of the "clique," the subject of Rosalind Wiseman's book *Queen Bees and Wannabes*, the inspiration for the movie *Mean Girls*. The purpose of cliques is to give members a feeling of belonging and value. The group solidifies itself by having a common enemy: those they exclude and put down. According to Wolf, "To an appalling degree, girls' day-to-day feelings of self worth are directly tied to a sense of their own popularity ... And all this transpires on a day-to-day, literally minute-to-minute, basis."[57]

Meg is the castaway, the loner, the misfit. Being adolescent, she can't help but conclude that the reason she has no friends is because she is fundamentally flawed as a person. John Bradshaw calls this "Toxic Shame." "Healthy Shame" is realizing we have done something wrong. With "Toxic Shame," we think that *we are* wrong. Meg has difficulty seeing that popularity is a game in high school, with the "unpopular ones" often arbitrarily chosen. She doesn't see that the girls who look so sure of themselves are masking their own fear and insecurity. Young adolescents do not have much experience of life. They see only their day-to-day experience, and they absolutize it. They use the words "never" and "always," as in "I'll never make any friends; I'll always be a loner." They can't compare this experience to previous experiences, when this is the first of its kind. With no lessons from the past to draw from, and unable to imagine a better future, they are stuck in the now with nothing.

Putting the present into a larger perspective is a skill that will come in time, but for people like Meg, the water is rising rapidly around them, and no one can see it but her. Teens often suffer alone, guys even more so than girls.

We need to be on the lookout for the "Megs" in our school. Religion class should be a refuge for them. Meg will gain much solace and hope from expressing her pain and being heard by her Religion teacher. That God can and does use our life experiences to make us into stronger and better people is a truth that can be accepted only later in life; in the meantime, Meg needs someone to express a sincere interest in her troubles.

When Dr. Ruth Arden was in high school, she experienced being "The Misfit," the title of an article she wrote in *Christian Home and School* magazine. After telling her story, she concludes,

> My teen experiences made me a different person than I would have been had my dreams of social prominence come true. The lessons I learned are similar to what others tell me they learned through similar experiences. Those of us who survived junior high have adopted the following goals:
>
> • To never intentionally disregard another person's feelings
> • To become loving and caring to a wide range of fellow human beings
> • To ache with those who ache and feel a real empathy with the rejected
> • To look beyond what society sees and to look into the heart
> • To recognize all human beings are created in the image of God, equal in his eyes, and called upon to serve him and others
> • To serve God above all, and to love our neighbor as ourself.

Could these lessons be just the result of growing up and looking at the world as an adult? I don't think so. The influence of early experiences is indelibly etched on each of our lives. We remember social and emotional pain from our early years, and this pain helps shape the adults that we become. I hope that we, young and old, can turn these experiences to our profit and the profit of others.[58]

Friends are everything in high school. A young person's sense of self, their happiness, and often their academic progress is inextricably bound up with having friends. As Meg says in the conclusion of her essay, "Now I can take smoking or leave it, but I know that I have friends that accept me for who I am ...."

Matt: The cry for respect

Matt smoked marijuana. His drug life existed somewhere between occasional experimentation and chronic use. There were no family horror stories in Matt's life, but home life was rarely a topic in his conversation. One sensed the family connections became strained when adolescence appeared.

Matt transferred to the Catholic school because, as rumour had it, he hadn't gotten along with his peers at the old school. Unfortunately, the pattern continued in his new high school, though not as severely.

Matt tried to stay upbeat, tried to look unperturbed, tried to act like he fit in, but some of the guys in his Grade 10 class saw through the act, and aimed their most pointed barbs at Matt's flagging sense of self. Putting down, making "fun," and generally tormenting Matt became the pastime of a few "jerks" in the class. In high school hallways, they always had an audience.

He tried to come back with insults of his own. He tried to laugh it off, tried to think, "This high school will be better," but inside the rage was deepening.

Something was happening, however, that Matt could not have suspected. A spiritual wrench was about to be thrown into the machinery of Matt's tormented social life. One of the most abusive "jerks" was experiencing the discomfort of an awakened conscience. He was tempted to disregard the inner prompting, but grace won out, and he listened. Something new was stirring within him: something called compassion.

When the Grade 10 retreat came around, Matt's desire to be a part of the class event was constrained by the fear of having to spend two and a half days in a confined environment with "those guys." Somewhere behind the school building, before he embarked on the school bus, he toked up. Getting high would provide the temporary courage he needed and would put that virtual smile back on his face.

The retreat progressed, as it always does, to a breakthrough point of openness, honesty, and authentic soul-searching. An opportunity came for anyone to speak, and one of Matt's tormentors, the one with the newfound conscience, took the stand. He thanked his friends for always being there for him even though "I acted like a jerk." He spoke about some of the stupid things he'd done throughout the year, and how he regretted hurting people. He looked around the room and personally apologized to a few students by name. Then he looked at Matt, paused, and said, "Matt, I want you to know that I think you're a cool guy, and I want to apologize for all the hell I've given you over the year, and part of last year. I'm sorry, man." Matt, who was sitting on the floor, nodded his head and put his thumb up. "Okay," he said, "you're off my to-kill list."

In Barbara Coloroso's book *The Bully, The Bullied, and the Bystander*, she makes note of a study of 37 school shootings that took place since 1974 in the US. Over two-thirds of those who did the shooting had been "persecuted, bullied, threatened or injured." In the aftermath of Columbine-like incidents, high schools in Canada and the United States are scrambling to put together a bullying policy. Barbara Coloroso's book should be a major resource.

She explains,

Bullying is not about anger. It's not even about conflict. It's about contempt – a powerful feeling of dislike toward somebody considered to be worthless, inferior, or undeserving of respect ....

Bullying is arrogance in action. Kids who bully have an air of superiority that is often a mask to cover up deep hurt and a feeling of inadequacy. They rationalize that their supposed superiority entitles them to hurt someone they hold in contempt, when in reality it is an excuse to put someone down so they can feel "up."[59]

After Matt mentioned his "to-kill" list on the Grade 10 retreat, I began to wonder what other "Matts" with other lists are feeling in high schools across the country.

According to youth advocates David Overholt and James Penner, in a study of contemporary youth entitled *Soul Searching the Millennial Generation,* "Adults need to be sensitive to the fact that serious abuse is happening on a daily basis in some of our schools at a far higher level than anything they themselves experienced."[60]

One Catholic high school where I taught had the most cunning bully I'd ever met. I came to the school when he was in Grade 10. I taught two Religion 10 classes, and he was in one of them. I did not have as much knowledge of class dynamics and "the bully" as I do now. I noticed, however, that one class was more relaxed, more open and more fun to teach. The other class was stiff, cautious and repressed. The bully was in this class.

Two years later, when they graduated, the class was half its former size. Students had been driven out of the school because of the toxic atmosphere. Their friends, in solidarity, had joined them.

What must Religion class feel like for a student who is harassed and demeaned in the hallways, yet minutes later sits a few rows away from his tormentor and listens as this person gives the expected pious answer to the teacher's question? In one Catholic high school, a ring of boys was sexually harassing girls in the school. As is unfortunately typical, the harassment had to reach a level of perverse intensity before one of the girls made an official complaint. When this behaviour was finally uncovered, the boys' Religion teacher was shocked. These boys were some of his finer students. There are many reasons why we have a persecuted Christ on a cross in our classrooms.

When 14-year-old Dawn Marie Wesley of Mission, British Columbia, took her own life, she left a note for her parents, naming three girls at her school she said were "killing her" because of their bullying. "If I try to get help, it will get worse," she wrote. "They are always looking for a new person to beat up, and they are the toughest girls. If I ratted, they would get suspended and there would be no stopping them. I love you so much."

Dawn Marie and her family are Aboriginal. Her parents moved off their reserve because they thought they could get a better education for their children elsewhere. To this immense tragedy in their family, they brought traditional Aboriginal wisdom to bear. As Barbara Coloroso writes,

> … the teenager who was convicted of threatening and harassing fourteen-year-old Dawn Marie Wesley before she committed suicide agreed to participate in an aboriginal healing circle with Dawn Marie's family to determine what her sentence will be. The dead girl's mother suggested that the healing circle be used because she was frustrated with the traditional justice system that didn't allow the families of the offender and the victims to communicate. Any sentence imposed by the healing circle will include actions that will invite healing and restoration.[61]

Catholic schools can offer more than a written policy against bullying. They can offer a process for repentance, restoration and reconciliation, before the bullying reaches tragic proportions. As someone who organizes retreats for every grade in the school, I have never met a class that did not need the sacrament of Reconciliation to evoke a change of heart and behaviour in the area of student relations.

On that Grade 10 retreat I described, Matt's bully had a chance to come clean, and Matt had the opportunity to "out" his list. I suspect this was the most significant Religion lesson Matt experienced that year.

Sean: The cry for belonging

Sean was a tall, good-looking Grade 12 student, and as shy as the first sign of spring. He was reserved, deferential and mannerly, and when he spoke, the volume seemed slightly above a whisper. He was friendly enough, everyone liked him, but he acted with that kind of self-effacement that says, "You're not interested in what I have to say, are you?"

We were interested, especially now, since it was Sean's turn to speak. Sean had joined the leadership team for the Grade 12 retreat. That alone was a surprise to the other members of the group. Sitting in a circle, we began to break down barriers with this question: "How have I changed the most over my high school years?" When it was Sean's turn to speak, he looked up and said, "You probably won't believe this …." He said it with such a steady and measured pace that I braced myself for the unexpected. "In Grade 6," Sean continued, "I was the class clown. I was the most popular and most outgoing kid in the class. I cracked all the jokes; I had everyone laughing. That's the way I was in Grade 6. Then one day, at dinnertime, my dad said to the family, "I have good news and bad news; I'll give you the good news first. I've been promoted at work. They are giving me a big raise in salary. The bad news is we have to move out of state in two weeks – I've been relocated."

Two weeks later, Sean and his family moved. On the first day in his new school, the principal took Sean to his new Grade 6 class. "I stood there in the front of the room with the teacher and the principal and I looked around the classroom. And then I saw it – this class already had a class clown. I was unemployed."

Slowly but steadily, Sean retreated into himself. The outgoing, exuberant parts of his personality atrophied and fell off. The descent was steady; Sean became painfully shy. "You probably find it hard to think of me as an outgoing kid like that, but I was. And it is only now, in Grade 12, that I'm getting that confidence back."

Sean's story reminds me how being affiliated (connection and belonging) is of immense importance to young people whose confidence and sense of security is often teetering on the brink. Anything can tip the balance: the death of a loved one, the loss of a close friend, divorce of one's parents, moving, even the death of a pet can jettison a kid's emotional well-being. Some young people exhibit a greater level of resiliency to changing circumstances in their lives. They grieve; they have support; they move on. Others repress the pain, put on a facade of confidence, and pay for it later in life. Some, like Sean, are deeply sensitive, and take longer to recover from a stressful jolt. One thing is true, however, for all teens: contemporary society is not teen-friendly.

We move too much, marriages end, and new people "blend" into our families. The neighbourhood changes, familiar places give way to housing developments, and friends close by move away. There used to be a time when neighbourhoods were composed of neighbours we knew and some we were related to. In the bygone, multi-grade, one-room schoolhouse, your siblings and cousins would be in the same classroom, and your teacher was a family friend or perhaps a relative. Contrast this with the mega-high school or middle school of over a thousand students. Governments build immense schools because it is financially efficient. It is not, however, soul-efficient.

Prior to 1963 in the United States, according to Jane Nelson and H. Stephen Glenn, authors of *Raising Self Reliant Children in a Self Indulgent World*, academic achievement, motivation and self-discipline had been increasing for years.[62] Suddenly, in 1963, these positive attributes declined and were replaced, over the next 20 years, with rising negative behaviours – drug use, teen sex and youth crime. What happened? Was it the fluoride they put in the water, the ban on prayer in public schools, the assassination of John F. Kennedy, the trauma of the civil rights movement, the emerging pervasiveness of TV? The answer, according to Nelson and Glenn, is less the 1963 content and more the seventeen-year context.

The high school graduates of 1963 were the first baby boomers to finish high school. In 1946, their parents – for most of their fathers were returning war veterans – left the small towns and neighbourhoods of their youth to "upsize" in the anonymous suburbs. What families gained in financial support, they lost in personal support. Seventeen years after they gave birth to their first child, that child graduated, in 1963. This was the first child to grow up without those small town or neighbourhood support systems people had taken for granted: ethnic traditions and rituals, extended family close by, parishes as the hub of social life, and familiar places where one's personal history had roots – "That's where my grandfather worked." It wasn't so much dealing with difficult changes that caused the turmoil. There were difficult times like the Great Depression and the war years that didn't reverse national academic and behavioural trends. It was the loss of a widespread support system to deal with life's vicissitudes that changed things. We have since learned that people are more vulnerable than we thought they were. Cut off from avenues of support, youth may survive, but they don't thrive. We are not wired that way.

This is not to idealize the small, connected communities of the past. Along with rootedness came small-mindedness. Alongside close connections were racism and prejudice. Still, the roots that nourish spirituality are found in the particular (my hometown), not the universal (the planet), and people need private sacred places (the woods I played in as a child) in order to appreciate public sacred places (Lourdes). Where we grow up is more than just a familiar place: it is magical, even mystical – something we see more clearly as age advances. It makes the impersonal planet personal, and it provides a tangible testimony of my life's passages: that is where I got into a fight, that is where I went fishing with my grandpa, that is where I played soccer, this is the school I went to and that was my classroom in Grade 2 – I belong! "The soul prospers in an environment that is concrete, particular, and vernacular," says Thomas Moore in *Care of the Soul*. "It feeds on the details of life, on its variety, its quirks, and its idiosyncrasies."[63]

To be sure, the great spiritual pilgrimages of sacred history begin with leaving – such as Abraham's "leave your home, your country, your own kinfolk" – but this leaving, paradoxically, is easier when the bond is stronger. An adolescent can more easily move to individuation when the bond with parents is deep. A strained bond, which would logically seem easier to leave, is just the opposite. We need a strong bond to give us the inner strength to leave.

Those who transplant flowers appreciate the sensitivity of roots to the trauma of change. Teens today, sensing the impermanence of society, may arrest their own personal development when their roots are severed or strained. Bonding to people and places *is* the support network that has been weakened in our economically driven, mobile society. Most adults just expect teens to adjust unscathed.

It took a while for society to catch on: peer counselling, parent support groups, Block Watch, mentoring programs, children-of-divorce support groups and community civic initiatives have all tried to fill the vacuum. Parenting courses have flourished, with parents doing their best to make up for the support their child is lacking from the village it takes to raise a child.

Teens have always been hungry for connection, for belonging, for a sense of permanence; teens today seem even hungrier for these things. When they feel a rumbling under their feet, they instinctively look for something strong to hold on to. This is where Religion class can help. First, it can give Sean a place to express his grief. Teens often express how much they appreciate just being heard during their time of need.

Second, a Catholic high school in general, and Religion class in particular, can help Sean make new connections and new bonds in a school community that seeks to "love one another as I have loved you" (John 15:12).

Third, we can lead Sean to the One who knows what it feels like to be uprooted. "Foxes have holes and birds of the air have nests, but the Son of Man has no place to lay his head" (Matthew 8:20).

After Sean gave his talk on the Grade 12 retreat, many of his classmates personally thanked him because what he said reflected their own experiences. He helped them to feel "normal," and they helped him to feel more connected.

Kaitlyn: The cry for significance

Every school needs a Kaitlyn, if for no other reason than to get through the February blues. Every day when Kaitlyn comes to school, you never know which Kaitlyn it will be. Hairstyle changes, makeup is undergoing continual experimentation, even her personality morphs, depending on which pop star she has decided to clone.

Kaitlyn, unlike most teens, does not want to "fit in," if that means being normal. She likes being different. Not only can Kaitlyn sing, dance and act; she can also draw, paint and construct graphic designs on the computer. Kaitlyn lives in her imagination, which is lively. She likes attention; she likes to be on stage; she likes to be seen. Popularity, which she publicly eschews, but privately craves, comes easily. When Kaitlyn is at a party, everyone knows she is there. Her exuberance is already in the room before she walks through the door.

But there is another side to Kaitlyn. Inside, though her admiring peers don't know it, she harbours a deep vein of self-doubt, self-criticism and a lack of self-acceptance. Though her sensitive soul longs for a love relationship that can dispel her inner pain, she doesn't feel she's good enough, pretty enough or attractive enough to make that happen.

One day, Kaitlyn sat down at the computer and refashioned herself. She gave herself a pseudonym, bumped her age up more than a few pegs, re-scripted her life story, and did a makeover of her photograph. The result was a new creation, which Kaitlyn dangled at the end of a line as she went fishing in cyberspace. On the other side of the country, a university student took the bait. After a few weeks of "chatting," she led her cyber-lover to quit school, empty his bank account, and set off in his car on a 3,000-kilometre journey to unite with the girl of his dreams.

Too bad she didn't exist. And too bad Kaitlyn's parents, belatedly discovering the amorous plot, had to meet him on his arrival, and disclose that their daughter was not 19 years old; she was 15; and that was only the tip of the iceberg. Oops, thought Kaitlyn, I guess I let my imagination go too far this time.

I have never met a high school student who did not go through a time when they saw only liabilities in their own life circumstances – family, looks, temperament, ethnicity – and only assets in many of their peers. You, the teacher, may see a lovely, congenial and gifted person, but they don't see it in themselves. They see themselves with muddied glasses; they see others with rose-coloured glasses. They count what they lack, not their blessings.

Why am I not as pretty, talented, popular, confident, intelligent and happy as "them"? This is a dangerous time for a young person, because they will be tempted to discard their values and principles for the chance to be like others, to be popular. It is a time of personal shame, when they will often take out their negativity on others – siblings, parents or some student they can make fun of. And it is a time, for some girls, when they are led to believe that their sinking self-worth will be saved only if they have a boyfriend.

How long a young person will wander in this land of self-negation is a mystery, but I gave up, some time ago, being surprised at who I see there. Many teens struggle daily with self-acceptance.

Self-acceptance, as a spiritual goal, does not mean you forsake self-improvement. Self-acceptance means being the best person you can be – not being the best person someone else can be. The emphasis is on the "you" – being the person you were called to be, gifted to be, meant to be, to bloom, as the saying goes, where you are planted.

Adam and Eve were planted in the idyllic Garden of Eden, but even that was not good enough for them. They were tempted to be something they were not – "like gods." Lack of self-acceptance is the original sin. "Be a first-rate version of yourself, rather than a second-rate version of someone else," said Judy Garland, who, like so many film stars, struggled with this very goal.

Self-acceptance begins by accepting the particulars of our lives. Teens think: I am too tall, too short, too fat. My hair is too curly, not curly enough, I suck at basketball, I can't carry a tune, I am too shy, I don't like the colour of my skin, or my lack of colour, I don't like the genes I inherited – I don't like me.

Self-acceptance is a lifelong spiritual goal, but the first real crisis of acceptance happens in adolescence. For Kaitlyn, the crisis of acceptance, like everything else in her life, assumed grandiose and Technicolor proportions – as did her response. But Kaitlyn has one thing right. The crisis of self-acceptance should not be endured passively. It demands an active response. The act of self-acceptance involves reflection and self-examination to discover "who I am," which is the task of adolescence: identity. Almost every question teens ask, every conversation they have with their friends, every activity they engage in is, at its heart, an attempt to answer the ultimate question: Who am I?

The problem, however, is that this question cannot be answered directly. Discovering one's identity, like happiness and self-esteem, is a by-product of discovering a vision, a mission and a purpose in life. You cannot stand in front of a mirror and ask, "Who am I?" and expect an answer. You need to stand before the world and ask, "What is this all about; what does this world need?" Then you need to stand and look within yourself, and ask, "What is going on in there? What are my gifts and talents?" Then you must bring both your outer and inner world to the Creator and say, "Show me the way; what should I do with my life?" The Christian path is all about following a call (vocation) to one's destiny, not autonomously constructing one's own "image." We receive our identity as much as we choose it.

The most important skill we need in the search for self is the gift of discernment. Discernment is like archeology; it entails the slow and patient process of sifting through the sand of our life in order to discover the treasure hidden within.

Discernment should be unhurried, prayerful, free of excessive pressure, almost playful in its abandonment to the search – elements all out of vogue in a culture that wants you "on track," "focused" and building your resumé with specific career goals in sight. The Christian tradition is to go into the desert (retreat), and listen to the whisper of your heart in order to decipher the passion within. The Religion teacher needs to help young people hear a call, not just choose a career; to lead them to their destiny, not just a place of financial security.

In his book *Theories of Adolescence,* Rolf E. Muuss uses the research of James Marcia to identify four identity states in young people: identity diffused, identity foreclosed, identity moratorium, and identity achieved.[64]

"Identity Diffused" are those who are confused about who they are and seem overwhelmed with the task of identity formation. It is easy to see how, in our pluralistic and media-dominated society, youth can be stuck in a state of observation and postpone the soul-searching needed for the formation of one's identity. Some youth are so busy watching other people's lives on TV and the big screen that they hardly ever ponder their own. Identity-diffused youth stand at the threshold of the search for self, but are unable or unwilling to take a discernible step forward. They keep turning the channels of their life, wondering what else is "out there."

"Identity Foreclosed" are those who have prematurely ended their search for who they are by adopting someone else's identity for their own. It is normal for youth to "try on" different personas and model themselves on a friend, a group, a parent or a celebrity for a while. This usually doesn't last long as teens come to admit, "I wasn't myself" – a realization that I find generally happens toward the end of Grade 10. Identity foreclosure is more than a temporary "try on," it is avoiding the necessary pain and self-examination that must accompany authentic growth by latching on to an identity with one's mind rather than allowing it to emerge from the heart. Foreclosing one's identity search may provide a temporary sense of security and lead others to see one as "all together," but it doesn't foreclose one's deeper yearning for an authentic self. This task will have to be renewed later in life, which often causes trouble in relationships when a friend or spouse says, "I thought I knew you."

"Identity Moratorium" are those who postpone a commitment to values and beliefs as they question and search to make those values

and beliefs truly their own. This corresponds to the Searching Faith stage of development mentioned earlier.

Identity Moratorium involves putting values and beliefs to the side, not in the waste bin. The values and beliefs handed on to youth by parents and teachers must be personally chosen by youth before they can make them integral to their identity. You cannot choose something you already have. Keeping beliefs at a psychic distance in order to question them and see them with new adolescent eyes may appear to parents as rejection when it is the beginning of integration and appropriation. The Religion teacher is in a good position to help guide youth though this moratorium period.

"*Identity Achieved*" are those who have taken significant steps in their identity search and have made an initial commitment to a vision, a moral code, and a direction in life. An exterior locus of control, which allowed others or the culture to determine who they are, has finally given way to an interior locus of control, taking its cue from one's own conscience. Stephen Covey said it best: "Integrity is a higher value than loyalty." When teens choose integrity over loyalty to their "friends," you know they have "identity achieved." Integrity, they will discover later, is actually a deeper form of loyalty. I cannot nourish my friendship with you while denying the calling of my own 'heart' – the biblical word for conscience.

The four identity states become, for many youth, identity stages. John A. Sanford and George Lough, in their book *What Men Are Like*, write:

> Adolescents typically go through a progression in these identity states from confusion to insecure fixation, then through conscious searching and rebellion to the ultimate integration of the personality into a new identity.

> The establishment of ego identity demands that an adolescent be self-preoccupied for a time. He may need to see himself as the center of the universe, to focus his energy on himself to get a sense of who he is. Narcissism is age-appropriate in adolescence. Consequently parents cannot realistically expect their adolescent to

show much appreciation for them, or sympathy for their struggles. The adolescent expects his parents to take care of him and may take them for granted when they do. Or he may give them double messages about his need to be taken care of. For example, one adolescent insisted that his mother tuck him in bed each night, but complained bitterly to her that she was overprotective when she wanted him to be home by midnight.[65]

Kaitlyn doesn't know who she really is, and is seduced by the image she portrays because sometimes it seems to work. This is where Religion class can help. We can teach Kaitlyn that personality is no substitute for character, nor image for identity. We can help Kaitlyn, and countless other teens, to see their life as half full, not half empty. To see what they do have and not what they don't. We can help Kaitlyn turn resentment into gratitude.

You are not what you buy or wear or own. You are not that illusory label that you crave so much – "cool." You are who you love. When we help youth to love God, we help them become like the God they love. In loving God, youth discover who they are, and have the confidence to serve others, as Jesus did, with the gifts God gave them.

Jesus' spiritual principle – in giving, you receive – is as true for your identity as for many other things in life.

Kaitlyn is in the throes of an identity search. It was not only her parents who bore the brunt of her narcissism, but also a gullible young man driving his car across the country. Kaitlyn, like so many teens, thinks she has to be other than herself to be "somebody," to be "significant." The road to self-knowledge and self-acceptance is long, but it leads to the sublime discovery that God is working in us and through us. God's will for us and our deepest longings for ourselves are ultimately the same. And God does not need us to be perfect; God only needs us to be ourselves. "If you are willing to bear serenely the trial of being displeasing to yourself, you will be to Jesus a pleasant place of shelter," wrote St. Therese of Lisieux.

In the meantime, Kaitlyn will be a hit in your classroom. She will bring life and energy and humour and she will make class discussions seem like a California talk show. She will have no shortage of things to say; just make sure you get "The Word" in edgewise.

Liam: The cry for God

Liam had wavy blond hair and an infectious smile. He didn't say much in class, but there was an intensity to his presence. Liam was in Grade 10.

When the schedule rotation put Religion class at the start of the day, I began to notice a pattern. Liam came to class 10, 15, sometimes 30 minutes late. He'd walk in and drop the late slip he received from the front office on my desk – always with that signature smile of his. Eventually, instead of coming late to the first class of the day, Liam didn't show up at all. Finally, he stopped coming to school altogether.

When I checked with the administration, I discovered why. Liam was an alcoholic; he'd gone for treatment.

There are three things about Liam's story that struck me. One: I didn't know that Liam's smile was alcohol-induced. Two: I didn't know, back then, that a 16-year-old could be an alcoholic. Three: I didn't realize that the well-being Liam was seeking in alcohol was also the "product" I was seeking to dispense in my Religion class. If I had known that back then, I would have been more aware of the pastoral urgency of my lesson. As it is, I suspect Liam hardly remembers my class.

Over the years, I have learned much more about this issue. Gerald G. May, M.D., author of *Addiction and Grace,* taught me that addiction is a problem we all struggle with. "To be alive is to be addicted and to be alive and addicted is to stand in need of grace," he says.[66]

May's explanation goes something like this:

- We have a built-in desire for God.
- God planted this desire in us that we may know love and experience well-being.
- The inescapable bumps, bruises, wounds, and pain of this life – and the fear and anxiety that ensue – incline us to:

- Repress this desire and go it alone – trusting God's love makes one too vulnerable, or

- Attach this desire for God to certain behaviours, things or people wherein we receive a pseudo-virtual and ultimately false sense of well-being. This is addiction. The number of possible addictions seems endless: alcohol, drugs, gambling, shoplifting, negative thinking, fantasies, eating, work, sex, power, "religion," even "being nice." Recently, in Spain, two young students were sent to therapy to overcome their addiction to cellphones. What addictions all have in common, however, is they are substitutes for the love of God.

- Yet, our addiction can lead us to grace. Says May, "Addiction is not something we can simply take care of by applying the proper remedy, for it is in the very nature of addiction to feed on our attempts to master it … understanding will not deliver us from addiction, but it will, I hope, help us appreciate grace. Grace is the most powerful force in the universe … Grace is where our hope lies."[67]

Those with obvious addictions in our society are the upfront ones revealing a problem we are all dealing with. We all try substitutes for God's love. Liam's erratic presence in my class was the beginning of this lesson for me.

Liam has not only taught me a few lessons, he has caused me to ask a few questions.

As Catholic school educators and ministers to youth, are we effectively engaging the drinking and drug culture that seems to be recruiting more and more of our students at progressively younger ages? Are we building a network where parents can consistently support one another in the values they share? For example, not turning a blind eye to the drinking parties taking place in our own homes. Does the slogan of a spiritually impoverished culture – "We cannot have fun without alcohol" – have our tacit endorsement?

I hope not.

Our teens need spirit, not spirits. They have a built-in desire for God. Grace is the high they are looking for, and Religion class is a treatment centre that can help.

Recently, I attended a talk by Dr. Gabor Maté, the doctor who set up shop in Vancouver's Downtown Eastside, which is home to many addicts. His latest book is *In the Realm of Hungry Ghosts: Close Encounters with Addiction*. When he asked one of his patients why he kept using drugs, the response came quickly: "It's where I get the hugs, doc. It's where I get the hugs."

When asked what a good prevention plan is, Maté told us, "An emotionally tuned, non-stressed available parent."

Parents, grace, hugs – I'm starting to see the connection.

Can Religion class be grace-filled?

I believe it must be. I believe we need to see Religion class as a graced environment – God's hug – and not just a place to dispense religious information.

Your religion class is not just a place to deliver a message; your class *is* the message.

I realize that this definition broadens the parameters somewhat. I realize that this way of looking at Religion class takes us to the humble realization that we can't do it alone. We need grace. And that is something that you and the Liams in your class have in common.

Every teenager has a story. If you want to know what it is, ask your students three questions:

1. What is the most important lesson you have learned in your teenage years?
2. How did you learn it? (The story)
3. What would you tell younger teens to help them in their high school journey?

Why did the Samaritan woman whom Jesus met at the well feel compelled to announce to the townfolk, "Come and see the man who can tell me everything I've done" (John 4:29)? Was it her great delight to be known and Jesus' great delight to know her? Was knowing this woman's story a sign of God's love?

"When kids tell their stories," as youth advocate and clinical psychologist Fr. Lucien Larre explained to me, "they have to face their stories. It is very therapeutic." Listening to the stories of our students is an expression of love that they deeply appreciate. Fortunately for Religion teachers, we have months to hear their stories, and not just a moment at a well.

7

Parents

Foundation for Faith

Religious educators have discovered that close bonding with parents is a greater foundation for faith than religious education.

—Martin Lang

Parents – "*In loco Deus*"

People need love the most when they deserve it the least.

—John Harrigan

Recently, on our school's Grade 9 retreat, one of our Grade 12 student leaders, Patrick, gave a talk. He sat on a chair before 65 Grade 9 students clustered together on cushions and mats. This was the heart of the retreat, the student leadership talk.

Patrick was about to tell his story, share what he had learned, and conclude his talk with a challenge to those who are where he once was. He was nervous, but with the support of the other 11 members of the leadership team, he dove in.

> Hi, my name is Patrick. I'm in Grade 12 and I've been at this high school for the past five years. I have a brother, Gareth, that you all know, for he's sitting right over there. In Grade 8, I remember being nervous. There was the cool group, the uncool group and many in between. I was in between, but I wanted to be in the cool group. One day, I think it was in October …

Patrick proceeded to tell how he started smoking marijuana. How he did it to belong, and how it gradually became a central part of his life. Then he spoke of his mother.

When his mom found out what he was doing to himself, she confronted him in tears; she poured out a litany of all the things he already knew, had heard before and had actually come to realize himself – "your future, your health, your grades, your little brother who looks up to you," etc. Then Patrick lifted his eyes from his notes, and looking at the Grade 9s, said, "And then it hit me. Not *what* my mom was saying – that was nothing new. What hit me was this: it was my mom *who* was saying it … it was *my mom*." What "hit him" changed him, and Patrick has been drug-free since.

Patrick's talk touched me, as most retreat talks do. His talk got me thinking again. How does one teach Religion to teens? How do we teach the beliefs, traditions and values of our Faith in a way that doesn't stay on the "I've heard all that before" level, but moves into the heart and out into life? When Patrick said, "It was my mom," what was he saying? That a bond of love is the wire through which the charge of faith can alone transmit. That a relationship of care and commitment is the only vehicle through which faith can be passed. The familiar truism speaks of this idea: faith is caught, not taught.

At the most sensitive place in the hearts of youth, you will find their parents. Because parents don't believe this, they try to assert themselves to gain their rightful place, a place they already occupy. Contrary to appearances, the door to a teen's heart is always open to their parents. But parents, not believing this, feel they have to barge in. Have you ever tried to barge through an open door? You look very foolish.

Why, then, do parents and teens fight and argue and yell and have conflict and end up saying mean things to each other? Religion teachers are *in loco parentis*: we take the parent's place. Parents are *in loco Deus*: they take God's place. Being in God's place is not an easy job.

As one teen said, "I argued a lot with my parents. They told me this stuff about me, and I didn't like what they said. So I argued with them. Well, I knew they were right, but I argued anyway."

"It is so hard to believe," said Kierkegaard, "because it is so hard to obey."

That teens see their parents in God's place may be difficult to believe when the teen seems to want parents around less, not more, and parents' importance in their life appears to be on the wane. Parents, however, do not diminish in importance in a young person's life; they just diminish in a young person's attention. A newly emerged self-consciousness gives more attention to what peers think about them and what teen culture dictates as "cool." It's not that parents are purposely pushed out to the periphery of a teen's life; they are inadvertently crowded out. It is no coincidence that faith and parents are crowded out simultaneously. It is important for parents to know that teens feel the pressure and pull of the group, and are calling out to them for help to navigate through it. Teens value their friends highly, but when it comes to naming the most influential persons in their lives, parents top the chart.

Parents represent God to their children, and children by nature are open to the revelation of God in their parents. For younger children, the power, authority and wisdom (omnipotence, omniscience) of God are all mirrored in those large adults who pick them up and mysteriously solve their problems. In adolescence, parents still need to be that "rock of ages" youth can lean on, stand on and even push against to test its solidity. Teens may wander after the false gods of our culture, or temporarily compromise their integrity for peer acceptance, but they still want their parents on the throne of their heart. In youth retreat talks, the mention of parents always strikes the deepest chord, touches the rawest nerve and evokes the most heartfelt desire.

Angela's story

I want to talk about my relationship with my dad (*tears begin to well up, and are held in check*). In Grade 10, we used to fight a lot (*a tear escapes and is wiped away*). He'd always come in my room and give me a lecture. I'd be sitting on the bed and I wouldn't say anything; I'd stare at the floor. And he'd stand there with his arms crossed, going on and on and on.

Then, one day, he came in again and instead of standing (*she tries to hold back the tears*), he sat down on the bed next to me (*pause*) and instead of giving me another lecture, he said, "Can we talk?" (*she reaches for Kleenex; the tears are cascading*).

Teens expect their parents to love them the way God does. Their hearts are always open to that love. Substitute the word *God* for *mom* in Patrick's story.

"What hit me was this, it was my God who was saying it … it was my God."

Now substitute the word *love* for *God*, as St. John does (1 John 4:8).

"… it was my Love who was saying it … it was my Love."

Eric's story

Eric was telling his peers about his long struggle with drug use. His girlfriend left him because of it; even his friends left – except the hardened users. His mom railed against him, but he was too sneaky for her. He was good at hiding, for a while. Eventually, he ended up hanging onto his soul by his fingertips. He finally turned himself in for treatment.

When he concluded his story, Eric said something with such sincerity and passion that I've thought about it often, trying to capture the full import of it. "There is only one thing for which I will always, always be thankful. I'm so glad … so … so glad that my mother never said to me, 'I told you so.'"

Teens cannot endure being shamed by their parents. They cannot bear it. It is like being shamed by God.

Adults often have no idea how close to the abyss of self-hatred many young people are. When life chips away at the last remaining stronghold of a young person's sense of well-being, they always have one ace in the hole – their parents. But when they lose that card, a tightness begins to form in their chest, and their mind freefalls into a self-condemning mantra that is difficult to silence. They begin to think in absolutes: "I'll never be good enough; I'll never pass the grade; I'll always be a loser." They feel like they are on a treadmill, always trying to get to that place of contentment, but never gaining any ground. Anger erupts, outward against others, or inward against one's self. But there was a net to catch Eric. His parents were there. Their love and support were expressed, as he interprets it, by not saying, "I told you so."

Eric may not realize it yet, but he met Jesus in his mother that day. It is the same Jesus who wrote in the sand rather than facing and shaming the woman caught in adultery. "Has no one condemned you?" asks Jesus, as the stone throwers depart. "Neither do I condemn you. Go and sin no more" (John 8:3-11).

Youth today draw their parents close to their hearts because they need a shelter from the pernicious messages they so often hear in youth culture: You are not cool enough, good enough, worth enough; you don't fit in. Without a parent to find refuge in, a student can suffer through a very lonely ordeal, as Cara's story reveals.

Cara's story

Cara received daily messages on her free web page telling her that she was ugly, useless, fat, and that she'd never have a boyfriend. She was told with assorted expletives how wasted her life was, how the future would be worse, and that there was no good reason to continue living. She felt that she couldn't tell her mom what was happening because she had disobeyed her parents by setting up the free web.com in the first place. Every day at school she had to face the girl and her friend who tormented her in cyberspace.

Cara soon developed suicidal thoughts that were more than impressions or feelings. They seemed like words from outside her, directed personally to her. She began to record them in a "suicide journal." Soon, the words and thoughts became obsessive.

Cara's lonely struggle escalated on a daily basis until the day she went to school and discovered everyone crying. A makeshift shrine had been erected for a boy who had accidentally taken his own life the previous evening. The outpouring of grief for this boy revealed to her how much people really do care, and how much a life is worth. Her suicidal thoughts began to recede. When the two girls who had tormented her left the school and Cara developed healthy friendships with other girls in her class, her healing was almost complete. One more thing remained to be done, and she did it. She told her mom about the "living hell" she had gone through at the beginning of the school year.

Attachment: A Faith Foundation

When the *Catechism of the Catholic Church* calls the family a "domestic church" (#2204) and speaks of parents as the "principal and first educators of their children" (#1653), and calls on them to "receive the responsibility and privilege of evangelizing their children" (#2225), most parents respond with a twitch of guilt and a mental survey of what more they should or could be doing for their child. They conjure up a mental snapshot of what a perfect Catholic teenager must look like, and compare the ideal to the one playing Wii in the living room. Parents, like religious educators, initially think of a product, not a process; they accentuate content, not context. Gordon Neufeld and Gabor Maté's bestseller *Hold on to Your Kids* is especially helpful to Religion teachers because, unlike most parenting manuals (helpful in their own right), this book addresses primarily what parents need to *be*, and only secondarily what they should *do*.[68] Christian tradition has always maintained the primacy of parents in the transmission of faith to children: this primacy is located in the relationship, rather than in any method or program of discipline employed. The Catechism uses rather pointed words when it says, "the role of parents in education is of such importance that it is almost impossible to provide an adequate substitute" (#2221).

It is "almost impossible" to recreate a relationship like the one between parent and child. If parenting was all about techniques, skills and methods, an adequate substitute could be provided with the proper training. But parenting is not primarily about these things. It is about attachment and relationship. "For a child well attached to us," write Neufeld and Maté, "we are her home base from which to venture into the world, her retreat to fall back to, her fountainhead of inspiration. All the parenting skills in the world cannot compensate for a lack of attachment relationship."[69] The words that Patrick's mom said to him seemed irrelevant; what mattered most was who was saying it – *it was his mom.*

A similar dynamic unfolds in Religion class. Our impact on our students is determined more by the relationship we have with them than the words we say to them. To put it a better way, the words we say penetrate only as deep as the relationship.

Hold on to Your Kids describes what every Religion teacher experiences as the biggest obstacle to teaching teens Religion: the phenomenon that Neufeld calls the "peer-oriented" teenager. The authors use attachment theory to explain how the natural attachment teens should have with their parents and other nurturing adults (e.g., Religion teachers) has been usurped for some teenagers by their peers. The book describes the harm this situation causes, explains why it happens, and offers ways to "reclaim our kids."

The malevolent effects of peer-oriented teens include shutting down vulnerability and looking to peers for direction (what the authors call "orientation") about what to believe, what to value and how to behave. On both scores, the Religion teacher is up against formidable barriers, because Religion is all about vulnerability (being open to one's deeper self) and being oriented towards values that are not highly esteemed in pop teen culture. When teens are unattached to their parents, they become more dependent and enmeshed in their peers. The same ratio will hold in the classroom. The more a student in Religion class is attached to her parents, the more she will be receptive to the Religion teacher. The peer-oriented student has no such desire. He or she watches carefully for cues from peers about how to regard Religion and how to respond to what you are trying to teach. The greatest resource that a Religion teacher has is not the curriculum, the textbook or any audiovisual materials – it is the parents of the students.

Be a Person Who Blesses

Then they brought little children to him, that he might touch them; but the disciples rebuked those who brought them. But when Jesus saw it, he was greatly displeased and said to them, "Let the children come to me, and do not forbid them …. And he took them up in his arms, laid his hands on them, and blessed them.

(Mark 10:13-16)

As the stories of Patrick and Angela and Eric and Cara reveal, there is a dynamic going on in the lives of students that is more foundational for their faith development than anything we do in the classroom. Knowing this, Religion teachers will avoid treating students as blank slates upon which to write Religious truths. Teachers will realize that we can't work with young people outside their family context; instead, we must attempt to deepen the connection teens have with parents, or help to repair damaged bonds.

You can almost bet that if a student expresses bitter resistance to what you are doing in Religion class – I'm not talking about honest, positive questioning here – he or she is projecting onto you the pain of a strained and conflicted family life. Your first response to a negative teenager needs to be inquiry, not criticism.

Some students will turn to you for support to make up for what is lacking at home. Although you can do much for this student, you will sense that it is never enough. Trust that what you do will be used by God in the broader providential plan that God has for this young person. As the Catechism puts it,

Family ties are important but not absolute. Just as the child grows to maturity and human and spiritual autonomy, so his unique vocation which comes from God asserts itself more clearly and forcefully. Parents should respect this call and encourage their children to follow it." (#2232)

Sometimes it is the Religion teacher who first sees and respects this call and encourages a student to follow it. I know of a student in my own high school who, having no religious upbringing at home, was drawn to faith by his Catholic high school and the parish youth group his Catholic friend invited him to join. He enrolled himself in RCIA and plans to be confirmed at Easter.

If parents come to you, the professional religious educator, for advice regarding the faith of their adolescent child, you can of course talk about the curriculum and about devotion at home and in the parish. But if you want to go to the core, the foundation, encourage the parents you represent to bless their children – your students. This is something that can easily get lost in the predictable storms of parent/teen relationships.

Blessing/Affirmation is the prerequisite course for high school Religion programs because it gives students what Conrad Baars calls a "felt faith" – an openness to what you are teaching because it resonates with the Affirmation/Blessing they received from their mom and dad.

What is Affirmation/Blessing? I owe a big debt to Baars, the author of *Born Only Once*, for teaching me the meaning of affirmation, and to theologian Fr. Ron Rolheiser, OMI, for a talk he gave on Catholic education where he equated the biblical word "blessing" with affirmation. This is what I learned.

Affirmation does not give the person "skills" or "knowledge"; it is not something you can put on your resumé. *Affirmation gives the person the gift of his or her own self.* It is in the receiving of ourselves as a gift that we experience the giftedness of our life. We cannot do this alone. Baars describes affirmation as three movements.

1. Awareness

I see you; I am aware of you.

Picture yourself walking alone along a busy city street. Everyone seems intent on his or her own business, and conscious of the march of time. From across the street, you hear your name called. You look up, and an acquaintance waves at you. You wave back. The concrete no longer feels so hard, and you no longer feel so insignificant. You are seen.

Young people are amazed when they are noticed. Some may react with suspicion: "What do you want from me?" Mostly they react with a sense of elation and wonder, "She remembered *me*; she even knew my name." We fail, as adults, to understand the sense of "unworthiness" that many young people carry around with them. To be noticed, to be seen, to be chosen is an uplifting revelation to them.

2. Being Moved

I am moved inwardly by you.

On a warm spring day, you go for a walk in the park. You see a child run across the grass, then stop to watch a duck waddle towards the pond. This child, so full of life, curiosity, attentiveness and presence, moves you.

Teachers see a student in class whom they have taught for three and a half months. This time, however, they are moved inwardly. It is hard to exactly explain why. They sense the student's uniqueness; he or she is not just "a student." It is not what the student has done – an essay, a test, a homework assignment – that moves the teachers; it is not his or her doing; it is his or her being.

Being moved within means finding delight in the other's goodness and worth without the desire to use them, possess them or change them.

3. Revealing

I express what has moved within me.

This may look like the "doing" part. Look again. Have you ever received a note of congratulations or a word of praise on the level of information about you, not affirmation of you? Have you ever received a word or note of praise from someone who you felt was doing it out of duty, or a workshop taught them to go around spreading random words of praise? Affirmation is a gift given out of the movement of the heart, not a task dictated by the head.

It can be a word or an action, and as simple as a smile or a hug. Pope John XXIII went to visit the inmates of Regina Coeli Prison in Rome. He spoke of God's love, God's mercy and the hope we have in God's promise. One of the inmates yelled out, "Are those words of hope you have given us for such a great sinner as I am?" John walked through the group, found the man, and threw his arms around him. Conrad Baars writes, "Whether it was in direct personal contact or via the television, young and old, men and women, Catholics and non-Catholics alike all over the world have been touched and opened by John's affirmation of everyone around him."[70] As a teacher of Religion, I may, like Pope John XXIII, speak beautiful words about God's love and forgiveness; but students will want to know, like the prisoner, if what I said is meant for them.

I remember being affirmed. I was in Grade 8, and the braces on my teeth exacerbated my normal shyness and self-consciousness. The usual epithets "tinsel teeth" and "don't smile; you're blinding me" were enough to reinforce my natural disposition, and convince me to keep my mouth closed most of the time. One day, I was walking alone by the gym when a popular senior student stopped me and said, "I notice you don't smile that much [he saw me]. Is that because you are embarrassed about wearing braces? [he is moved inside] Don't let that bother you; you're okay – just be yourself." [he reveals what moves him and shows acceptance of me as a person]. It was that quick; then he walked on. When I turned, he had vanished. He was an angel sent by .... Just kidding. He was a real human being – a teenager, too.

Why is it that I can hardly remember anything else from that year? Why is a 30-second conversation from so many years ago still fresh in my mind? Because that student, whose name I didn't even know, gave me the most important gift I received that school year – the gift of myself. Of all the students walking around the school, he was the one who stopped me. He told me I was okay. Slowly and imperceptibly, I began to believe it.

Someone might ask, weren't you taught that in Religion class? Isn't learning about God's love for you part of the curriculum? I was taught this point, but I didn't learn it. I was taught faith as a noun, but I needed to receive it as a verb. I needed a felt faith, the result of being affirmed, of being blessed. I needed to receive the gift of my own goodness in order to trust the goodness of God – i.e., faith. As Conrad Baars explains,

> A truly felt faith and trust in a loving God are essential if we are to become open to the goodness of all being, and to live without fear. However, the presence of this felt faith and trust depends on and develops only as a result of emotional affirmation. Non-affirmed individuals are capable of directing their will towards God when their intellect discovers the necessary reasons for doing so. However, purely intellectual orientation towards God does not stimulate their feeling of love for God, and does little to open them to knowing and feeling the goodness of all being. In fact, in times of severe emotional stress this spiritual orientation may collapse easily and reveal the underlying fearful self-centeredness.[71]

The love that Jesus gave the world originated in the affirmation he received from the Father, his Abba. When Jesus stood before John the Baptist in the Jordan River, his Father affirmed him: "This is my beloved Son in whom I am well pleased" (Matthew 3:17). I see you, my son, I see you. You are my beloved son; in you I take great delight. Youth today still seek this blessing from their father – and their grandfather, as Eli's and Gaurav's stories reveal.

Eli's story

> Losing my grandpa was the biggest challenge in my life and I will always keep his name in my heart. A simple sentence my grandpa would always say to me that always keeps me thinking about him is, "You're gonna be a boxer one day." What keeps me going is not the words but what the words mean to me. To me it means he thought I was worth something and I could do anything I put my mind to.

Gaurav's story

My dad was always a little more religious than the average Joe. He also had great values that I believe everyone should have. One day, after a muddy soccer game, Dad came to pick me up in his Mercedes. I said, "Do you have a towel or something to put over the seat so it doesn't get muddy?" Dad replied with, "Son, I can replace the seat, and even the car, but I cannot replace you. Get in!"

That day, I saw God in my dad, and I do every time I see him.

God has called parents to bless their children. When they don't or can't do it, God will call others. But the child will never stop grieving that it wasn't his or her parents who did so.

Lisa's Story

When I was smaller I used to lie to my parents about small things. I knew though that they knew that I was lying. So it didn't really matter that much. But ever since I can remember, my parents have lied to me.

At first about small things like, "I'll get you this next time." But that "next time" never came.

And now, too, If I ask them to spend more time with me, and we set a date, something would always come up, and they would say, "Oh, next week" or "When it warms up" or "I'm busy right now, we'll see tomorrow."

But the "tomorrow" or "next week" never comes along.

Usually now, when my parents tell me this, I don't believe them, even if it might be true that particular time.

I know that I'm not perfect in telling the truth. I know I shouldn't doubt this, but whenever they say that they love me, which is rare when they do, I don't believe them.

I ask them lots of times why they don't spend time with me and they say, "It's hard with a baby in the house." But it was the same even before my brother came.

I remember noticing Lisa's intense interest in Franco Zeffirelli's film *Jesus of Nazareth*, parts of which I sometimes show my class. It was the person of Jesus that won Lisa over. She asked me if she could borrow the film to watch on the weekend. She saw in Jesus the love she so deeply desired. One day Lisa will have to grieve the pain in her heart – a necessary step in healing. I hope she does this while being held in the strong arms of Jesus.

Often, when parents can't affirm and bless their children, it is because they were not affirmed by their own parents as children. This is when they need to bask in the lavishness of the Lord's blessing, because we cannot give what we have not received. There is no doubt about it; a parent's enduring presence will remain in the heart of a child. It is meant to be a light that guides, a fire that warms, and a love that never ceases.

I conclude this chapter with part of an essay that a girl in Grade 11 wrote. This girl was an open and receptive student in Religion class. It is no surprise why. Being blessed at home, she possessed a felt faith. Religion class merely gave her the words, images and stories to express what she had already experienced.

Cecile's Story

"Lose five pounds by summer."
"How to be a success at school."
"Accentuate your eyes, cheeks, lips so he'll notice you."
"Only three exercises to a newer, happier you."
On the cover of fashion magazines this is all young girls see today. So much is based on improvements. Improvements in your appearance, personality, lifestyle. All this to make you more appealing, lovable, affirmable.

All my life I have grown up listening to and absorbing this prevalent message like a sponge absorbs water. It came as a surprise to discover that affirmation of my self-worth would be born out of nothing but love for who I inherently am.

It seemed odd that anyone could love me before I gained any of these attributes that society deems desirable. Then I realized that my parents have done this all along.

It always reminds me of *How the Grinch Stole Christmas*. The Whos had nothing in Seuss's story. The Grinch stole all the materials associated with Christmas, yet Christmas still existed because of the unconditional love and sense of community. It was a love that came without "boxes, ribbons, or bows."

When I picture the idea of unconditional affirmation and self-worth, I can then just picture myself without "boxes, ribbons, and bows." Before a certain point in my life, I would have considered myself "unlovable" without all these trimmings. However, now, as I mature, I realize that a person is perfectly lovable in herself. To have love for myself though, I had to be repeatedly affirmed by others. Of course, my parents were the first to do this.

I remember in Grade 9 when I brought home a less than stellar mark, my parents did not care. They noticed, but did not harp on it. They knew I had put much of myself into the work. My mom even instituted mother-daughter Friday dinners. Not as a reward or even a celebration for an achievement or goal. The dinners were just "because" – because we are mother and daughter. No amount of achievement or underachievement would change that.

Quietly, in homes across the continent, teenagers are being affirmed by their parents. It doesn't make the evening news. It is not the subject of "shocking life experiences" in the non-fiction section of the library. It is not the stuff of rumours circulating in the neighbourhood and in the hallways of our high schools. It goes unnoticed, except in the hearts of the young who turn off the light when they go to bed at night and experience the serene contentment of being blessed as they drift into blissful sleep – the way I imagine Jesus went to bed when he was young.

8

Sin

Moral Erosion or Reconstruction?

We acquire a sense of sin only when we receive
the revelation of God's faithfulness to us.

—Cardinal Suenens

It happened ten years ago. A few teachers and I were in a candlelit room on a Saturday night. We had prepared a retreat for the Grade 9s; this was the hour set aside for Reconciliation. Student leaders from Grade 12 acted out the parable of the prodigal son, and we read aloud an examination of conscience. Then we put on soft music and encouraged the students to confess their sins to God through the priest, who sat facing an empty chair in the corner of the room. We also recommended reconciling with each other, if needed. That's when it happened.

Long line-ups formed to see the priest. Heart-to-heart forgiveness ensued between class adversaries. Tears and hugs were shared lavishly among classmates. Two hours later they were still hugging, crying and confessing. I looked across the room at my colleague. Our facial expressions said it all: This is incredible. This is Grade 9! Since then, every year, at every grade level, it's been the same. Reconciliation is the highlight of youth retreats. On their evaluation forms, students explain why:

Well, I know everyone was tearing up, including me. And it was very deep. Reconciliation really opened my eyes to what I was doing wrong.

Very refreshing.

It helped me to become a better person and to become a better friend to everyone. I no longer want to talk bad or mean about anyone. I just want to treat others with respect.

I really should have gone up, but I didn't. Now, thinking about it, I kinda wished I did.

I suspect this last student will "go up" on the Grade 10 retreat.

I don't know about you, but when I was young, I never thought of Reconciliation (we called it Confession then) as a celebration. I didn't look forward to being dropped off at the church on Saturday morning during Lent to "go to Confession." It certainly wasn't something to prolong – it was something to get over with quickly.

Young people today are experiencing the fruit of a renewal of Reconciliation, which began with Vatican II. The renewal came, providentially, just in time, because the ability to "avoid the near occasion of sin" has, for many youth today, become extremely challenging. The seduction of sin in our culture is more than near – it's in your face. If in the past you had to search for pornography, just the touch of a key will deliver it today. When our students' great-grandparents watched *Gone with the Wind* in movie theatres 70 years ago, they were shocked when Clark Gable declared at the end of the film, "Frankly, my dear, I don't give a damn." Today, trash talk, incessant swearing and sarcastic put-downs are just part of the language of both sexes, in the movies and in everyday conversations.

Theft is a problem in my school. Students are afraid to leave anything anywhere or it could be "gone in 60 seconds." Lying, today, seems something you just have to do to get what you want. Moral dilemmas have assailed all generations, but I think it is harder being good today.

"There have been more ethical scandals in the last five years than the previous five decades combined," writes Patricia Hersch. "In every field of endeavor – business, political, entertainment, sports, law … religion, prominent organizations, and famous people have found their name in the news because of illegal or unethical conduct …. They [youth] have grown up in the quicksand of an ambivalent, amoral society."[72]

My wife and I were given a striking example of this when we purchased a cellphone. On page 17 of the operating manual, we were told how we can win $666 by text messaging our best sin. I'm not making this up.

SIN 2 WIN

At Virgin Mobile, we know nobody's perfect. Heh, some of us are downright wicked. That's why we created SIN 2 WIN. So all you sinners can get your worst (and most entertaining) sins off your chest. Why carry around all that emotional baggage when you could just as easily share it … and have the chance to win $666!

How it Works:

1. Do something sinful.

2. From your phone, text your sin 4746 (I-SIN).

3. Check the VXL SIN 2 WIN page on your mobile each Wednesday to see if we posted your sin. If we do, you win $25 credit on your account. Remember to check back often – there's a new winner every week.

4. Vote! Every few months, the sin with the most votes wins $666.

The Bible says, "the wages of sin is death," but this ad says the wages of sin is hard cash, so keep it up!

Jesus never dismissed sin as a normal mistake we all make because "nobody's perfect." He saw sin for what is it: utterly destructive, the great lie propagated by the "father of lies who was a liar from the beginning" (Luke 8:44), the thief of humanity's inheritance as children of the King.

And he said to his disciples, "Temptations are sure to come, but woe to him by whom they come! It would be better for him if a millstone were hung round his neck and he were cast into the sea, than that he should cause one of these little ones to sin." (Luke 17:1-2)

Teens today are often perplexed when a rule is laid down with the express purpose of helping them, in the words of the old Baltimore Catechism, "avoid the near occasion of sin." Curfews, dating restrictions, chaperones and rules governing time and place may elicit a vigorous protest that tests a parent's or teacher's resolve. "What's the big deal?" teens will bellow. I once had to stand my ground at a senior youth retreat with my "unreasonable" directive forbidding the sleeping arrangements the students had anticipated: guys and girls in the same cabin with very limited supervision. "But you are going to ruin this whole retreat," one student told me. I was willing to take that risk. I have an acute aversion to swimming with millstones. Fortunately, as it turned out, neither the retreat nor my conscience suffered. As Peter Maurin, co-founder of the Catholic Worker movement, was fond of saying, I tried to "make a society where it is easier to be good."

Where sin abounds, said St. Paul, grace abounds more. And this is what is happening today. Young people are seeking God's grace to live moral lives, and have become the spearhead of a moral resurgence in society.

Michelle Borba, author of *Building Moral Intelligence: The Seven Essential Virtues that Teach Kids to Do the Right Thing*, notes, "The close of America's twentieth century could well have been called the Decade of Moral Erosion."[73] If this is so, then there are signs that the first decade of the 21st century could be called the Decade of Moral Reconstruction. "A renewed concern for character is one of the most important ethical developments of our time," says Thomas Lickona, author of *Raising Good Children*.[74] The immensely popular *The Virtues Project*, founded 20 years ago by Linda Kavelin Popov, Dr. Dan Popov and John Kavelin, has since spread to more than 95 countries worldwide. The proliferation of books on morality and character development in children, the use of the traditional word "virtue" for value, and the receptivity of young people to moral principles are signs in our culture of a moral resurgence.

The Religion teacher needs to be on the front lines of this movement. To the predictable calls for more rules, harsher penalties and zero tolerance, the Religion teacher can provide a wider and deeper perspective by doing three things: teaching the primacy of God's love, teaching principles, not values, and teaching forgiveness.

1. Teach the Primacy of God's Love

In 1973, Karl Menninger wrote a book with the provocative title *Whatever Became of Sin?* The book evoked much interest because Menninger was a psychiatrist, not a clergyman or Church spokesperson. In 1973, many were hailing the social sciences as the sole remedy for our inner woes. Here was a distinguished doctor and founder of the world-renowned Menninger Institute reminding the Church that the welfare of humanity depends on the role Religion has always played— shedding light on the reality of sin, and on a greater reality that can save us from it.

The reality of sin was foremost in the minds of our students' grandparents. The greater reality (God's love) is foremost in our student's minds. The two need to go together. The experience of God's love is primary, however, because this experience enables us to see our sin. The following familiar gospel account can help our students understand this point.

> When he had finished speaking he said to Simon, "Put out into the deep water and let down your nets for a catch." Simon answered, "Master, we have worked all night long but have caught nothing. Yet if you say so, I will let down the nets." When they had done this, they caught so many fish that their nets were beginning to break. So they signaled their partners in the other boat to come and help them. And they came and filled both boats, so that they began to sink. But when Peter saw it, he fell down at Jesus' knees, saying, "Go away from me, Lord, for I am a sinful man!" (Luke 5:4)

What prompted Peter's confession of sinfulness, and at such an awkward moment? The boats are brimming with fish, even sinking; the men are trying to save the catch. Their minds begin to calculate what this windfall will garner at the fish market. Suddenly, Peter turns to Jesus and says, "Go away!"

It is as if he is saying, "Your presence, Lord, has revealed my sin. Your love, Lord, has caused my shame to surface. Your light, Lord, has illuminated my darkness."

"Do not be afraid," Jesus says to Simon. "From now on you will be catching people."

Fr. Richard Rohr put it this way:

Nine out of ten people start with the premise: If I behave correctly I will one day see God clearly. Yet the biblical translation is saying the exact opposite: if you see God clearly, you will behave in a good and human way ... We almost all think that good morality will lead to a mystical union, but in fact, mystical union produces correct morality – along with a lot of joy left over. And the greatest surprise is that, sometimes, a bad moral response is the very collapsing of the ego that leads to our falling into the hands of the living God.[90]

Other methods I use to convey this message to youth are through clips from the films *Jesus of Nazareth* and *Dead Man Walking*.

Jesus and Mary Magdalene

In Franco Zefferelli's monumental film *Jesus of Nazareth*, Mary Magdalene is cast as the prostitute who has no friends. "Ah," says one of her clients. "Yes, you have – Jesus, friend of outcasts and sinners ... he thinks nothing of eating and drinking with thieves and whores ... if you have to go around on business as I have, you can't help seeing him. You turn a corner or go into a tavern and there he is. Have you never come across him?"

"I sleep during the daytime," says Mary.

Mary is curious about this Jesus. As the film continues, she stands on the outskirts of the crowd on the hillside listening to him. His words are puzzling, yet have a compelling force. Jesus' apostles suggest that the crowd be sent away. There is no food to give them, only five loaves and two fish. "Give it to the people," Jesus commands. Mary witnesses the multiplication of the loaves and fish – the outpouring of God's love.

Zefferelli does something at this point in the film that captures the core conversion experience – *metanoia*, turning around, turning to God from sin. Mary is eating the miraculous bread, and suddenly the tears begin to fall. She is weeping inconsolably. I freeze the frame and ask my students, "Why is she crying? She just got a free meal!" They do not know.

Then, gradually, Mary begins to look up again at Jesus, who is in the distance. Her tears subside; a hint of joy breaks through; a faint but growing smile emerges. What is happening here? She moved from tears of shame to the joy of new-found love. The experience of God's love in the miracle brings bread to her stomach, but pain to her heart. It reveals to Mary her sins and her remorse – so she weeps. But if love is the X-ray that reveals our sins, it is also the laser that destroys the tumour of self-hatred. Sensing hope, Mary's grief is consoled and joy breaks through. In the film, the shift takes place in moments; in life, it may take moments, too, or hours, days or years.

The next time we see Mary in the film is at Simon the Pharisee's home. A small crowd from the Pharisaic all-boys' club has gathered for a meal. Jesus is present as well. They want to question him, test his theology, and scrutinize his mission. Suddenly, the woman appears. Mary has found her way in. Simon says to her, "This is no place for you, woman. Leave quietly and at once." Then he whispers to a friend, "If this man was really a prophet he would know what kind of woman this is."

"Simon," says Jesus, "you see this woman? When I came into your house, you did not give me any water to wash the dust off my feet. This woman has washed my feet with her tears, and has dried them with her hair. You did not anoint my head with oil. She has anointed my feet with perfume." Then Jesus, lifting Mary's face to meet her eyes, says, "Daughter, your sins, and I know they are many, are forgiven you because of the greatness of your love. Your faith has saved you; go and sin no more."

Your faith has saved you?

Faith in what?

Saved her from what?

Mary has faith; no woman of her time, especially a prostitute, would have crashed the men's luncheon unless she had faith. Her faith, her belief was this – God's love for me, personally, is real; it is revealed in that man Jesus, and nothing will prevent me from going to him.

Your faith in God's great love for you will save you from sin; it will give you what sin has falsely promised; it will fill the emptiness that sin had tried to occupy. Now that you know this, not just in your head, but have experienced it in the depths of your heart, now you *can* go and sin no more. As John Steinbeck once said, "Sin is just an attempted shortcut to get love." Teaching the reality of sin without the primacy of God's love is like giving a drowning man a book on water safety. It is nice to know, but it won't save him from going down. When it comes to avoiding sin, Jesus does not just command us, *he empowers us.*

Sister Helen Prejean

The film *Dead Man Walking,* based on the book and ministry of Sister Helen Prejean, CSJ, tells the story of a young man (called Matthew Poncelet in the film), on death row for the murder of a teenage boy and the rape and murder of the boy's girlfriend. Two men have been arrested, and now Matthew, one of the two, awaits the death penalty – only he denies he committed the crime. "I'm innocent," he tells Sister Helen, and asks for her help.

The film is a reflection on crime, justice, punishment and the death penalty. It juxtaposes the desire for retribution and the bottomless grief of the slain youth's parents with the life of this death-row inmate – his soul, his conscience, his fate. But the film is more than this. It is about God's love as revealed through Sister Helen, the only one who can reach out to Matthew, the only one who can wait in love with him, the only one who, by her presence more than anything else, reveals something to him that he has long forgotten or perhaps never knew: love exists, love is real … he is loved. And finally, Sister Helen is the only one to whom he can tell the truth:

> "The boy … I killed him," says Matthew, tearfully confessing his guilt shortly before his execution.
>
> "Did you rape the girl?"
>
> "Yes, ma'am."
>
> "You have dignity now, no one can take that from you. You are a son of God, Matthew."
>
> "No one has ever called me a son of God before. They called me a son of a you-know-what lots of times, but never a son of God. Figures, I have to die to find love. Thank you for loving me."

Matthew goes to his death, and the parents of the victims watch through a large plate-glass window as the lethal injection is administered. Sister Helen prays behind the glass barrier while fixing her eyes on the eyes of Matthew Poncelet. Your faith has saved you, now go where sin does not even exist.

Loving the Sinner, Hating the Sin

It doesn't take much life experience to realize that every truth, no matter how sublime, will be distorted; every ideal, no matter how fervently proclaimed, will be tarnished and compromised. How is it, for instance, that freedom has become licence, tolerance has become endorsement, intimacy has become sex, and rights have become indulgence?

So it is with the truth of God's unconditional love. What is meant to be a rallying cry of God's grace for virtuous living has, in the minds of some today, become a rationale for indifferent living. If God loves me no matter what I do, goes the logic of many youth, then it doesn't really matter what I do. This attitude resembles what Dietrich

Bonhoeffer called "cheap grace." As veteran religious educator Fr. James J. DiGiacomo, SJ, said, "A God who makes demands or who calls for sacrifice or restraint is problematic for students who have heard only of a God who loves them just the way they are."[75]

If we really knew God's love, however, we'd realize how it matters very much what we do. We are God's child, and God has given us moral laws because God loves us. God gives us these moral laws so we do not harm ourselves or others – God grieves to see God's children hurt.

Pam Stenzel, an inspirational speaker on the virtue of chastity, told this story in one of her presentations:

> A mother drives to the supermarket with her young child. "Do not run in the parking lot," she demands. A week later they go again. "Do not run in the parking lot," she exhorts. This continues until one day, ignoring mother's directive, the child runs in the parking lot, and is hit by a car. What does the mother do? Does she stand there and yell, "I told you so – you won't listen to me; now look what happened."
>
> No, she runs to the child, calls 9-1-1, goes into the ambulance and stays with her child until she is well. There is nothing she wouldn't do to help her child … but *I wish you had not run in the parking lot.*"

The God Mother will love us – no matter what. But we need to understand that God's laws are not capricious; God's commandments are not frivolous. No one ever really "breaks" the law of God; we just demonstrate it.

Explaining to youth that God's unconditional love means "God will love you anyway, no matter what you do" is fraught with all kinds of misunderstandings, and gives excessive leeway for rationalization. I find it more helpful to explain God's unconditional love as love that has *no hidden agenda.* God loves you – not to get something from you, to manipulate you or to control you. God's love is not that of a greedy marketing executive, a macho player checking you out, or a fair-weather friend who leaves when the crowd turns its back on you. God's love does not want something from you; God's love wants something *for* you. God loves you unconventionally.

One student asked, "Then why does God, in the first commandment, command us to worship God alone. Isn't that wanting something from us?"

"You become," I tell my student, "like the God you worship. If you worship money, you become greedy and hard of heart like Scrooge. If you worship pleasure, you become shallow and self-absorbed. If you worship power, you become paranoid and incapable of loving. God wants us to worship God alone so that we can be like God – all good and all loving."

God's love wants what is best for us, and God will never stop wanting it. God's love is not like a parking meter. It doesn't run out of time.

As one student wrote, "God will never break up with us, or stand us up, or die, or move away."

2. Teach Principles, Not Values

When the best-selling author of *The 7 Habits of Highly Effective People* was asked what he had learned since the book's publication, Stephen R. Covey said something that is worth quoting in its entirety:

> [I have relearned] the importance of understanding the difference between principles and values. Principles are natural laws that are external to us, and that ultimately control the consequences of our actions. Values are internal and subjective and represent what we feel strongest about, what guides our behaviour. Hopefully we will come to *value principles*, so that we can get the results we want now in a way that enables us to get even greater results in the future, which is how I define effectiveness. Everyone has values; even criminal gangs have values. Values govern people's behaviour, but principles govern the consequences of those behaviours. Principles are independent of us. They operate regardless of our awareness of them, acceptance of them, liking of them, belief in them, or obedience to them. I have come to believe that humility is the mother of all virtues. Humility says that we are not in control; principles are in

control; therefore, we submit ourselves to principles. Pride says that we are in control, and since our values govern our behaviour, we can simply live our own way. We may do so, but the consequences of our behaviour flow from principles, not our values. Therefore, we should *value principles*."[76]

Youth today are strong on values but weak on principles. Covey's admonition to value principles can serve as a mission statement for those of us who toil at the moral education of the young. A very useful and practical tool for this task is the book *The 6 Most Important Decisions You Will Ever Make: A Guide for Teens* by Sean Covey, Stephen's son.

I always look forward to teaching morality to teens. It is an easy topic to engage them in because they are so keenly interested in it. Generating discussion (Step 1 in the learning process) is best accomplished by presenting students with a moral dilemma. I teach the topic of conscience by showing clips from the film *A Man for All Seasons* and asking my students if St. Thomas More lost sight of his obligation to the king or his family by remaining steadfast in his convictions. Students come to see that conscience, properly formed, is the deepest voice within us. We cannot give another person or group control over our conscience. It is the call of God within us. I ask my students if nurses have the right to a "conscience clause" in their contract that allows them to refuse to participate in an abortion procedure when it violates their beliefs. I read them the story of two sisters, twins, age 15 at the time, who turned in their crack-smoking parents to the police as a last resort to gain some stability and order in their troubled family life. I have my students read a *Time* magazine article about how a teenager in New York City "borrowed" his friend's dad's car to go on a date, and how a minor accident led to armed robbery, death, and a cover-up involving the driver and four of his friends. We trace the evolution of bad choices: choices based not on principles but on feelings.

We read the story of Reena Virk, a 14-year-old girl who was killed by her peers on the Gorge waterway a few kilometres from my high school, while a group of teens looked on and remained silent even days later as news of the killing spread in school hallways. And we read a story of a Florida teen who found $1,100 dollars in a lost wallet but returned it to the owner, to the shock and surprise of adults who could not believe that anyone, much less a teenager, would do the honest thing.

When the unit is completed, students have an adequate understanding of the difference between forming one's conscience and following one's conscience, a belief in objective morality (principles) as opposed to subjective morality (values), the seven capital sins, seven virtues, and an ability to define sin and explain the conditions that render an act sinful. Then, in Step 3 of the learning process, they write their essay.

> My conscience tells me to follow what is right. For example, one day at lunch I was sitting with my friends as usual. I remember a girl, about my age, eating her lunch all by herself, in the corner of the field, looking very lonely. My conscience told me to go and eat my lunch with her. My friends thought what I was going to do was a waste of time … I found out that she was having an unpleasant day … and I was filled with joy to help her. That day I showed many virtues.
>
> Jessica

> I went to one of my friend's house for a party. We were having so much fun that we didn't know we were making a huge mess. I was the first to notice the mess and I started to clean up a bit. My friends were looking at me weird and the host of the party said, "Dude, my mom can clean this up. You don't have to clean this." I just ignored them and continued doing what I had to do. My friends felt sorry for me doing all the work, so they helped me clean up the whole room. It was weird because we had more fun cleaning up than we did when we were messing everything up. The host of the party's mother came into the room and was so impressed that she took us to a mini-golf course as a reward …
>
> Ryan

3. Teach Forgiveness

In our sister diocese next door, they have a youth event each year called *Freedom* – a diocese-wide Reconciliation service for youth. Priests of the diocese are gathered, testimonies are given, praise and worship music is sung, scripture is read, and teens confess and are set free. We don't teach young people about sin because it is interesting, to get them talking or because it is part of the curriculum. We teach them about sin so they can be set free – saved. Francis MacNutt, known widely for his preaching and healing ministry, writes in his book *Deliverance from Evil Spirits*,

> The entire New Testament shows us that Jesus was not primarily a Teacher (although He was an extraordinary teacher), but that His chief title is *Saviour* or *Redeemer*. The traditional title *Saviour* means, of course, that He actually saves us; He rescues us from a real danger, from something evil.[77]

Youth go to the sacrament of Reconciliation today because they know that the teacher who taught them about sin cares about their soul. They know that the priest cares about them, and their family and friends who support them care, too. They come to realize that all of these are reflections of God's great love for them. They confess their sins because they want to experience God's love. And when they do, they feel great.

Learning about sin and guilt is not doom-and-gloom theology. Nor will it lead to a negative self-concept. On the contrary, it is the beginning of grace and freedom, and the restoration of our dignity as children of the King. As with Peter, Mary Magdalene and Matthew Poncelet, we discover that the love that enabled us to see our sins is the same love that lifts us out of them.

High school Religion teachers are among the first to witness this new moment of openness to God among youth. Young people are less afraid to look into the darkness of their sin, because we have shown them a light at the end of the tunnel.

The topic of sin is broad, deep and multi-dimensional. Finding the right balance and exercising wise pastoral practices are not always easy, but youth stand in great need of your efforts.

In the end, it is not the list of moral rules or reasonable explanations of them that helps teens to turn away from sin. It is the strong relationship with those who truly love them – and the One Who is Love – that keeps them on the moral road.

9

Sex

The Catholic Revolution

Contrary to popular opinion,
most young people engage in sexual activity for psychological reasons
rather than hormonal ones.

—David Elkind

I am standing in front of my Religion class with my hands behind my back. I'm about to begin a new unit on sex. The kids are pumped. This should be swell, groovy, funky, out of sight, right on, radical, awesome, wicked, stella, bad, sweet, the bomb, c'est fabuleux – epic! (Pick your adjective according to your age or attitude.) Provoking student interest is a piece of cake.

I say, "Behind my back is a picture of one of the sexiest men and sexiest women of modern times – who wants to see?"

The guys yell out, "Yeah!"

The girls look at each other, then at me, and put on that inscrutable teenage-girl look that says, 'That don't impress me much!'

"Okay, ladies and gentlemen," I continue, "the award for the sexiest people of modern times goes to … Voilà!" In one hand I whip out a *Time* magazine "Man of the Year" picture of John Paul II; and in the other hand a *Time* portrait of "Modern Day Saint" Mother Teresa.

Some students think it's funny. A few laugh. Many just look at me – still not impressed. "Everything that happens in this classroom has a point, a meaning, is educational," I tell them, repeating my once-a-month assurance that they are receiving a religious education and are not just at the mercy of a wannabe comedian or village prankster. "Pope John Paul II and Mother Teresa are two of the sexiest people of our time; and I'll prove it to you by the time this unit is completed, Anyone want to place a bet on it?"

There are no takers, but I proceed anyway. "It all depends," I say, "on what you mean by 'sexuality.' So let's start there."

Thus begins a unit on the theology of the body for teens.

Sexuality education is a "must see – must do" topic for every year of high school. It should be one of our most effective units. It should feature good theology, animated discussion, engaging films, powerful guest speakers and uncompromising Church teaching. It can be done; it should be done; and if we are not doing it in the Catholic high school, we should be sued for malpractice.

Teens need it; teens want it; and we got it – so why don't we give it?

Teens Need It

Hello, it's a mess out there. "Girls Gone Raunch" is the title of an article in Canada's national magazine, *Maclean's*.[78] Below the title it reads, "Increasingly, young women are treating themselves and each other like pieces of meat." You read about a group of girls in short skirts and low-cut tops showing a group of boys the words they have written on their breasts and upper thighs, about girls flashing their breasts and butts for the *Girls Gone Wild* videos advertised on late-night TV, and about how girls no longer aspire to be just pretty and popular like their female forebears, but instead want to be "hot" – often translating as skanky or slutty.

The comic strip *Zits* by Jerry Scott and Jim Borgman offers a sociological heads-up for any adult wanting to know what is going on at teen dances. Parents are shown reading the "Winter Mixer Guidelines" for the upcoming school dance. "Provocative dress and lewd behaviour are discouraged," it reads. "Grinding, bumping, moshing, mashing, licking, squeaning, shoving, sledging, rolling, kicking, wallowing, freaking, pronking, booty dancing, fondling, and whole or half-body knurling will not be permitted." The parents stare dumbstruck as their kids leave the house. Says Dad, "High school dances have changed." Mom adds, "And I was worried about Jeremy's tie matching his pants."[79]

Freaking, for the uninitiated, is when the male partner is behind the female and is simulating penetration. Grinding is rubbing pelvises together. Both are a form of sexualized dancing where the dancers put their genitals and butts very close together, and rub up against each other.

The virtual world is of course in on the act. Recently, in my corner of the world, concerned Canadians, in an effort spearheaded by Archbishop Raymond Roussin of Vancouver, convinced Telus Corporation, Canada's second-largest phone company, to rescind plans to offer pornographic material for a fee on their cell phones. Sleaze was about to go mobile.

If you want to know what is going on in the teenage world where you teach, take an anonymous survey. I gave teens at a Catholic teen summer camp this sentence to complete:

"What I see going on in my high school in the area of sex, sexuality, relationships, etc., is …"

Here are some of their responses.

In my high school I see girls about 13 or 14 having sex because they "love" the guy.

My best friend at the beginning of this year (Grade 11) thought she was pregnant. She was really scared … The guy … told her to have an abortion. I see these results in my high school and it makes me think.

There are also people that I am friends with that have had relationships over a year that are sex-free and plan to stay that way till marriage. These people are far more mature than the people who are sexually active.

Most people I know who have experienced sex were taken advantage of when they were drunk or high at a party, which in my opinion is no excuse.

What I see at my high school is the guys always talk about which girl was easy to get in bed and who did the best job in bed and stuff like that; and the girls talk about who is the nastiest guy and who is a big **** to them and stuff like that.

At my high school it seems like everyone is having sex from Grade 8 to 12 and it just doesn't seem like that big a deal anymore. I think it is super cool to wait till you're married – but I think if you find the right guy and are ready, just giver ... I dunno, that's what I think.

What I see is people using people. Girls using their bodies to get guys to date them; guys using their popularity to get girls.

Their relationship is all about image. I want to be with this person because they make me look cool. It's all about image.

All of my friends are having sex with their boyfriends and they always tell me about the good – none of the bad. I thought about the bad but it didn't click in so my boyfriend and me started having sex. It didn't feel right at all, it hurt me, so I told him I want to stop so he agreed. It wasn't love; it was curiosity.

I am proud to say I have friends with positive values and have seen these values slowly and gradually spread to other people.

I've tried to stay as pure as I can but it is so hard.

I wish my whole school could hear the presentation we receive at camp so that they would have some sex-sense knocked into them.

What they didn't mention, and what many may not know, is that their sexually active friends are exposing themselves to viruses and bacteria that can result in infertility and lifelong incurable infections. Chlamydia, known as the "silent disease," is the most common sexually transmitted infection (STI) in Canada and the United States; 50% of infected males and 70% of infected females have no symptoms. The disease is silently doing great damage while the infected, unaware, pass it on to others. Our students often do not know that some STIs are transmitted by skin-to-skin contact. Years ago, I opened the *Time / Life Medical Advisor* and discovered in the second sentence, under the STD section, that one in four American adults has a sexually transmitted disease. I thought it was a misprint.

Over ten years ago, Dr. Stephen Genius, an Alberta physician, gave a presentation to my Grade 10 class on the risks of teen sex. That was my first heads-up. I have used his book, *Teen Sex: Reality Strikes Back,* and his video ever since with my students.

Let's face it: things are so bad out there, maybe we should network and bring back the arranged marriage system like our not-so-distant forebears – or at least the arranged date. Actually, this did happen to a former student of mine who is now in his mid-20s. Andrew – good-looking, intelligent, Christian – was just minding his own business one day when the phone rang.

"Hi, you don't know me, but my daughter is interested in you and I'd like to ask you a few questions before I let you meet her." It was her dad speaking. "Can we meet for coffee?"

Not your everyday type of phone call.

Feeling a bit unnerved, but realizing he had nothing to lose, Andrew agreed. Although he had never met this girl, he figured she must be somewhat mature to know what she is looking for in a man. It got him thinking about the kind of girl he would be interested in. He decided to meet with the dad and to be "open and truthful, because those are the traits that I value highly, and I did not want to give this man the wrong idea about who I am."

The meeting went well. It "wasn't nearly as stressful as I thought it would be," Andrew said. He and the dad decided to have another meeting to compare lists about what Andrew and the young woman were looking for in a future spouse.

Andrew reports, "So I thought about what I wanted and realized that if I wanted it to be the best list it could be, I would need God's help. So I prayed a lot. I found myself driving to and from work with the stereo off so that I could be quiet and I could think of what I wanted." The lists were very similar, so Andrew met with the daughter and they talked about their lists and their lives. But a few days later, she got accepted to a university in Sydney, Australia, and decided it was not the right time to begin a relationship. Afterwards, Andrew had a few things to say to God:

"God, what are you doing? Why have I gone through this whole process if it is not going to work out?"

But somehow I got this answer in my mind:

"Now you know what you're looking for."

What am I looking for? That's a good question for teens to ask.

When Andrew shared his story with a group of high school students, I could tell he had created a "teachable moment." Boy/girl relationships touch a deep wellspring in a teen's soul. They thirst for that water in a way they can't explain. Their young minds were working overtime, trying to wrestle a morsel of applicable wisdom from Andrew's experience. There was much for the taking:

- That relationships are not a "dating game," but important enough to send your dad to prepare the way.
- That you can't just "hope for the best" – "Mr. Right, Miss Right." You have to know what best is and actively seek it.
- That you need to be the kind of person described in Andrew's list: a person of honesty, integrity, one who will challenge me, one who is compassionate and hard working.
- That God needs to be involved in your discernment.

And finally, for guys:

- That every girl is some father's daughter, which is something you need to know from the start.

If you are a Religion teacher to teens, you will quickly discover one thing. Teens do not reject the faith or cease their walk with God because they disagree with papal infallibility or the virgin birth or the real presence or the assumption of Mary. They quit religion over sexual matters.

If a kid habitually responds adversely to what you are trying to do in the classroom, this might be why. Your very presence is a neon sign reminding him of his guilt. It is easier to pull the plug on the sign than deal with what it signifies.

If teens try to ditch religion over sexual matters, it is not because they have thought it out and can't agree with what the Church is saying. It is because they haven't thought it out and find it hard to obey.

This is where the battle lines are drawn. This is where we have to win students over. If we lose them here, we've lost them; and who's to tell how long the road will be that brings them back.

Teens Want It

At a youth conference held in a California sports stadium, young people signed cards promising to abstain from sex until marriage. There were enough cards signed to stack from the floor to the top of the dome twice over. Chastity speaker Pam Stenzel talks to 500,000 young people a year. Her talk is informative, inspiring and challenging; and teens respond to her strong message with sustained applause. I know. We had Pam come to our school. This is what teens wrote on their evaluation form after her presentation:

> The part of the talk that struck me the most was the part about guys with integrity and manners.

> It really has motivated me to keep being a virgin until I get married.

> I am determined to love and respect every woman in my life, especially my wife.

> Young people need to know that being promiscuous is not a no-danger form of fun, and that their decisions will matter when they meet their future husband / wife.

> There are many teens these days influenced by the media's view. It's important to know God's view.

> I did not believe in waiting until I heard this talk.

At my school, we've also had Brad Henning from Life Resources in Washington State.[80] The teens love him. They call him the "Sex Guy." They buy his book *Don't Take Love Lying Down*. One girl keeps it in her locker, and uses it to counsel girls who come to her for advice in navigating the whitewater of boy/girl relationships. One student, a guy, told me flatly, "I don't believe in God," yet had this to say about the "Sex Guy."

> His talk was the best, funniest, most perfectly worded talk I have ever heard. I learned more from that talk than in my whole student career. He makes his point perfectly. Is your future wife worth waiting for? The answer is "Yes." So I will wait until my wedding night.

Another student wrote:

> It taught you probably the most important thing you will ever need to know. I think he should definitely come to the school again.

And a girl wrote:

> I hope he comes back in the future so my brother can hear his talk.

Teens want to hear the Church's teaching on sex. They want to know how to have a healthy, chaste relationship in this sexual culture. They want you, the adult Catholic, to give them good advice. And when you do, the teens will be exceedingly grateful, and will tell you.

> These Religion classes have been very interesting. I learned a lot and I've decided to save sex for marriage.

> I would really like to thank you for teaching me these things. Without you I would have made so many wrong decisions about sex.

> It also finally cleared up why the Church does not believe in premarital sex, which was a mystery to me for a long time, but now seems clear and obvious.

> This unit has taught me so much about life, how I should treat others and should be treated. How to tell if someone really loves me and that there is someone out there for me, who will love me

as much as my parents. It's also taught me how fortunate I am to be loved so I don't have to be looking for love in people who will never love me. Thank you.

And, as only a guy could put it,

I'd like to start off by saying that before we started doing this section on sexuality, I hadn't really looked at girls as if they were gentle, kind, sharing, etc. But I looked at them as little whining wimps because they cried all the time. I have now progressed in my maturity by realizing that they aren't really wimps but just have good and deep feelings about certain aspects of life.

Teens want good sexuality education. Why? Because they have raging hormones? Because they're obsessed with sex? Because they're horny little creatures with no self-restraint?

Not!

Wrong!

Actually the reverse is true. Teens, frankly, are not into sex; the culture is. It's a sexual culture. Unscrupulous marketers are into sex, because sex sells. If you want to go see a movie, you have to be prepared for sexual scenes, sexual innuendo and sexual content. A lot of movies, even some very good ones, have to throw a gratuitous sex scene in because … I don't know why – Hollywood peer pressure?

A certain element in the adult population pushes casual sex and wants the rest of us to believe that teaching teens chastity is at best an impossible dream and at worst a complete waste of time. Better to promote condoms, give your girls a vaccine against HPV, tell them the pros and cons of teen sex, and provide abortion as a backup, they claim. The underlying attitude remains – teens are gonna do it anyway.

But those who work with teens directly on this issue discover otherwise. Teens are not into sex; they are into relationships. If they make bad decisions about sex, it is because they have learned somewhere (everywhere!) from the culture that guy/girl relationships include sex – it's a given. That's what happens in the movies!

The authors of *Soul Searching the Millennial Generation* write,

Despite what we think, teens do not spend every waking minute thinking about sex. A young woman came up to talk to me after a weekend retreat. She thanked me for not spending all the whole time talking about sex. She said, "It's important to know about, and all, but every year every speaker they bring in always talks about sex … there is a lot more to our lives …."[81]

I suspect that, as teachers and parents, if we offer guidance and support in the areas that make up the "lot more to our lives," then the problems around teen sex will be mitigated. If young people engage in sexual activity for psychological reasons, rather than hormonal ones, what are the reasons? Here are a few that I notice as I walk the hallways of my high school.

Looking for Daddy

I can almost point out the girls in school who have a distant or damaged relationship with their father. They are the ones always looking for a boyfriend. They are boy crazy.

Every girl needs a man in her life. For the teenage girl, that man is her father. No boyfriend can even come close. He's not in the same league. He's not even playing the same game. When the teen girl does not receive what she needs from her dad, she will try to get it from some other guy. This is a disaster in the making.

David Popenoe, author of *Life Without Father*, sums up what daughters learn from their fathers. Daughters learn

> how to relate to men. They learn from their fathers about heterosexual trust, intimacy, and difference. They learn to appreciate their own femininity from the one male who is most special in their lives …. Most importantly, through loving and being loved by their fathers, they learn that they are love-worthy.[82]

It is no wonder that girls with close bonds with their dad can see a player coming a long school hallway away, while those without will cling to the one who "really likes me" when even her girlfriends tell her she is being used. "Girls with uninvolved fathers," writes Popenoe, "commonly become obsessed with heterosexual relationships. In a desperate search for substitute forms of male affection, some have inappropriate sexual contacts, become overly dependent on men, and allow men to take advantage of them."[83]

Girls instinctively know they need their dad. In a heartfelt way, they want their dad. They know that he is an essential piece of their life puzzle. When this piece is missing, girls will lean on their mom, but missing their dad will sometimes feel like sitting all alone in an empty house.

Valerie's Story

When her mom and dad divorced, it was no big shock to Valerie. She knew "something was totally wrong" with having "fights every day." It was, however, a great relief to Valerie that her dad would be living in the same area, since "me and my dad were very close."

Her dad bought a new computer, and used it to find his next amour. He went off to visit his new cyber-girlfriend and soon returned declaring that he'd like to move closer to her. Valerie didn't pay much attention to this announcement, since "he always wanted to do new things, but he never actually did them." Then, says Valerie, "the worst thing happened to me."

After school, I decided to walk to my dad's house, which was a long walk. It was winter, so it got dark early. I was coming up his driveway, but I didn't hear music, which I usually did. Okay, I said to myself, he must be sleeping; I'll just play on the computer. When I got in the house everything was gone. He packed up all his things and left just like that. The only thing left were some boxes in one part of the house with some of my things in it. I didn't know what to think. I was in shock. I called my mom and sat in the empty house until she came.

I have not seen my dad in five years. Yes, I do talk on the phone, but he asks dumb questions all the time like he doesn't know me anymore. It's not the same. It is almost like not having a dad. It's like he's alive but you wouldn't know it.

When you lose something special no one ever really gets over it "just like that." One thing that I have lost is my dad. He has not passed away, but he might as well be.

Michelle's Story

I knew my mom and dad would end up getting a divorce. I knew it for years. All the arguing and yelling and the awful silence, all the tension.

I thought, I'm prepared for this, I can handle this. But when the day came and my dad actually walked out of the house and closed the door behind him, I could not believe how much it hurt. I cried and cried and cried.

(And Michelle cried again when she told this story, a year later.)

Looking for Love

Teens are not into sex. Younger teens even think it's gross. But relationships touch their hearts. They just love loving relationships. Show up to chaperone a high school dance and slow dance with your husband or wife. A group of teenagers (mostly girls) spy on you from a distance. Awww! they sigh. They love to see married couples in love. If you want to get a collective sigh in class, tell them a love story. One of the best is *The People with the Roses*, by Max Lucado, which I read every year to my class.[84]

In keeping with the four-step learning process, I never start my unit on sexuality with answers. I spend a lot of time provoking the questions. And the best question to start with is this one: What is Love?

Figure that out, and everything else falls into place. Ask your students to write out what love is. Collect the papers, read them out, summarize what is said, and your lesson is launched.

Here, condensed, is what the rest of the three- to four-hour lesson plan looks like:

- Love is not a feeling; it is a decision.
- A decision to want what is best for the other person (*agape*).
- There are three "types" of love:
  - *Eros* – erotic attraction
  - *Philea* – friendship
  - *Agape* – self-sacrificing concern for the other.
- *Agape* is the foundation of all relationships.
- Ask your students, "Why do some teens have sexual intercourse before they are married?" Here are some responses I receive:
  - curiosity
  - it's fun
  - he/she will leave me if I don't
  - a good stress reducer
  - inexpensive / cheap date
  - to get some practice
  - it's a hot chick
  - I was bored
  - to score points
  - to feel grown up
  - to be cool
  - to brag
  - to be like James Bond
  - sexercise

Do these reasons pass the "Love test"? Are they expressions of *agape* love?

- Why is the Church against premarital sex?

Because the Church promotes love, and premarital sex is not loving. The Church believes in premarital love, not premarital sex.

- God is love (the title of Pope Benedict XVI's first encyclical, *Deus Caritas Est*).

After this unit, a girl wrote, "This year I really learned a lot about what love is. It was really helpful to be able to put it into one sentence, it helps me to really think about it." The sentence she memorized was this: "Love is wanting what is best for the other person." The *General Directory for Catechesis* has called for the return of memorization in Religion class. Memorization is not necessarily a substitute for thought. This student discovered that memorizing a definition helps to "really think about it."

If, in the past, people repressed their sexual feelings, today's teens are in danger of repressing their deep desire to love and be loved. One of the worst consequences for sexually active teens is that they lose a belief in love. Some want to keep the word, so they change the meaning. Instead of something that is real and lasting, "love" becomes something momentary and self-induced. They take their cues from tabloid stories of pop stars who testify that love is "real" but fleeting; you believe in it when you have it, but like a beautiful snowflake in your hand, it soon melts.

Teens learn to repress their belief in love because they force themselves to stifle the feelings they have when they get involved in casual sex. Feelings are the doorway to deep thoughts. Repress them, and you close the door. Teens have picked up the cultural mantra that sex is no big deal, no matter if your feelings are indicating otherwise. I heard one author say, "Your head can always lie to you, but not your body." Teens let their heads keep lying and try to repress their body's felt emotions, which contradict the lies in their head.

"Researchers have found a statistical link between teen suicides and premature sex," writes Clayton Barbeau in *How to Raise Parents*. "When girls and boys give themselves away sexually and the affair breaks up, many are left with profoundly damaged feelings of self-worth."[85]

Adolescence is a time for ideals and dreams. High aspirations are what give youth the energy and courage to begin the construction of their life. Sex undercuts their dreams because they sense (correctly) that sex is related to something ideal, some aspirational dream – true love! This is why there is a relationship between adolescent depression and teen sex.

Depression is about loss: in this case loss of a dream – the beloved, the one and only. It is also about the loss of one's own self-worth and dignity. After sex they realize they gave the deepest part of themselves away, and gave it cheaply. "It's no big deal," they are told, but something gnaws within them saying otherwise. A vague feeling of depression sets in, and since most teens see painful emotions as something to escape rather than befriend and understand, they quickly find ways of staying out of touch. A hardened, jaded, cynical crust around their wounded heart does the trick. Another method is to keep things jovial, distracted or superficial. The result, however, is that the search for one's deeper self (the task of adolescence) is delayed. Identity work is heart work, and that is where they do not want to go. In Religion class, these students' defences are tangible. You will try to lead them to a deeper reflection on life, but they just won't go there. These students need a lot more than information in your class; they need healing.

It is sad to lose these students in Religion class, but it is a much greater tragedy to see teens lose themselves and become cynical about love. "There is no sadder sight," Mark Twain once wrote, "than a young pessimist."

The Christian, however, holds onto a belief in real, true, lasting love. That is the heart of our faith. This is why the Church says no to premarital sex. Sexual self-denial is not self-negation or anti-sex. Self-denial is choosing to say no to sex to increase our capacity to say yes to love, and yes to the beauty of our future beloved, and yes to the One who created sex in the beginning. A guy should not be reaching out to caress a girl's breast until her heart is indelibly etched in his soul. Do you want safe sex? Slip on one of these – a wedding ring.

Looking for Intimacy

My son had a revelation in Grade 12. One afternoon, he was hanging out with three of his male buddies from school. When he came home, he told his mom, "It was awesome. We just walked and talked. I never had that experience before. It was great – we talked about everything, what was going on in our lives. We want to do this every month."

Teens are not into sex; they're into intimacy. Intimacy is revealing your deepest self. If they could get away from iPods and Facebook and videogames, and just talk about their lives, a great hunger and need would be met. Their desire for intimacy is so strong, it "drives them to drink," for when they drink, "their tongues are loosened." The problem in a sexual culture is that when alcohol enters the scene, much more is loosened: their inhibitions, their natural sense of modesty, their hold on their virtues, their clothes. The vast majority of teens' regrettable sexual behaviour begins with "we were drinking and …."

Teens want to get close to each other; they want to really know each other; they want to bond. Yet they are afraid of opening up because they fear rejection, judgment and loss of respect. Others might not think they're cool.

Religion class can contribute to meeting this need. It should be a place where teens feel safe opening up. In my experience, however, it is the retreat that can best facilitate this process. A retreat, I tell my students, is not an escape from life but a journey into the heart of life. Teens want to make this journey, but some have bought the societal line that sex is a suitable shortcut to get there. Premarital sex, however, does not create intimacy; it kills it.

Before sex, a couple is getting to know each other emotionally, intellectually, socially and spiritually. That is the whole purpose of dating, courting and the engagement period before marriage. These steps build a strong foundation for marriage. Such a foundation requires constant maintenance, even within marriage – one of the benefits of Natural Family Planning, which involves periodic abstinence from sex.

For the unmarried, especially the teen, once sex enters the picture, all the other expressions of intimacy recede. Sex becomes the focus and intimacy dies – as does the relationship. Brad Henning's book *Don't Take Love Lying Down* addresses this issue in a thorough and engaging manner. Chap Clark's book *Next Time I Fall in Love: How to Handle Sex, Intimacy, and Feelings in a Dating Relationship* is another book that has helped me to teach this unit to teens.[86]

When it comes to Religion class, teens don't want just a "why to" lesson; they want a "how to" lesson. This is especially the case when teaching about sex. They want to know *how* to deal with strong sexual feelings if they're not supposed to have sex. This is where the wise counsel of Mary Rosera Joyce can help. Her little book *How Can a Man and Woman Be Friends* offers helpful insights on every page. Here are some examples:

> [A man says], "I have such strong erotic feelings when I think about Laurie. I notice that if I think about her as someone who causes these feelings, I want to possess her right away. But if I think about her as Laurie, as the person who she is, I don't feel so possessive. I feel my feelings just as they are. I let them be what they are. Soon I feel a warmth and a glow in my mind. My original sexual feelings are doing something different inside me now. They are helping me feel good about who I am as a person, about my potential for developing my own meanings and values in life. I also notice I feel more tender toward Laurie, not so urgent. I feel more interested in finding out from her what her philosophy of life is all about, what means most to her, and what she values in herself and other people."

> You can learn to receive your erotic feelings into your mental hands, holding them gently and encouraging them to find *their* centre ….

> Touching and holding without possessing. Without manipulation. Just receiving. This is the source of tenderness.[87]

By locating the centre of our sexuality in our minds rather than in our genitals, Mary Rosera Joyce is helping young people to find true sexual freedom by avoiding the sexual repression of an older generation and the sexual impulsiveness of the present. This is where calling John Paul II and Blessed Mother Teresa the sexiest people of modern times starts making sense to students.

Sexuality, according to Ronald Rolheiser, OMI, in *The Holy Longing*, is an energy inside us. It is a drive – a force for love, communion, friendship, family, affection, wholeness, joy, delight, creativity, self-transcendence.

For this reason sexuality lies at the centre of the spiritual life. A healthy sexuality is the single most powerful vehicle there is to lead us to selflessness and joy, just as unhealthy sexuality helps constellate selfishness and unhappiness as does nothing else. We will be happy in this life, depending upon whether or not we have a healthy sexuality.[88]

Chapter 9 in *The Holy Longing*, entitled "A Spirituality of Sexuality," is fruitful reading for high school Religion teachers. The sexual energy of teenagers is meant to be a holy fire, not one that burns the house down. Teens need someone to help them build a fireplace so that their sexual energy can bring light and warmth to themselves and others. That is what John Paul II and Mother Teresa did, and that's why they are very sexy people.

Looking for Mentors

When Pam Stenzel came to our high school, I saw what else teens need. They need adult heroes, spirit guides, mentors. Pam gave our students wisdom, and they gave her their hearts. A small crowd gathered around her after she spoke. When she left, they would e-mail her. Teens need adults. They want your words more than the worn-out lines from their boyfriend or girlfriend.

On the evaluation form, I asked the students if they wanted to say something I could pass on to Pam. Here is what they said:

Thanks, Pam, you are my hero.

You are my hero. Never stop giving your message. You save us from pain and heartache.

I know in my heart that I have been raised to be a good man. You have influenced me to be a greater man.

You opened my eyes and you felt like the mother I never had.

Pam, you deserve an award, like the Nobel prize thingy.

Thank you, Pam, you are a wonderful inspiration. Since Grade 8, when I watched your video in Religion class, I have always wanted to meet you. I hope you set others on the right path like you have set me.

Teens need adults; they need mentors; they need Religion teachers. But when adults are absent or silent or lack integrity, then teens will turn to their peers, seeking to fulfill some deep need from their boyfriend or girlfriend, and wondering why it doesn't work.

There are two tracks in high school: the educational track and the social track. Both are important. Sexuality should be a big priority on the educational track, or teens will seek the answers from their peers – the social track. If that happens, the pastoral mission of your school will surely derail, and that's a tragedy you want to prevent.

We Got It

In my journey toward a Christian sexual life, I have had many mentors. Jesuit Father John Powell taught me about love and *The Secret of Staying in Love.* Engaged Encounters, Marriage Encounters, and presentations on Natural Family Planning have enriched my understanding of love, sex and relationships. I have already mentioned Mary Joyce and Fr. Ron Rolheiser. In recent times, Pope John Paul II's Theology of the Body, popularized most notably by Christopher West, has become a theological tour de force for me and many other Catholics. Yet all these mentors entered my life while I was in my late 20s and beyond.

In high school, except for the occasional "don't," which I picked up from the Church, my sexuality education was nil, even though I attended a Catholic school. I had some good general Catholic training, both in the domestic church (the home) and the universal one. I credit both for keeping me free from what I consider grave sexual sins. Yet I consider it no cliché to admit, "There but for the grace of God, go I." Sexual temptation is, and I suspect always has been, huge. It is more so for youth today, who inhabit a more intensely sexualized society. I was never their age!

When I was in high school, I went out with a girl named Mary. If people pointed her out and asked me who she was, I'd say that "she's my girlfriend." They and I would think that I therefore knew her well, this person – "my girlfriend."

But I didn't know her well. And looking back, it bothers me that I didn't know her, or her brother who had Down's syndrome, or her older sister who was married to a Vietnam veteran who would wake up with nightmares, or her parents who cordially met me at the door, and to whom I gave only short, non-descriptive responses to their polite questions. I didn't really *know* that she was somebody's sister and somebody's daughter, or even who her friends were; if I had, I would have shown some interest in what was most important in her life. But I only knew that I "liked" her and I was attracted to her.

When I look back, I'm very glad I didn't do anything really stupid, but I regret that I didn't do anything really good. And I ponder how it was that I was so unaware. I think of young people today who have sex with their girlfriends or boyfriends and I realize they have no idea what they are doing. They have no idea how one day they will have to reflect on their past, because memory is a vibrant, living thing that we can't chop up into little bits, discarding the pieces we do not want. And they have no idea how everything is connected; how our lives touch, influence and change others, and how we live in their memory, too.

When I broke up with Mary, because I had gone away to university and had another "interest" in my life, there was, I suspect, some temporary sadness on both our parts, but no long-term hurts. I am exceedingly happy about that, since she was a wonderful person.

Some years later, there was another girl, Janet. Janet liked me, but I did not like her in the same way, although I enjoyed the attention she gave me and the fledgling friendship we had. One day, when we were alone, I kissed her. Then, over the next few days, I spent time with yet another girl whom I actually did like.

Janet came to me, and with a puzzled and hurt look in her eyes, asked, "Why did you kiss me?"

There are some questions asked of us at certain points in our life that help us break through to another level of consciousness. This, for me, was one of those questions. At the time, I had no answer and just stared blankly at her – duh! Days later, unable to justify or rationalize an edifying answer, I had to admit the truth to myself. I kissed her because I felt like it.

"I felt like it" – not "I cared, I loved, I was concerned about your best interests, not even because I like you, just, I felt like it." I was stupid, and since sin is doing something stupid on purpose, I also call this a sin, though I can just hear some modern kid laughing – "Ha ha ha, kissing a girl; that ain't no sin."

When I kissed her, I crossed a boundary I did not respect. I stole an intimacy without the requisite commitment. And when that happens, people get hurt. I did not understand then, nor do many youth understand today, that every encounter with another human being, especially every intimate encounter, affects that person's ability to trust, to love, to believe, and to be the person God created them to be. We influence others to have open hands or closed fists, hearts of flesh or hearts of stone. Every time you interact with another person, you are building the Kingdom of God or tearing it down, revealing God or concealing God.

Older generations remember that there were set rules in courtship. Break the rules and prepare to get slapped. If she wore your ring or your sweater or you were seen holding hands, you were "going out," "going steady." This meant others were to back off, because he was "my guy." Kissing meant something, an engagement meant something else, and marriage was the final step crossed, with new and permanent boundaries thereafter.

Teens today may try to explain: this is the girl I'm going out with; this is the girl I'm with; this is the girl I'm making out with … well … it's complicated. "It's complicated" has become a euphemism for having no relationship boundaries, no borders, no lines, no rules – no integrity. One teen responded, "We're not going out; we're friends with privileges." Or benefits, as it is also called – sexual benefits.

Heather, 19, booked an appointment with the campus psychologist – Miriam Grossman, M.D., author of *Unprotected*. Heather had moodiness and crying spells, the cause of which escaped her. She also felt withdrawn and worthless, and at times experienced self-hatred. Normally upbeat, Heather was both perplexed and anxious about her sudden unexplained loss of mental health. After much probing of her recent past, Heather said,

> "Well, I can think of one thing: since Thanksgiving, I've had a 'friend with benefits'". She went on to explain. "Well, I met him at a party, and I really liked him, but there's this problem. I want to spend more time with him, and do stuff like go shopping or see a movie. That would make it a friendship for me. But he says no, because if we do those things, then in his opinion we'd have a *relationship* – and that's more than he wants. And I'm confused because it seems like I don't get the 'friend' part, but he still gets the 'benefits.'"

> "Do you think," asks Dr. Grossman, "that these moods you have, when you are unhappy and critical of yourself – do you think they may be related to this?"[89]

Friend with benefits?

A young couple who were living together were asked at a party, "Are you two single?" The man answered, "Yes," and received a sharp elbow to the ribs. Single to him meant unmarried; living together was a form of marriage to her. The boundaries have been erased, and young people get burned by a fire that they can't even see. "It is no coincidence," writes James Taylor, author of *Sin: A New Understanding of Virtue and Vice,* "that the traditional wording of the Lord's prayer, as it is used in most churches, defines our sins against each other as 'trespasses' … It's about overstepping bounds."[90]

Where do teens learn to trespass sexual boundaries? Some learn it in the privacy of their own home, online. Behaviour in chat rooms, for instance, is very sexual. Cyberspace provides the anonymity to play at pushing sexual boundaries. It's a thin line between saying it in virtual life and doing it in real life.

Every once in a long while, in my dreams, I meet Beatrice, Dante's Beatrice. I can only gaze at her, for when even the slightest hint of consciousness arises, she vanishes. Her beauty holds me. It is a numinous dream, a vision so uplifting and pure that psychic turmoil and conflict seem eons away. Being in her presence seems a foretaste of heaven. But when she fades, as all dreams do, I realize she is not gone. She is my wife who sleeps beside me. God has renewed my wedding vows, and taken me back to the moment when the beauty of my beloved transfixed me.

Brad Henning relates how a man came to see him after Brad's talk on love, sex and relationships. The man was weeping as he explained that all the women he had had sex with – and there were many – were ruining his marriage. He kept seeing them in his head while he was making love to his wife. "I love her," he said, "and I don't want these other women in my head; but I don't know how to get rid of them." Then he wept some more.

This man had lost his Beatrice, and he wanted to find her – the one and only, his beloved, his wife.

The Church does not want teens to lose their virginity before marriage, because they will also lose their Beatrice as well.

Catholic teens today who wish to chart a loving and life-fulfilling sexual course must delve deeply into the wealth of the Church's teaching, as promoted by authors cited above (and many others), and take part in the Church's spiritual life through prayer and sacraments. Even then it will be a struggle. When the older priest was asked by the younger priest, "Tell me, Father, when do you stop thinking about sex?" the older priest replied, "About an hour after you're dead." Sexual purity is a struggle, but a struggle worth every effort.

Some students will hear your message and think, "Too late." Once, when serving as a parish youth minister, I sat in a small circle of teens in order to introduce to them the topic for that particular meeting – sexuality. I was an inexperienced and unskilled religious educator at the time. I was learning to swim by being thrown into the lake. There were about half a dozen youth in the circle, grades 10 to 12, guys and girls. They knew each other but did not know what to expect from me, the new youth minister. So they sat there, bantering little jokes back and forth, but mostly looking at the floor, nervously waiting for me to start.

I said, "I'd like to discuss some of the reasons why waiting until you are married to have sex is a good idea." Their heads did not move, but their eyes shot around the circle. I had the sense that some cryptic text-messaging of the eyes had just taken place between them. To my left, a big Grade 11 boy must have picked up the ocular signal that he was the spokesman. He lifted his head and said out loud, "Too late."

I don't start lessons like that anymore, but in my high school Religion classes I do, in the course of the unit on sex, address this boy's implied question: "What happens when it is too late, when you've already had sex?"

I fumbled for a response back then, but now I tell my students about a young girl who came up to Pam Stenzel and said, "I'm a recycled virgin." She explained that having sex at fourteen had left her so much pain and trouble that she made a pledge to wait, no matter how long, for the man she marries.

I tell the story Brad Henning relates in his book, about a young man who came to the same conclusion, and sat down and wrote a letter to his future spouse, leaving a blank for her name to be filled in. In the letter, he explained the mistakes he had made, how he did not want his past to ruin his future marriage, and how he would now wait for his true lover, his wife.

On the day of his wedding, years later, he slipped the letter out of his side pocket and gave it to his wife. It was a sign of love as deep as the vows he had just taken and the ring he had put on her finger. She cried when she read the letter.

I talk about Reconciliation, how it is never too late; about beginning again; about how much you are worth as a person; and about how

215

SEX

someone out there is waiting for the gift of their life to love them and honour them all the days of their life.

That's just too sappy for me, a cynical baby boomer might respond – get real!

No, I say, get ideal!

Just as I believe there is a new moment in adolescent catechesis, so I believe we have a momentous opportunity for a fresh presentation of the Church's teaching on sexuality. For many reasons and in many ways, we have failed in this area in the recent past. Catholics of an older generation complain that they were given rules with no depth of explanation, and somehow sensed that the goodness of sex and the body was suspect. Younger Catholics have grown up with the Church under a colossal shadow due to scandals of sexual abuse. Still, the individual student who will enter your classroom tomorrow morning is willing to give you, the Church's representative, another chance to offer the kind of wisdom to build a life on.

I believe the Church has that wisdom:

- sex is good, our sexual complementarity reveals God, our body is sacramental – a visible sign revealing the invisible person
- the plan of God is found in the body; the plan is love
- uncommitted sex does not signify God's love, it obscures it
- marriage is the primordial sacrament revealing God's covenant with us
- sexuality is God's energy within us
- there is a way to feel sexual while not acting on it – it's called sexual freedom
- you can still be pretty and modest
- we are not controlled by our hormones but by our choices
- the gift of a chaste life that is promised us is no less than a foretaste of the beatific vision – "Blessed are the pure in heart, for they shall see God" (Matthew 5:8).

This is what we can share with our students. They see all around them the results of sexual decisions at variance with God's plan:

loneliness, pain, infection, heartache, shattered lives. They want a fresh voice, something different: a revolution.

When it comes to teaching sexual morality in the Catholic high school Religion class, here are three questions for Religion teachers:

1. Despite whatever sexual decisions I have made in my own life that are at variance with Church teaching, do I now see the teaching of the Church as true and wise counsel?

2. Am I willing to teach and promote the Church's teaching on sexuality to the best of my ability?

3. Am I willing to continue my own prayerful study and reflection on the sexuality teachings of the Catholic Church?

If you answered "yes" to all three questions, you can move forward, confident in God's grace, to recruit youth to a new sexual revolution – a Catholic one.

You cannot teach what you do not believe, and you cannot believe what you do not live. It is the task of every generation to lift the one coming up to a higher place than its own.

10

Social Justice

Jesus' Seamless Robe

If you want peace, work for justice.

—Pope Paul VI

I was driving a bus of Grade 11 students to Cloverdale to attend the Archdiocese of Vancouver's annual Youth Day. Cloverdale was once a small rural community southeast of Vancouver, but now the older homes on acreage are slowly giving way to housing developments. My students were both excited and anxious because they were about to meet their billets – local parishioners whom they would stay with for two nights while they attended the conference during the day.

Before embarking on this class trip, I had given my students the billeting pep talk.

- Decide now that you will accept whatever accommodations you are given.
- Be polite and courteous.
- You will be with another student or two, but you will not be alone.
- Here is my number; call if you have any concerns.

Christine and Megan, who sat at the front of the bus, kept chatting about their billet expectations and fears. "Don't worry," I said. "People don't usually offer their homes to billet youth unless they are youth-friendly."

Like a general who encamps with his troops, I was billeted as well, in the same house as three of our Grade 11 boys. The expansive home looked new, and was graced with a very hospitable couple with teenage boys of their own. We greeted each other, exchanged a few trivial observations, and then, suddenly, the conversation paused. A few moments of silence ensued as I, and no doubt others, looked around for some topic to reignite the cordial banter. That is when the dad piped up. "You boys want to watch a movie?" They had a home entertainment centre with a big-screen TV and surround sound speakers. Before I could decipher my better instincts – which was to scuttle the idea – his boys and my boys marched off to the home theatre and spent the evening in semi-darkness, exchanging hardly more than a few grunts. So much for my private hopes that billeting would be an experience to help my students break through another layer of personal insecurity and gain a larger Church perspective by encountering other pilgrims on the journey.

The next morning, when I saw Christine and Megan in animated discussion with a small circle of girls, I knew something was up. When they approached the bus, I braced myself for what might come next. I got an earful.

"She's an older woman; she lives on a farm; her house is … old; it doesn't even have a shower, just a bathtub!" All the other liabilities, both large and trivial, were cited. The two girls were not just mildly disappointed – they were livid.

"We're not going back there tonight; we're not!"

I listened to everything they had to say and then I responded.

"Is it unsafe?"

"No."

"Is it unhygienic?"

"No."

"Is she mean?"

"No!"

"Then you are going back. That's the plan we agreed on, and we have to stick to it."

Question: Who had the better billet, the boys (first world) or the girls (third world)?

In the first world, people are initially very friendly: "Hi, how are you? Come on in." Soon, however, possessions and technology get between people and prevent any real encounter and communion. In the third world, there are fewer possessions to buffer personal relations, and people discover that they have only themselves to share.

In the first world, we end up bored, suppressing a feeling of loneliness with more media distractions. In the third world, we sit in the kitchen drinking tea and telling stories – our stories. I said to the boys, "How was the billet?"

"Okay, I guess."

I said nothing to the girls. But when we returned home in the early evening of the last day, Megan and Christine lingered by the bus. Then they came up to me and said, "Mr. Brock, we're sorry. When we heard how everyone else had all this stuff and private bathrooms and game rooms and all the snack food, well, we felt we had lost out. But the second night, we sat and talked to our billet and, well, she's really nice and she showed us some old photographs and things, and, I don't know, it was … cool. I think, really, we had the better billet."

Charity and Solidarity

Charity is when I leave a gift on your doorstep or some money in your mailbox. Solidarity is when I billet with the poor and become enriched by their presence. This is what Megan and Christine experienced without expecting it. They entered the world of the other, the foreigner, the labelled, the stereotyped, and began to relate as persons, fellow travellers on the journey. They connected with a person, and came to see that in many ways that person is just like them. That weekend, they entered into solidarity, and discovered it was "the better billet."

If there is a hidden meaning to Jesus' saying "the poor will always be with you," it is because the wealthy need them, to billet with them. "Having material goods and name brands equals happiness" is the message teens hear in the culture. But a recent story in Victoria's *Times Colonist* states, "Adolescent materialism is connected to low self-esteem, researchers find."[91] Social justice education helps students question the culture's message. Wealth does not give worth, because self-worth is an inside job. In giving, you receive – that is Jesus' advice for gaining self-esteem.

Solidarity as Bonding

Billeting with the poor is a good description of solidarity. A teenage word for solidarity is "bonding."

Teens are always looking over their psychological shoulders wondering what other teens are saying and thinking about them. They worry about peer judgment. The slight comment, the turning of a head, the raising of an eyebrow, is considered evidence more alarming than the signs of global warming. They ponder it, fret over it, react to it – it creates enormous internal stress. They long for an experience that can dissolve the stress, banish the fear, and free them from the pervasive disquietude they live with. They long for one thing – bonding.

Teens will say, "The class trip was great. We bonded." "The retreat was awesome. We bonded." Bonding is a primal need for teens. The pastorally wise teacher and retreat director will facilitate the bonding process. It's not that difficult, because teens want it. You're working with the grain.

The task of the Religion teacher is to push the bonding initiative through yet another threshold of comfort – to bond with the other, those of a different race, religion, nationality, economic status, culture. The Religion teacher can open students' eyes to the encounter with God in our loving service to others. Whenever you do this to the least of my sisters and brothers, said Jesus, you bond with me.

Bonding, ultimately, is both a lateral and vertical endeavour. In bonding with others (lateral), we bond with God (vertical). The shape of Christian bonding is a cross. I read a story once about Jesus hanging on the cross. A crowd appeared and said, "Jesus, let us take you off the cross." And Jesus said, "Go, get everyone in the world, bring them here, then you can take me down." When the whole world becomes bonded, Christ's work is done.

Solidarity as Knowing One Another

Solidarity fuses helping a person with knowing that person. As much as we need a helping hand, we crave an understanding heart. We need to be known. We want others to empathize, to feel, to know what it is like to be us, to walk a mile in our shoes. When people call but are refused a hearing, wait but are endlessly stood up, write but receive no response, their quest to be known turns to a quest for revenge: "I will make you feel what I feel." Revenge, however, never mitigates the pain of not being known.

Solidarity is a movement of the heart to help someone by entering into a relationship with him or her. It is a mutual relationship in which both sides give and receive.

"I've taken three showers just today," one teenage girl told me, beaming with a squeaky clean freshness and smelling like flowers. I thought – okay, junior-high self-indulgent body obsession. Three years later she was working at Tim Horton's to earn enough money to go back to Latin America to do mission work. She told me how much the volunteer work had changed her. I could see the transformation in her. In giving, she received.

God entered into solidarity with us when "he sent his only begotten Son" (John 3:16) to be one with us. Jesus didn't walk just one mile in our shoes, he walked many miles; and he walked them not only in our shoes, but in our skin. When we are in solidarity with others, we are most like God. The solidarity of the Incarnation is not just an event, it is a *way*. It is *the* way, the only way, to bring peace, reconciliation and justice to the world. The wounds of the world will never be healed otherwise; there is no other way. When Jesus said, "I am the way … No one comes to the Father except through me," he was closing all the ideological doors that we have constructed for finding a way in this world. There is no other way but the way of compassion, the way of mercy, the way of dialogue, the way of solidarity – the Jesus way.

We may call people terrorists, communists, secularists, enemies of freedom, Islamic militants, Godless atheists, criminal trash that deserve to die, but as long as we refuse to walk even one inch in their shoes, we have slammed shut the door that Jesus is trying to open. We not only "refuse to go in ourselves, but prevent others from going as well" (Luke 11:52). Abraham Lincoln once said, "I do not like that man; I must get to know him."

After the deaths of 58,193 Americans and 500,000 Vietnamese in the Vietnam War, Secretary of Defense Robert McNamara lamented America's mistake. We did not know them, he said. We did not know their history, their culture, their beliefs, their loves, and their hates. We did not know that they had fought colonialism by a foreign power for hundreds of years and were willing to fight another hundred. We did not know that they saw America as colonizers. We did not know them.[92]

Greg Mortensen's 2006 book *Three Cups of Tea: One Man's Mission to Promote Peace … One School at a Time* strikes a similar note today. Speaking to military brass in Washington, Mortensen said,

> And if you tell them, "We're sorry your father died, but he died a martyr, so Afghanistan could be free," and if you offer them compensation and honour their sacrifice, I think people will support us, even now. But the worst thing you can do is what we're doing – ignoring the victims. To call them "collateral damage" and not even try to count the numbers of the dead. Because to ignore them is to deny they ever existed, and there is no greater insult in the Islamic world. For that, we will never be forgiven.[93]

Solidarity is getting to know one another in a heartfelt way. It is a lesson we keep having to learn. It is the God-message Jesus taught us.

Are our students capable of solidarity? A student of mine went to Auschwitz, the former Nazi concentration camp in Poland. She told me that when she was looking at the photographs of prisoners that were mounted on the walls of the prison, she suddenly began to see the faces of her own family and friends superimposed upon them. She began to weep. It was a profound spiritual moment for her. This is the kind of experience the Catholic school was created to foster.

"Family, culture, religion, community, and friendship are all realities that are vital for human growth," writes Jean Vanier in *Finding Peace*.

But we need to learn how not to remain enclosed or imprisoned in such groups. We have to cross boundaries and meet others who are different .... To create peace we have to go further than just saying hello. We have to discover who the other person is and reveal who we are. As we listen to and really meet one another, we begin to see the work of God in the beauty and value, in the deepest personhood, of those who are different.[94]

Then Vanier describes what I have heard many times from youth returning from a spring break mission service, or a summer service project, or even weekend volunteer hours at St. Vincent de Paul.

I am touched to see the many young people today who leave their homes and go to live with and serve disadvantaged people. Their shared life with people of another culture breaks down their prejudices and calls them to discover the beauty and value of different cultures and of our common humanity. The waters of understanding and compassion for individuals rise up within them. They are starting on the road to peacemaking and wisdom.[95]

A friend of mine, Paul from Wisconsin, told me of his experience overseas. It was the summer of 1999. He was working in the border area of Georgia, Armenia and Turkey on an Economic Assistance Project: restocking and improving cattle herds in small, remote villages.

On my first visit to a small village consisting of about 30 households, an old woman (nearing 100 years old) asked to speak to me through my translator. She was stooped and frail, but able to walk from her home to my car. She explained to me that she had never met an American before, but that American food aid had saved her and her family from starvation after World War I. Because I was the first American she had met, she wanted to thank me for the food (even though she received it long before I was born). Later that summer, I was honored to be present at her funeral.

Genuine charity has a long memory.

A few months ago, I stepped out the door of my home and saw a former student of mine and a few of his friends walking by. I invited them in for tea – and food, the door to a teen's heart! We reminisced about the school he had graduated from three years before. His family was not religious, but somehow he ended up in the Catholic high school. He admitted to being a real pain in the early years of high school, not just to teachers, but to students as well. Then he said, "The biggest thing that St. Andrew's taught me was compassion for other people; that's what I learned from the Catholic high school."

Compassion for other people – that's what makes a person, a school and a nation great.

Over 1.2 million votes were cast in a national contest sponsored by the Canadian Broadcasting Corporation to discover who was "the greatest Canadian of all time." Canadians chose the former Premier of Saskatchewan, the father of medicare, the inspiration behind Canada's national healthcare safety net: Tommy Douglas. "My friends," Douglas once said, "watch out for the little fellow with an idea."

Catholic Social Doctrine: A Seamless Robe

In December 1983, Cardinal Joseph Bernardin of Chicago travelled to Fordham University in New York to give a talk. "Because we esteem human life as sacred," he said, "we have a duty to protect and foster it at all stages of development from conception to natural death and in all circumstances. Because we acknowledge that human life is also social, society must protect and foster it."[96]

The Cardinal explained his position. Catholics, he said, must have a "consistent ethic of life." During the question-and-answer session after the talk, he used an expression that captured the imagination of many Catholics. He referred to John 19:23, to the seamless robe of Jesus, which his executioners did not tear apart. Human life comes from God; it is sacred; and all issues that affect the dignity of human life form a "seamless robe." It is one cause, and Catholics are pro-life in the largest sense of the term.

What are pro-life issues? There are many.

Abortion is the primary life issue. Attack on human life at its conception, at its most vulnerable stage, is, in the words of the Catechism, a "grave offense" (#2272).

I hardly ever hear a debate anymore about whether the fetus is a human being; I believe we all know it is. Canada has no law protecting life in the womb at any stage, but Health Canada puts this warning on cigarette packages:

Cigarettes Hurt Babies

Tobacco use during pregnancy reduces the growth of babies during pregnancy. These small babies may not catch up in growth after birth, and the risks of infant illness, disability, and death are increased.

I don't spend any time in the classroom trying to prove that unborn babies are human beings. The students all know it is true. If they don't, show them the Michael Clancy photograph of Samuel Alexander Armas. At 21 weeks in his mother's womb, an ultrasound revealed Samuel had spina bifida. The parents opted for pre-birth surgery to treat his condition. The surgeon cut a small incision in the mother's uterus. Through that incision came a miniscule hand that wrapped itself around the surgeon's finger. It was Samuel's hand. That is what you see in the photograph.

In my class, I show them a picture of Gianna Jessen when she was 13 years old. It's a colour photograph of a smiling and beautiful young girl sitting in a wicker chair cuddling her pet puppy. Underneath the picture is the word "Survivor." I ask my students to write down in their notebook what they imagine she might be a survivor of. They must guess and write something.

They write: cancer, AIDS, child abuse, car crash, skiing accident. Keep thinking, I tell them. Fell out of an airplane, was trapped in a sinking submarine, was wounded in a drive-by shooting, was caught in a tsunami, was attacked by a terrorist. When everyone is finished guessing, and no one has guessed correctly, I hand out the March 1995 edition of *Focus on the Family* magazine. They read the story of Gianna Jessen, survivor of an abortion attempt.

They learn how her seventeen-year-old birth mother, who was over six months pregnant, sought a saline abortion. She ended up giving birth to a baby girl, ten weeks premature, who would develop cerebral palsy as a result of the attempted abortion.

They learn how, at 12 years old, Gianna asked her adoptive mother about her cerebral palsy. Before her mother, Diana, could fully explain, Gianna said, "I was aborted, right?"

"How did you know?" asked Diana.

"I just knew," she replied.

They learn how, after a talk at a church about her life, a woman came up to Gianna and said, "I had an abortion … nobody knows; I confessed to God; but I still feel guilty."

"You didn't know what you were doing," responded Gianna.

They learn how her audience wipes away tears when Gianna concludes her talk. "I have cerebral palsy – but that's okay, because I have God to keep me going every day. It's not always easy, but He is always there. He's there for you, too."[97]

But the primary thing students learn is that abortion is about real people – in this case, Gianna – and she is a teenager, "just like me."

But abortion as a pro-life issue, as one of the issues in a consistent ethic of life, includes an examination of the systems that make abortion widespread rather than rare or non-existent. Because we all know that it is a human life we are taking in abortion, no one, really, wants an abortion. No one wants an abortion like they want a vacation or a car or a new computer or new clothes or a condo in the city or cottage in the country. No one wants an abortion.

I once showed a pro-life film that was hard-hitting, but not graphic, to a group of teens. Three First Nations girls walked out halfway through. After the film, I asked them why they left. They were not bitter or angry or upset. They left because abortion was so foreign to them, so unnatural, so unimaginable, that they just had to leave – it jarred them.

What they felt is what everyone feels deep down, but covers with layers of hurt, distrust, pain, anger, resentment and fear. Aboriginal people in Canada do not live idyllic lives. Elders and leaders are trying to solve enormous problems in their communities. But the spirituality of Aboriginal people goes to the heart of this land, because God was with them long before anyone else arrived on these shores. When the girls walked out of my presentation, I wanted to walk with them and drink from the well they drank from.

The question is this. What about our culture perpetuates the abortion mentality? Ours is a culture of competitive individualism where poverty often nips at the heels of those who have not learned the ropes; a culture that promotes casual, uncommitted sexual hook-ups, leaving anxiety and stress over a possible unanticipated pregnancy; a culture that produces the kind of panic that leads to "looking after #1." This is the cultural system that undergirds the rhetoric of abortion rights. A consistent ethic of life perspective looks not only at the rights of the unborn, but at the cultural systems that make abortion not excusable but understandable.

Author Frederica Matthews-Green, in an article included in *The Best Christian Writing 2002*, described how she had set out to discover the main reasons women had abortions and subsequently how best to help them. "Thus when I asked women, 'What would you have needed in order to finish the pregnancy?' repeatedly they told me, 'I needed just one person to stand by me.'"[98]

"Stand by me" – that's a good definition of solidarity, and a suitable mission statement for Religion class.

Like Gianna Jessen, we need to help our students see other people in the world as "just like me" and part of the fabric of Jesus' seamless robe. After all, pro-life means much more than anti-abortion.

People "just like me" include the curious children who pick up a "butterfly" land mine, with a shape and colour that make it look like a toy, until it explodes in their hand and face.

People "just like me" include the victims of cluster bombs, a weapon that former Canadian foreign affairs minister Lloyd Axworthy called "a vicious and indiscriminate killer of innocent people."[99]

And people "just like me" include detainees who are imprisoned for years without trial, and are called "unlawful enemy combatants" in order to circumvent the Geneva Convention on the rights of prisoners of war.

Pro-life issues include industry's effect on the environment; global warming; the stockpiling and proliferation of nuclear weapons around the globe; economic policies that perpetuate poverty; corporate policies that place concern for greater profits over regard for workers; a government budget that prioritizes weapons as opposed to health and education for its own citizens; and the suffering of the one billion children who live in poverty around the globe and the 400 million who have no access to safe water.

"Who said the following?" asks Paul William Roberts in *A War Against Truth*. "Gandhi? Che Guevera? Karl Marx? Martin Luther King?"

> Every gun that is made, every warship launched, every rocket fired, signifies, in the final sense, a theft from those who hunger and are not fed, those who are cold and are not clothed. The world in arms is not spending money alone. It is spending the sweat of its laborers, the genius of its scientists, the hopes of its children.

It was President Dwight D. Eisenhower, in *The Chance for Peace*, a speech to the American Society of Newspaper Editors, in Washington, DC, April 16, 1953.[100]

Inspiring youth to global solidarity is accomplished more through showing them pictures and films and telling them stories than through articulating ideology. A survivor of the nuclear attack on Hiroshima tells her story in *Our Hiroshima*, a National Film Board release. Another NFB film, *Aftermath: The Remnants of War*, reveals the post-traumatic stress of war victims in Bosnia; the perilous occupation of French de-miners who attempt to uncover and defuse unexploded ordnance left over from the First and Second World Wars; and the children in Vietnam who are born with severe birth defects due to the toxic chemical Agent Orange, which is still present in the ecosystem. Show the film *Romero*, *Gandhi*, *The Fog of War*, *Emmanuel's Gift*, or the latest version of *Twelve Angry Men*. Rely mainly on the power of narrative, as Jesus did, to convey the principles of the social gospel – the good Samaritan, the rich young man, the rich man and Lazarus, and the gospel reading that continues to comfort the afflicted and afflict the comfortable.

"When, Lord, did we see you hungry, naked, in prison, sick? … When? Please tell me."

"Whenever you did this to the very least, you did it to me."

Years ago I showed my students a film called *Kibbutz on Tall Grass Mountain*, about Father Ian McDonagh in the Philippines. Fr. Ian was an Irish missionary of the Columban order. He served the people of the Philippines during the repressive regime of Ferdinand Marcos. They decided to purchase land to grow sugar cane, and, on Tall Grass Mountain, they formed a collective, a community, a kibbutz. Fr. Ian was at the centre of this activity.

I don't know what became of the kibbutz, but I remember reading, years later, how Fr. Ian was jailed and eventually deported by Marcos. Back in Ireland, Fr. Ian was a household name; his triumphant return was given a hero's welcome on O'Connell Street in Dublin. Young and old alike hailed him. Here was someone to look up to, to emulate.

Not long ago, while teaching a World Religions course, I showed another film, *The Spirit of Tibet* – a National Film Board release featuring the life of a Tibetan Lama named Rinpoche (senior teacher). Having spent years in a cave mastering meditation, Rinpoche was shown being escorted through the villages of Tibet. Young and old flocked to see the holy man. Children were squeezing between adults to catch a glimpse of the Rinpoche as he passed by.

On O'Connell Street in Dublin to the hamlets of Tibet, these are the villages it takes to raise a child – spiritually. What villages do our youth live in today? Who are the heroes they line up to see? The answer to this question is often found on the inside door of their school locker.

Social justice education is needed in our high school, because teens need heroes. On the wall of my classroom, I hang pictures of Oscar Romero, Dorothy Day, Martin Luther King, Mahatma Gandhi, John Paul II, the Dalai Lama, Mother Teresa, Jean Vanier and others. I want my students to see models of those who are "visionaries without borders."

We need social justice education in our schools, because it speaks to the very best in us. It does not appeal to our baser instincts for self-preservation, fear of the other and exclusive identification with our own clique. Social justice education appeals to the higher qualities and aspirations of our human nature. It speaks to the transcendent potential of our soul. It is the stuff of dreams and it calls forth prophets.

Look at the students in front of you. They all have the potential to be Mahatmas – Great Souls.

Catholic Pro-life: Global Solidarity

Have you noticed what I have noticed? I keep running into Catholics who accept wholeheartedly the Church's teaching on sexual morality, but resist the Church's teaching on social justice. "The Church should stay out of politics," they say. Or, as I remember reading from a Catholic magazine editor years ago, a response to Pope John XXIII's encyclical *Mater et Magistra*: "Mother – yes, Teacher – no!"

And I continue to encounter Catholics who are zealous for the Church's critique of economics, war and peace, capital punishment and the rights of workers, but consider the Church's view on sex unsupportable and outdated.

Bishop Sheen said it years ago: very few people reject Catholic teaching; they reject what they *think* is Catholic teaching. When it comes to the Church's social teaching, many Catholics are so out of the loop, they are not even sure what the questions are.

The *new moment* in adolescent religious education is a *new movement* – the coming together of all the threads in the Church's teaching ministry into a single "Tapestry of Faith," which was the theme of a recent

Catholic Schools' Week in British Columbia. There are distinctions in Church teaching, but not divisions, for the Church has a consistent view on the sanctity of human life that is not just the seamless robe of Jesus, but Jesus' seamless, undivided, all-inclusive heart.

I remember Fr. Richard Rohr once saying that Catholics should be value conservatives and pastoral liberals. I believe it was Dorothy Day who remarked that when it comes to sexual morality, we should go all the way to the right; when it comes to social justice and peacemaking, we should go all the way to the left. I figure if we go all the way to the right and all the way to the left, we'll eventually cover the whole world. That's what the word "Catholic" means – universal, international, global. God bless everyone – no exceptions.

Catholic high schools should be at the forefront of social justice advocacy. As Catholics, we do not subscribe to the late-great-planet-earth theology of those Christians who misuse the Book of Revelation to predict the end, something they seem to welcome. Enthusiasm for the coming of the end is not a sign of Christian vitality; it is a sign that insulated, "gated community" Christianity needs renewal. Catholics, instead, should take their cue from Pope John Paul II's *Crossing the Threshold of Hope* and Pope Benedict XVI's encyclical on hope: *Spe Salvi – Saved in Hope*.

Catholics have a rich heritage of social justice literature in the papal encyclicals and national episcopal letters. "In the social documents of the universal church," writes Father Michael T. Ryan in *The Social Attitudes of a Catholic* (a great resource for Catholic high schools in Canada and the United States), "and in the social documents of our bishops here in Canada and in the United States, we have a treasure. So it is important to be familiar with them."[101] According to the dictionary, a treasure is wealth or riches stored up. The social teaching of the Church seems more stored away than stored up. In our high school Religion classes we can unlock the treasure and show it to the world.

High school students have heart. They care. Over and over again I have seen their generosity. Students in my high school, of their own volition, founded V.O.I.C.E. (Volunteer Outreach In Catholic

Catholic Schools' Week in British Columbia. There are distinctions in Church teaching, but not divisions, for the Church has a consistent view on the sanctity of human life that is not just the seamless robe of Jesus, but Jesus' seamless, undivided, all-inclusive heart.

I remember Fr. Richard Rohr once saying that Catholics should be value conservatives and pastoral liberals. I believe it was Dorothy Day who remarked that when it comes to sexual morality, we should go all the way to the right; when it comes to social justice and peacemaking, we should go all the way to the left. I figure if we go all the way to the right and all the way to the left, we'll eventually cover the whole world. That's what the word "Catholic" means – universal, international, global. God bless everyone – no exceptions.

Catholic high schools should be at the forefront of social justice advocacy. As Catholics, we do not subscribe to the late-great-planet-earth theology of those Christians who misuse the Book of Revelation to predict the end, something they seem to welcome. Enthusiasm for the coming of the end is not a sign of Christian vitality; it is a sign that insulated, "gated community" Christianity needs renewal. Catholics, instead, should take their cue from Pope John Paul II's *Crossing the Threshold of Hope* and Pope Benedict XVI's encyclical on hope: *Spe Salvi – Saved in Hope*.

Catholics have a rich heritage of social justice literature in the papal encyclicals and national episcopal letters. "In the social documents of the universal church," writes Father Michael T. Ryan in *The Social Attitudes of a Catholic* (a great resource for Catholic high schools in Canada and the United States), "and in the social documents of our bishops here in Canada and in the United States, we have a treasure. So it is important to be familiar with them."[101] According to the dictionary, a treasure is wealth or riches stored up. The social teaching of the Church seems more stored away than stored up. In our high school Religion classes we can unlock the treasure and show it to the world.

High school students have heart. They care. Over and over again I have seen their generosity. Students in my high school, of their own volition, founded V.O.I.C.E. (Volunteer Outreach In Catholic

Education). This year, for Lent, at an all-school assembly, they enacted a skit showing the inequitable distribution of food among the world's population. Members of V.O.I.C.E. raise funds for local and international causes, raise our school's awareness of social issues, and call their peers to global solidarity. Compassion for others was the reason Catholic formal education was founded centuries ago. Catholic education has a deep and enduring tradition of outreach and a preferential option for the poor. It is beautiful to see this tradition continue in the hearts of our students. When Jesus said, "I thirst," the words Mother Teresa placed beside the crucifix in her chapel, he identifies with all those who thirst for dignity, bread, medicine, peace, clean water, health and a planet to bequeath to their children and grandchildren. We teach social justice education because that is where we find the thirsting Jesus.

Checklist for Social Justice Advocacy in Catholic High Schools

Read through the following checklist. What are you already doing in your school? What needs work?

☐ 1. We have, especially in the upper grades of our high school, Religion teachers with thorough knowledge and understanding of the social justice teachings of the Catholic Church.

☐ 2. Considerable time in Religion class, particularly in the upper grades, is dedicated to social justice education.

☐ 3. Our school enlists guest speakers to address social justice issues with our student body.

☐ 4. We have a large collection of media resources that support and supplement our social justice component in Religion class.

☐ 5. We have an annual Mission Trip for our senior students that offers hands-on, live-in experience in a developing country or a domestic area in need.

☐ 6. We participate in national and diocesan mission appeals or projects (Development and Peace, St. Vincent de Paul, Catholic Charities, etc.).

☐ 7. We foster awareness in our Religion program of missionary religious orders and foundations (Maryknoll, Scarboro Foreign Missions, etc.).

☐ 8. We make known to our Grade 12 students various volunteer opportunities for young adults, particularly Catholic organizations such as the Jesuit Volunteer Corps (Catholic Network of Volunteer Services, www.cnvs.org).

☐ 9. Our students are informed of the goals of organizations that work for protection of the environment, eradication of world hunger and disease, and advancing the cause of world peace, such as:

- Pax Christi: www.paxchristiusa.org
- Human Rights Watch: www.hrw.org
- Kairos: www.kairoscanada.org
- Canadian Catholic Organization for Development and Peace: www.devp.org
- Bread for the World: www.bread.org

☐ 10. We practise, among our entire school community – students, staff, administration, maintenance – the same level of justice, fairness and respect for the dignity and welfare of others that we teach in the classroom. We show concern and take measures to address exclusive cliques, bullying, sexual harassment, racist or sexist put-downs, or demeaning comments about the poor.

Doing justice, loving kindness and walking humbly with your God (Micah 6:8) may not be a requirement for graduation, but it should be a Religion teacher's earnest prayer for all our students. As Catholic religious educators, our great desire should be "Blessed are those who attend Catholic schools, for they shall be peacemakers."

11

Commissioning

Sent on a Mission

One looks back with appreciation to the brilliant teachers,
but with gratitude to those who touched our human feelings.
The curriculum is so much necessary raw material,
but warmth is the vital element for the growing plant
and for the soul of the child.

—Carl Gustav Jung

So, do you still want to teach teens Religion?

Not sure?

Take the following test.

For a) to f) below, rate yourself from 4 to 1:

(4) That's me completely.

(3) I give myself a C+ in this area.

(2) This is new to me, but I'm progressing quickly.

(1) I haven't a clue about this.

I have ...

a) ____ A thorough knowledge of Catholic theology, as outlined in   the Universal Catholic Catechism.

b) ____ A familiarity with current youth culture.

c) ____ A strong desire to teach teens Religion.

d) ___ A knowledge of the theory and principles of religious education methodology and youth ministry

e) ___ A faith life animated by prayer and a commitment to Jesus and the gospel.

f) ___ A love for young people.

___ **Total score**

Rating

Above 20   You are overqualified; get a desk job at the chancery.

16 – 19   There are Catholic high schools across the country looking for you.

12 – 15   Believe, begin, and they will come.

8 – 11   Fools rush in where angels fear to tread – rush in anyway.

0 – 7   This is how Daniel felt in the lions' den – but he survived.

At the end of every school year, I pray, "Lord, do you want me to continue teaching teens Religion?" Then I look for the Lord's answer in my feelings, thoughts and memories of the year. I look at my family, my marriage, and my energy level. All sorts of inner voices vie for my attention: "Drive a truck for a living; pick daffodils; pound nails into a piece of wood so that you can enjoy the thrill of something doing exactly what you want it to do, without talking back." I give every voice a hearing (except the one that says, "Teaching teens Religion – ha ha ha ha! That's the most ridiculous thing I've ever heard of." That voice comes from Old Scratch and merits only one response: "Be gone!").

I try to get that deep-down sense of it all, to see if it still "fits." And if I feel my skin becoming sensitive to an inner joy, and suddenly experience a depletion of energy – a sort of holy inertia, as if the Lord had put his hand on my shoulder to give me his blessing – and if, at this point, a feeling of deep gratitude spills over for being chosen as an envoy to a teen's soul, then I take these as confirmations that Jesus is still saying, "Come!"

And when I respond with, "Yes, Lord; Yes, Lord; Yes, Yes, Lord," I realize that it is not just for the students' welfare that I accept this ministry, but for my own as well. I am a much better person for being a Religion teacher.

But I must warn you, if you say "Yes" to teaching teens Religion, and give it your all, your students will take the life out of you. It will happen. You will carry these teens in your heart, you will grade their essays on weekends, you will rack your brain inventing engaging lesson plans, you will work the phones recruiting guest speakers and organizing class trips, and after all the provocations, antics and spiritual surges in the classroom, you will be spent. You will crawl through the door of your home on Friday afternoon, and your spouse will accuse you of being with your mistress once again – School. You will plead, "But honey, I work with wildlife." You will receive little sympathy.

But if you look a little closer, you will notice something else happening. New life is coming into you as the old life is drained out. The teens will give it to you. They have it to spare. And that is what we need, after all, to stay spiritually alive – *new life*.

New life – from day to day, from dawn to dusk, from the beginning of our life to the very end – we need it. Old teachers or young teachers, it doesn't matter, for the old will "dream dreams" and the young will "see visions" (Joel 2:28).

Believe me, teaching teens Religion will keep you youthful, fresh and abundantly alive, and the child within you will still be playing long after the street lights come on. It was Religion teachers, I believe, whom Jesus was also talking about when he said, "Unless you become like one of these, you cannot enter the kingdom."

To end the year with my Grade 8 class, we sat in a circle and prayed, shared some thoughts and feelings, and affirmed each other. When we were finished and the bell rang, the students said their goodbyes and left. Two girls lingered. They came up to me and gave me sweet little-girl hugs as they said, "Thank you, Mr. Brock."

They blessed me. That is enough to live on for at least a week, a month, or perhaps several months – maybe longer. How long can we go without being blessed? How long can we drive on empty?

What can compare to a genuine expression of teenage gratitude? All year long I try to cajole, provoke, encourage and hassle teenagers to choose the higher ground. Then they thank me. It's like giving your dentist a hug after he has drilled your teeth. It's like giving a police officer a gift card for Tim Horton's after he gives you a ticket for running a yellow light. I'm not sure what to compare it with, but it is so sweet. It is so sweet to touch the hearts of teens. It is so sweet to help them on their spiritual journey. A Japanese exchange student, who disagreed with some of what I taught during the year, came up to me at the graduation banquet, put his hands together and bowed to me as he said, "Thank you for teaching me about love."

Sweet!

It really is worth all the effort to make Religion class a favourite class. But if you don't agree with me, fine. If you don't want to make it a favourite class, make it the worst class ever. Here are some helpful hints:

Teaching Teens Religion:
How to Make It the Worst Class Ever

1. Spend most of your class having teens read aloud from the textbook.

2. When teens ask questions off topic, tell them you can't discuss that because you have to complete the curriculum and you don't have the time to explore other questions.

3. Tell the non-Catholics that they probably won't do very well in the class because they just don't have the background.

4. When a kid disagrees with something you teach, be sure to argue him down right away, so that this student and the whole class can see that he lost the argument and you won it.

5. Don't smile until Christmas. But if you really want to excel as a Religion teacher, don't smile until Easter, and tell them you are only smiling to be liturgically correct.

6. Say to the students who have older siblings in the school, "Your older brother is spiritually mature; why can't you be like him?"

7. Tell them that if they read Harry Potter, they are committing a sin because it is all about magic and the occult, and is just a bunch of New Age anti-Christian rubbish.

8. Tell your students stories about the old days that show how much better they were than the present. Be sure to begin the story with "When I was your age ...."

9. Keep telling them that they need to learn all this stuff, because they are the Church of the Future. When a student protests by saying, "Hey! I'm baptized; I'm the young church of today!", refer to #4 above.

10. Don't enjoy teaching Religion. There is nothing to be happy about. You are trying to train, discipline and teach a group of hormone-driven, pleasure-seeking, attention-deficit, media-crazed postmodern pagans. This is not fun; so don't try to make it so. This is your purgatory on earth. If it doesn't hurt, it is not good for you or them. And when you ask yourself at the end of the year, "Why am I doing this?" then repeat over and over again, like a mantra, the following answer: "Because somebody has to!"

Uncle Jesus Needs You!

In Chapter 2, I offered eight reasons why teaching teens Religion is difficult. Here are four reasons why you need to do it.

1. A Student Body with a Home-School Soul

In today's society, some parents choose for their teens what is becoming a growing phenomenon – home schooling. The enormous expenditure of time and energy that home-schooling parents give is all for one purpose – to provide a place where it is easier to learn, easier to discover one's blessedness in the eyes of God, easier to discover one's worth as a child of God.

Home-schooling parents remind us that our Catholic high school should be a "home school" as well, where youth experience a family atmosphere of respect and support, a community where they feel a sense of pride and ownership, an ecclesial community of real pastoral care.

Let us be honest; this is not always the case. As one student recalls from her elementary school days,

> I think everyone goes through a period of low self-esteem sometime during their life … The worst years of my life were grades 6 and 7. I know if you're in a Catholic school, it seems like everyone should be friends, or at least friendly. It's sad to say that was definitely not the way … It was a Catholic school so we wore a uniform. You think that would make it so that there was no competition regarding name-brand clothes. Well, there was. I can remember one time, I was wearing my hair in a barrette and this one girl came up to me and said in front of everyone, "Where did you buy that, Fields?" Everyone laughed. I started crying and ran away. Every day I would come home and cry. I thought I was the ugliest person who ever lived. I thought I was worth nothing.

It is these kinds of experiences that often prompt parents to home school. Catholic schools may defend themselves by saying, "This kind of behaviour is off our radar screen." In this case, we must upgrade our radar technology. Sometimes we can be tempted to say, "Oh well, teens will be teens," but that is hardly an inspiring mission statement. It is everyone's job in a Catholic school to help those who are hurting and to create a climate of goodwill; but Religion teachers carry a special responsibility because it is to them that teens will more readily reveal their wounds. This is part of the mission of being a Religion teacher; teens need you to accept that mission.

Every act of faith in God involves a corresponding act of faith in our own life – that it has meaning, purpose and significance. Every act of hope in God fosters the reassurance that our life is in God's hands. Every act of authentic love of God reverberates in a heightened love and respect for ourselves. Why is Religion class so important to teens? Because all teens, at times, doubt the significance of their lives, cannot see anything hopeful down the road, and sink into a debilitating lack of self-worth. It is not popularity, being on the honour roll, or being a celebrated athlete that will make the big difference in high school. A relationship with God will. Teens need Religion class; they need you.

Years ago I saw a bumper sticker that read, "I Survived Catholic Schools." I will know our mission has been accomplished when I see a bumper sticker that reads, "I Thrived in Catholic Schools."

2. The School Culture War

Okay, here is my theory. Every Catholic school has a culture, and it is either moving towards gospel values or away from them. It does not stand still. If it is to move towards gospel values, it will need the whole-hearted effort of the adult staff.

It's like my back. I have lower back pain, so I went to see Michael Phillips, the guru of physiotherapists in the city of Victoria. Within ten minutes, he had my diagnosis, prognosis and therapy. "You had a growth spurt in adolescence and your body grew disproportionately. It usually shows up at your age as back pain. Here is a sheet of daily exercises that will straighten you up. Your body will continually slide back to the old posture, so do these every day. You'll have this for the rest of your life. Have a good day!"

Ensuring the gospel culture of our Catholic high school is like my back – it's a daily grind.

If you want to do an initial assessment of the school culture, administer the following anonymous survey:

On a scale of 1 to 5, how comfortable do you feel expressing your religious faith, belief and values in this school?

1. ☐ Not at all. I'd be made fun of and put down if I did this.
2. ☐
3. ☐
4. ☐
5. ☐ I feel completely free and supported in my faith life.

I overheard one girl in a Catholic high school say, "I can't wait to graduate so I can live out my faith without fear." The primary reason why there is a culture war going on in your high school is that teenagers are always battling over popularity. Popularity – that ephemeral, morphic, bloodless, substance-deprived false god – is constantly trying to set the tone of the school. Most adults think that popularity is outside their sphere of influence. This is a mistake. After all, to God *everyone* is popular – a truth that undermines the popular meaning of the word.

There are some teens in your high school who reject the values of the school, and say so with their words and actions. They feel threatened by the "religion" of the school, and actively seek popularity because it gives them influence and power. These are the "cool" teens, a term that defies strict definition, although the following might come close: flippantly cynical, emotionally guarded, religiously detached, fashionably trendy and excessively narcissistic. If there are enough of these teens and the usual majority of "neutral" teens waiting to see which way the wind is blowing, there is a good chance your school will lose the culture war – so long as adults don't intervene.

What can adults do? We can be proactive. We can empower. We can be on the field and not on the sidelines. Those teens who reject the school's values are not necessarily the bad apples that rot the whole basket. They are lost teens needing to be found. We need to engage them. Carry one on a retreat team. Take a few to a youth conference. Affirm the positive qualities you see in them. Massage their spirit into a better place.

Teens who perpetuate the tyranny of the clique are full of fear. They need to be gently coaxed out of their hiding places and into a place of light. They may have retreated because of wounds experienced long ago. Still, the time of their deliverance may be now.

Teens who are trying to live their faith need your help, too. Encourage them; bestow leadership upon them; network them with others so there is a support team; commission them as teenage apostles.

Every student in the school needs help to buy into gospel values. Hire youth speakers to come to school assemblies. Invite young adults of faith into your classroom. Find ways to touch the common ground in all the students – the desire to be accepted and respected and loved beyond the image they so carefully project. If there is an anti-gospel system in the school, it is our job to disrupt that system. The greatest factor in determining the culture of a school is the diligence of the adult staff, not the presence of difficult and unruly students.

When we care enough to confront our students about the serious issues that are undermining our ecclesial community, the students respond appreciatively. The way teens see it, if teachers do not show concern about theft in the school, then theft is not a very big concern. It may be low on the morality discernment chart, but the way many teens view it is this: if adults are excited about something, it must be good; if adults are upset about something, it must be bad; and if adults are silent about something (e.g., theft, vandalism, swearing, sexual talk bordering on harassment, grinding at dances, racist put-downs, bullying), then the legal principle kicks in: *Qui tacet consentire*, or "silence means consent."

The Religion teacher can make an enormous difference in the school in this area, because he or she experiences the culture war every day in class. One of the worst things that can happen in a Catholic school is for students to arrive with an attachment to their Catholic faith, only to ditch it because it proves not to be a social asset. The world will test our faith repeatedly, but it should not be assailed in a Catholic high school.

3. T-E-A-C-H-E-R: A Teenage Mystic Maker

Of all the teacher-student stories in the genre, the story of Anne Sullivan and Helen Keller shines among the brightest. The 1962 movie *The Miracle Worker* depicts the early life of Helen Keller. Infected with an undiagnosed illness at 19 months of age, Helen became blind and deaf. Not able to see or hear words, Helen was cut off from knowing reality. Words are the symbols that represent reality to our minds. Truth is conformity of the mind to the real; and words are the go-between. For five years, Helen lived in darkness and silence. Then her 21-year-old teacher arrived.

In her autobiography, Helen tells us:

The most important day I remember in all my life is the one on which my teacher, Anne Mansfield Sullivan, came to me. I am filled with wonder when I consider the immeasurable contrasts between the two lives which it connects. It was the third of March, 1887, three months before I was seven years old.

Have you ever been at sea in a dense fog, when it seemed as if a tangible white darkness shuts you in, and the great ship, tense and anxious, groped her way toward the shore with plummet and sounding-line, and you waited with beating heart for something to happen? I was like that ship before my education began, only I was without compass or sounding line, and had no way of knowing how near the harbour was. "Light, give me Light!" was the wordless cry of my soul, and the light of love shone on me that very hour … I was caught up and held close in the arms of her who had come to reveal all things to me, and, more than all things else, to love me.[102]

Anne Sullivan began by trying to teach Helen the "manual alphabet" by spelling out words into her hands. The signing in her hand was the symbol she needed in her mind to *know* the reality of the doll in her arms; but to Helen, it was a "finger game," a meaningless gesture, not a symbol of anything. In Anne Sullivan's renewed attempts to teach her words, Helen became impatient and smashed the doll Anne had given her. Helen says, "Neither sorrow nor regret followed my passionate outburst. I had not loved the doll. In the still, dark world in which I lived, there was no strong sentiment or tenderness."[103]

Knowledge, when it came, would never be, for Helen Keller, a mere academic acquisition of facts. It would always entail an associated "tenderness" and "strong sentiment."

Eventually, Anne took Helen outside, to the pump in the front yard.

> … my teacher placed my hand under the spout. As the cool stream gushed over one hand, she spelled into the other the word water, first slowly, then rapidly. I stood still, my whole attention fixed upon the motions of her fingers. Suddenly I felt a misty consciousness as of something forgotten – a thrill of returning thought; and somehow the mystery of language was revealed to me. I knew then that 'W-A-T-E-R' meant the wonderful cool something that was flowing over my hand. That living word awakened my soul, gave it light, hope, joy, set it free! There were barriers still, it is true, but barriers that could in time be swept away …
>
> It would have been difficult to find a happier child than I was as I lay in my bed at the close of that eventful day and lived over the joys it had brought me, and for the first time I longed for a new day to come."[104]

The next morning Anne Sullivan wrote a letter to a friend. She described what had happened at the pump. Helen, she said, "was transfixed – a new light came into her face … and suddenly turning around she asked for my name. I spelled 'T E A C H E R.'"

Anne Sullivan concluded her letter with these words:

> Helen got up this morning like a radiant fairy. She has flitted from object to object, asking the name of everything …
>
> Last night when I got into bed, she stole into my arms of her own accord and kissed me for the first time, and I thought my heart would burst, so full was it of joy.[105]

I teach the story of Helen Keller and show clips from the film as part of a lesson plan on sacraments and sacramentality. Words, I explain, are symbols. They are more than the chalk or ink or sounds they are made of. They stand for, point to, symbolize and *make known to us* a reality we would otherwise not know.

I tell my students that we, too, are blind and deaf like Helen once was. We fail to see that everything that exists points to a greater reality beyond itself.

Who is going to teach our students to see ordinary things with new eyes? Who is going to "keep the morning dew in their souls"? Who is going to help them move out of that common teenage malady of taking everything for granted? Who will help them, as William Blake wrote, "see a universe in a grain of sand"? "A child can see a painting," wrote Fr. Erik Riechers, "but it takes a teacher to unlock the beauty that is contained within it." Who can help young people to sense "a misty consciousness as of something forgotten" – that we came from God, are children of God, and the Word came to reveal this to us? Who will teach our youth to be teenage mystics?

Everyone in the school, I hope, but especially the Religion teacher.

Knowledge, for Helen, was transformative. It evoked tenderness within her and deep gratitude for the one who revealed "all things to me, and, more than all things else, to love me." Teaching is an act of love.

4. And a Hero Lies Within You

Finally, here is why you should be a high school Religion teacher: the teens need you. They need a spirit guide, a mentor, a counsellor, a healer, an advocate, a hero. Somewhere along my training in youth ministry and religious education, I was told to make sure that I did not become a guru to teens, because the program was what mattered most, and it was the program that needed to survive when I moved on. I understood the theory, but in the ensuing years, I discovered it didn't work. Teens, I found out, want a guru. Teens need a guru. Why should it not be you?

Being a hero to youth is not a product you should seek, but it is a by-product you will experience when you are faithful to the Faith you are trying to teach. It happens. It happens because you are interested in them, you treat them as important, you ask them for their opinion and you make them feel significant, valuable, precious – "as if I am a child of God."

You became a hero because you helped them see in a new way, walk on a new path, and become the person they looked up to when they were younger. If teens make you a hero, accept it. Let it touch your heart and enlighten your life. Let it be their lesson to you. You will think, "Their idealization of me is not accurate; I'm a mixture of altruism and ego, insight and ignorance, sanctity and sinfulness." Let them idealize you anyway, because they need a hero, and you need to experience that mixture of gratitude and humility that will take you to the only person who could actually, without flinching, bear the ultimate hero title – the Son of God.

"Blessed is He who comes in the name of the Lord," the people in Jerusalem shouted. And when Jesus was told to stifle their praise, he said if they were silenced the stones would then shout out. Jesus accepted the adulation of the crowd, because the people needed to express their faith, and because what they believed was true – he is the Blessed One. When a student sees in you a reflection of Jesus, you will discover in a flash what I tried to express in this book. This is why you teach teens Religion.

Express to Jesus all that you feel, and let him continue to train you in this mission to which he has called you. You need to stay close to Jesus, because if you ponder this ministry long enough, you will be overwhelmed by the realization of the sacred trust you have been given.

A person may borrow their neighbour's hammer, and if they break it, say, "I'm sorry I broke your hammer; I'll get you a new one." Religion teachers borrow our neighbour's kids. We can't break them, because nothing can replace them. We borrow these kids for only a short time, and because their teenage life is a series of rapid changes, we will be a special hero for only a short time as well. So be it.

Soon, our students' universe will expand, making room for more heroes, other guides and new mentors. When the pantheon of their influential persons increases, you will be relegated to the back row. Remember that you filled a great need in these young people's lives at a time when they sorely needed it. When you filled the abyss of their life with hope and faith and love during a time of need, realize that the vacuum could have been filled with very different and destructive things. You were there to show them a better way, and in the process, they saw a little bit of Jesus in you.

Our faith tells us that God sees the depths of all that is. We will never know what effect we had on others until we experience that celestial embrace and hear the words "Come, good and faithful servant."

When the students we teach today enter their autumn years (a thought they cannot conceive of at present), I suspect they will reminisce, as the old are accustomed to do, on the days of their youth. Flipping through the pages of their high school yearbook, they will pause at your picture, and say to their grandchild perched on their lap, "This was my Religion teacher, and that was my favourite class."

Postscript #1

Memo: To Religion Teachers

Subject: Sweet Sixteen Points to Ponder

1. You are in charge in the classroom. Your authority comes from God. Your authority is not an end in itself, but a means to an end – service. So when you get your towel to start washing feet, remember, you decide how they line up, who will be first and how long it will take. You are the senior servant in charge.

2. Like the teens, encourage the teens, confront the teens – in that order.

3. Don't think that what you think is happening is actually all that is happening. God is making things happen through you and sometimes despite you.

4. The grade you give in Religion class should not be a judgment of a student's spiritual state.

5. You can't be doing God's will if you compromise God's word. Don't be a Cafeteria Catholic; serve your students a full-course meal, with all the trimmings.

6. Your students do not have to agree with you.

7. Use music; it is the universal soul language of teenagers.

8. If Religion can't speak to life experience, it can't be heard.

9. All religions and those with no religion are welcome in this class. No matter where we are on the journey, we all have a long way to go.

10. God sent you to teach these students. And God sent these students to teach you. Learn their lessons as diligently as you want them to learn yours.

11. Fun in Religion class is not off topic.

12. Live what you teach. No class can rise above its teacher. Raise the bar for yourself – be a saint.

13. Win an argument; lose a soul. Love them into faith, because teens will not follow your logic until they follow you.

14. Our judgment of teens is based on circumstantial evidence. Most of what is going on in their lives we just don't know.

15. Don't use teens to teach theology; use theology to teach teens. Don't use teens to teach the curriculum; use the curriculum to teach teens.

16. Young people need to see Jesus in someone before they see Jesus. You are that someone.

Postscript #2

Memo: To Religion Teachers
Subject: Students from Other Faiths

First, it is essential that the backgrounds and experiences, the personal integrity and religious beliefs of all who participate in the school community be respected. Secondly, it is imperative that the freedom of conscience of those who are present be respected. While the Catholic school is a community of Faith as well as an evangelizing and catechetical community it should never be concerned with proselytizing. The school should be viewed as a graced environment within which its participants, whether Catholic or non-Catholic, are invited but never coerced to accept the Good News, to incorporate its spirit and to manifest its values in daily living.[106]

Just before Christmas holidays, a Sikh student in my Religion class who wears the patka (turban) handed me a present. It was a leather-bound, gold-tinted, red-letter edition of the New International Version of the Holy Bible.

"I found it in my room," he said. "I got it at the Christian elementary school I went to. I'd like to give it to you."

Another Sikh student, a girl in Grade 11, wrote me a note:

Thank you so much for all you have done. I really appreciate the effort you put into retreats, getting Pam Stenzel to come to Victoria, and helping your students keep in touch with the important things in life. I also appreciate how you read each individual evaluation that you get back. It makes me feel like my opinion really counts. Even though I have never had the privilege of being your student I really enjoy seeing you at school.

In my part of the world, the Sikh community supports our school by sending their children. Their children support our school by allowing their hearts to be touched "by the important things in life." The Catholic school can support Sikh students by inspiring and encouraging them to be better Sikhs.

Sometimes it is the non-Catholics in our class who witness to the Good News with more sincerity and enthusiasm than the born and bred. This student may have you exclaiming, as Jesus did to the Roman Centurion, "I have not found such great faith even among my own" (Luke 7:9).

Students from other Christian traditions or other faiths are a blessing to our school. Whoever walks into your classroom in September has been sent to you by God. Some have come to bless you; others arrive as punishment for your sins – just kidding! All of them have arrived for you to bless. It is not the ones from other faiths or even those who doubt God's existence who present a problem in your school. It is the ones who are anti-religious. Even the anti-religious issue can be solved by either winning them over, or being such a spirited Catholic school that the student concludes on his or her own that "I'm not ready for this," and leaves. If a virulently anti-religious student feels "at home" in the Catholic high school, then they are not what they say they are, or the school is not what it says it is.

Postscript #3

Memo: To Religion Teachers
Subject: Parent–Teacher Interviews

When a parent arrives for a parent–teacher interview, don't sit behind your desk. Graciously meet them at the door, shake hands and sit down together – person to person. This is not a meeting; this is a rendezvous – two people on the same mission, sharing notes.

The parent will be quick to ask, "So, how is my son doing in your class?" Be quicker and ask first, "So, how is Nick doing?" Nick's mom and dad will know if he's happy in school or if he is going through a hard time. They know who his friends are, and what really seems to make Nick tick. By talking to his parents, you will get a bigger and clearer picture of Nick, and this will help you teach him.

These parents have put into your hands what is most precious in their lives. In the short ten minutes they sit with you, they will have a sense of your genuine concern for their child – or lack thereof. Start with your grade book closed, for although they will want to know what marks he has received, this should not be the focus of a parent–teacher interview. We want to talk about Nick, not just his grades. We care about him, not just his report card. A parent should not leave your classroom feeling beholden to the one who administers grades and judgments on their child. They should leave contented, having just had a good conversation with a friend – a family friend.

Notes

1   Pope Paul VI, Discourse to Members of the Council for the Laity, general audience, 2 October 1974, 1.

2   Most Rev. Leonard P. Blair, "Where Are We in Catechesis? *Situating the National Directory for Catechesis.*" www.usccb.org/education/ndc/blaireng.shtml (accessed March 5, 2009).

3   United States Conference of Catholic Bishops, *National Directory for Catechesis* (Washington, DC: USCCB, 2005), Section 48D, p. 201.

4   Brian D. McLaren, *More Ready Than You Realize: Evangelism as Dance in the Postmodern Matrix* (Grand Rapids, MI: Zondervan, 2002), 14.

5   Edward P. Hahrenberg, *Catholic Update*, "Treasures of Vatican II, Our Compass for the Future" (Cincinnati, OH: St. Anthony Messenger Press, September 2005).

6   James Mulligan, CSC, *Catholic Education: The Future Is Now* (Toronto: Novalis: 1999), 97.

7   Dean Sullivan, *Papal Bull: A Humorous Dictionary for Catholics* (Deephaven, MN: Meadowbrook, Inc., 1988).

8   Ronald Rolheiser, *The Holy Longing: The Search for a Christian Spirituality* (New York: Doubleday, 1999), chapter 1.

9   C.S. Lewis, quoted in Walter Hooper, ed., *The Business of Heaven: Daily Readings from C.S. Lewis* (New York: Houghton Mifflin Harcourt, 1984), 327.

10 A version of this text, entitled *To All the Kids Who Were Born in the 1920's, 30's, 40's, 50's, 60's, and 1970's*, was sent to me through cyberspace.

11 Russell Shorto, *Saints and Madmen* (New York: Henry Holt and Company, 1999), 53–54.

12 Luigi Accattoli, *When a Pope Asks Forgiveness: The Mea Culpa's of John Paul II* (New York: Alba House, Society of St. Paul, 1998).

13 Michael J. Bradley, *Yes, Your Teen is Crazy* (Gig Harbor, WA: Harbor Press, 2002), 8.

14 Bradley, *Yes, Your Teen is Crazy*, 8.

15 William Glasser, M.D., *The Quality School* (New York: Harper and Row, 1990), 47–48. (Italics mine.)

16 Glasser, *The Quality School*, 66.

17 John H. Westerhoff, *Will Our Children Have Faith* (Seabury Press, 1976, 1984).

18 Matthew Linn, Sheila Fabricant and Dennis Linn, *Healing the Eight Stages of Life* (New York Mahwah, NJ: Paulist Press, 1988).

19 Gabor Maté, M.D., *Scattered Minds: A New Look at the Origins and Healing of Attention Deficit Disorder* (Toronto: Alfred A. Knopf Canada, 1999), 90–91.

20 Linn, Fabricant and Linn, *Healing the Eight Stages of Life*, 41–42.

21 Joseph F. Girzone, *Never Alone: A Personal Way to God* (New York: Doubleday, 1994), 12.

22 Conrad W. Baars, M.D., *Born Only Once* (Chicago: Franciscan Herald Press, 1975), 49.

23 Danny Dutton. www.jaredstory.com/explain_god.html (accessed March 5, 2009)

24 John Powell SJ, *A Reason to Live! A Reason to Die!* (Niles, IL: Argus Communications, 1972, 1975), 162.

25 Deidre Sullivan, *What Do We Mean When We Say God* (New York: Doubleday, 1990), 32.

26 Mitch Finley, *Let's Begin with Prayer* (Notre Dame, IN: Ave Maria Press, 1997), back cover.

27 Thomas Merton, *Conjectures of a Guilty Bystander* (Garden City, NY: Doubleday, 1966), 140–41.

28 Henri Nouwen, *Lourdes: At the Beginning of a New Decade* (Cincinnati: St. Anthony's Messenger Press, 1993), 30–31.

29 Joseph F. Schmidt, FSC, *Praying Our Experiences* (Winona, MN: Saint Mary's Press, 1980), 15.

30 Michael Warren, *Youth and the Future of the Church* (Minneapolis: Winston Press, 1982), 42. This story is a retelling, originally from Marc Oraison, *Love and Constraint* (New York: Paulist Press, 1961), 72.

31 Pierre Babin, O.M.I., and J.P. Bagot, *Teaching Religion to Adolescents* (New York: W.H. Sadlier, 1967), 10.

32 Patricia Hersch, *A Tribe Apart* (New York: Ballantine Books, 1998), 365.

33 Diane Baltan, *Catholic Register*, May 1995.

34 Hersch, *A Tribe Apart*, 365.

35 Most. Rev. Donald W. Wuerl, "Reflections on the Content of the *National Directory for Catechesis*," USCCB. http://www.usccb.org/education/ndc/wuerlleng.shtml (accessed March 5, 2009)

36 Cardinal Leon-Joseph Suenens, *Nature and Grace: A Vital Unity* (London: Darton, Longman and Todd, 1986), 51–52.

37 This idea is inspired by the *Discovering* program booklet *Friendship*. *Discovering* is a parish-based religious education program for junior high students edited by renowned religious educator Tom Zanzig and published by St. Mary's Press. Teen friendly, highly effective and theologically engaging, it is a program that I highly recommend for the junior high years (grades 8 and 9) in the Catholic high school.

38 Doug Fields, *Would You Rather …?, 465 Provocative Questions to Get Teenagers Talking* (Grand Rapids, MI: Zondervan, 1996).

39 *Reader's Digest,* November 2003.

40 Barry MacDonald, *Boy Smarts: Mentoring Boys for Success at School* (Surrey, BC: Mentoring Press, 2005).

41 MacDonald, *Boy Smarts*, 55.

42 MacDonald, *Boy Smarts*, 95.

43 MacDonald, *Boy Smarts*, 92.

44 Jim Taylor, *Your Children Are Under Attack: How Popular Culture Is Destroying Your Kid's Values and How You Can Protect Them* (Naperville, IL: Sourcebooks, Inc., 2005), 10, 11, 14, 22, 12, 18, 19.

45 Taylor, *Your Children Are Under Attack*, 23.

46 Taylor, *Your Children Are Under Attack*, 23.

47 James J. DiGiacomo, S.J., *Teaching Religion in a Catholic Secondary School* (Washington, DC: National Catholic Educational Association, NCEA Keynote Series, 1989), 41–44.

48 DiGiacomo, *Teaching Religion in a Catholic Secondary School*, 41–44.

49 Steven R. Covey, *The 7 Habits of Highly Effective People* (New York: Fireside, 1989); Sean Covey, *The 7 Habits of Highly Effective Teens* (New York: Fireside, 1998).

50 Blair, "Where Are We in Catechesis?"

51 Hersch, *A Tribe Apart*, 29, 103, 374, 363, 364.

52 Schmidt, *Praying Our Experiences*, preface.

53 Schmidt, *Praying Our Experiences*, 33–34.

54 Merton P. Strommen, *Five Cries of Youth*, new and revised edition (San Francisco: Harper and Row, 1988).

55 Hersch, *A Tribe Apart*, ix.

56 Anthony E. Wolf, *Get Out of My Life – But First Could You Drive Me and Cheryl to the Mall?* (New York: Farrar, Straus and Giroux, 1991, 2002), 41–42.

57 Wolf, *Get Out of My Life*, 42.

58 Ruth Arden, "The Misfit," in *Christian Home and School Magazine* (September 1992), 12–15.

59 Barbara Coloroso, *The Bully, the Bullied, and the Bystander* (Toronto: Harper Collins Publishers, 2002), 20–21.

60 L. David Overholt and James A. Penner, *Soul Searching the Millennial Generation* (Toronto: Novalis, 2005), 118.

61 Coloroso, *The Bully, the Bullied, and the Bystander*, 197.

62 H. Stephen Glenn and Jane Nelsen, *Raising Self-Reliant Children in a Self-Indulgent World* (Rocklin, CA: Prima Publishing and Communications, 1989).

63 Thomas Moore, *Care of the Soul: A Guide for Cultivating Depth and Sacredness in Everyday Life* (New York: Harper Collins Publishers, 1992), 25.

64 Rolf E. Muuss, *Theories of Adolescence* (New York: Random House, 1975), 69–81.

65 John A. Sanford and George Lough, *What Men Are Like* (Mahwah, NJ: Paulist Press, 1988), 36.

66 Gerald G. May, M.D., *Addiction and Grace* (San Francisco: Harper and Row, 1988).

67 May, *Addiction and Grace*, 4–5.

68 Gordon Neufeld and Gabor Maté, *Hold on to Your Kids: Why Parents Need to Matter More than Peers* (Toronto: Vintage Canada, 2004).

69 Neufeld and Maté, *Hold on to Your Kids*, 6.

70 Baars, *Born Only Once*, 46.

71 Baars, *Born Only Once*, 53.

72 Hersch, *A Tribe Apart*, 101.

73 Michelle Borba, *Building Moral Intelligence: The Seven Essential Virtues that Teach Kids to Do the Right Thing* (San Francisco: Jossey-Bass, 2001), 46.

74 Thomas Lickona, *Raising Good Children* (New York: Bantam, 1994).

75 DiGiacomo, *Teaching Religion in a Catholic Secondary School*, 14.

76 Stephen R. Covey, *Living the 7 Habits: Stories of Courage and Inspiration* (New York: Fireside, 1999), 299–300.

77 Francis MacNutt, *Deliverance from Evil Spirits* (Grand Rapids, MI: Chosen Books, 1995), 32.

78 *Maclean's*, September 26, 2005.

79 Jerry Scott and Jim Borgman, "ZITS," Victoria *Times Colonist*, Sunday, Dec. 17, 2006, C6, distributed by King Features Syndicate, © 2006 ZITS Partnership.

80 www.bradhenning.com

81 Overholt and Penner, *Soul Searching the Millennial Generation*, 116–17.

82 David Popenoe, *Life Without Father* (New York: Simon and Schuster, 1996), 143.

83 Popenoe, *Life Without Father*, 159.

84 Alice Gray, compiler, *Stories for the Heart* (Sisters, OR: Multinomah Publishers, 1996), 125.

85 Clayton Barbeau, *How to Raise Parents* (San Francisco: Harper and Row, 1987), 190.

86 Chap Clark, *Next Time I Fall in Love* (Grand Rapids, MI: Zondervan, 1989).

87 Mary Rosera Joyce, *How Can a Man and a Woman Be Friends* (Collegeville, MN: The Liturgical Press, 1977), 40–41.

88 Ron Rolheiser, *The Holy Longing: The Search for Christian Spirituality* (New York: Doubleday, 1999), 192–93.

89 Miriam Grossman, M.D., *Unprotected* (New York: Sentinel, 2006–2007), 2.

90 James Taylor, *Sin: A New Understanding of Virtue and Vice* (Northstone Publishing, 1997), 91.

91 Victoria *Times Colonist*, "Adolescent materialism is connected to low self-esteem, researchers find," December 2, 2007.

92 *The Fog of War: Eleven Lessons from the Life of Robert S. McNamara*, a documentary film directed by Errol Morris, 2003.

93 Greg Mortensen and David Oliver Relin, *Three Cups of Tea: One Man's Mission to Promote Peace … One School at a Time* (New York: Penguin Books, 2006), 294.

94 Jean Vanier, *Finding Peace* (Toronto: House of Anansi Press, 2003), 41.

95 Vanier, *Finding Peace*, 77–78.

96 Joseph Cardinal Bernardin, Gannon Lecture, Fordham University, New York, December 6, 1983.

97 *Focus on the Family*, March 1995.

98 John Wilson and Eugene H. Peterson, *The Best Christian Writing 2002* (New York: Harper Collins, 2002), 144.

99 *The Globe and Mail,* March 31, 2008, A13.

100 Paul William Roberts, *A War Against Truth* (Vancouver: Raincoast Books, 2004), 136–37.

101 Michael T. Ryan, *The Social Attitudes of a Catholic* (Parkhill, ON: Solidarity Books, 2005), 107–08.

102 Philip Dunaway and George de Kay, eds., *Turning Point* (New York: Random House, 1958), excerpts from *The Story of My Life* by Helen Keller (New York: Doubleday and Company, 1903, 1931), 105–06.

103 Dunaway and de Kay, eds., *Turning Point*, 106.

104 Dunaway and de Kay, eds., *Turning Point*, 106–07.

105 Dunaway and de Kay, eds., *Turning Point*, 108.

106 James Hawker, *The School as an Evangelizing Community: Guidelines Regarding Teachers, Pupils and Parents* (National Catholic Educational Association, Department of Religious Education).

Want to continue the conversation?

Contact Danny Brock at
Dannybrock7@gmail.com

 This book has been printed on 100% post consumer waste paper, certified Eco-logo and processed chlorine free.